Know Your

50 Years

SHIPS

Guide to Boats & Boatwatching
Great Lakes & St. Lawrence Seaway

ISBN: 978-1-891849-12-1

© 2009 – Revised Annually

(No part of this book may be published, broadcast,
rewritten or redistributed by any means, including electronic)

P9-APR-431

Marine Publishing Co. Inc.

P.O. Box 68, Sault Ste. Marie, MI 49783

(734) 668-4734

OJIBWAY

Founder
Tom Manse, 1915-1994

Editor & Publisher
Roger LeLievre

kysbook@concentric.net

Researchers: Jody Aho,
Mac Mackay, Matt Miner, Gerry Ouderkirk,
Wade P. Streeter, Franz VonRiedel,
John Vournakis and George Wharton

Crew: Kathryn Lengell,
Nancy Kuharevicz, Audrey LeLievre,
Neil Schultheiss, William Soleau

KnowYourShips.com

Precious Cargo?

WE CAN HANDLE IT!

At Interlake Steamship we treat each and every shipment as if it were priceless. Whether it's coal, grain, taconite pellets or limestone we know how important that cargo is to our customers... and to their customers. And, we know how important it is that it be delivered in a timely manner with the utmost care.

With self-unloading vessel capacities ranging from 17,000 to 68,000 tons, you can trust Interlake Steamship with all your dry bulk cargo needs on the Great Lakes.

*Call Interlake Steamship – where all cargo is **precious cargo**.*

INTERLAKE STEAMSHIP

On the Great Lakes since 1913

ISO Certified

The Interlake Steamship Company
Interlake Corporate Center
4199 Kinross Lakes Parkway
Richfield, Ohio 44286
Telephone: (330) 659-1400
FAX: (330) 659-1445
E-mail: sales@interlake-steamship.com

CONTENTS

Front: *Stewart J. Cort,*
the first 1,000-footer,
on the lower St. Marys River.
(*Roger LeLievre*)

Back: *Edward L. Ryerson,*
from the Aerial Lift Bridge
in Duluth. (*Eric Treece*)

AMERICAN REPUBLIC

3

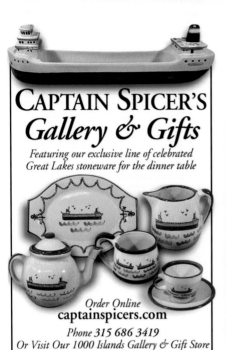

CAPTAIN SPICER'S
Gallery & Gifts

*Featuring our exclusive line of celebrated
Great Lakes stoneware for the dinner table*

Order Online
captainspicers.com

*Phone 315 686 3419
Or Visit Our 1000 Islands Gallery & Gift Store*
40467 NYS Route 12
Clayton NY 13624

Marine Navigation and
Engineering careers begin
at Georgian College's
**Great Lakes International
Marine Training Centre**.

Visit **marinetraining.ca**
for program information.

GEORGIAN
YOUR COLLEGE · YOUR FUTURE
**GREAT LAKES INTERNATIONAL MARINE
TRAINING CENTRE**

Founded in 1874
THE J.W. WESTCOTT CO.

**Ship Reporters and Vessel Agents
Foot of 24th St., Detroit, MI 48222**

Authorized Nautical Chart Agent
• U.S. and Canadian charts for the entire Great Lakes
and St. Lawrence Seaway • U.S. government publications
• Bookstore – books about the history and vessels of the Great Lakes,
plus maritime books and manuals for the professional mariner

**A RELIABLE AND DEPENDABLE
MARINE DELIVERY SERVICE**

*Serving the Port of Detroit via the
"J.W. Westcott II" diesel motorship*

*Ship-to-shore service 24 hours per day,
every day during the navigation season*

24-Hour Telephone
(313) 496-0555 **Fax** (313) 496-0628

www.jwwestcott.com

• *Water taxi service via
the M/V Joseph W. Hogan*
• *Pilot service via the M/V Huron Maid*

S.S. BADGER

HISTORIC
LAKE MICHIGAN CARFERRY

A little history, a lot of fun!

800-841-4243

www.ssbadger.com

MANITOWOC ★ LUDINGTON

Cruising
Port Huron
aboard the
Huron Lady II

Shipwatching Tours
from the
Home Port of Boatnerd
World Headquarters
810-984-1500
www.HuronLady.com

GLLKA
Great Lakes Lighthouse Keepers Association

☐ Preserving Lighthouse History
☐ Lighthouse Restoration & Preservation
☐ Education Programs
☐ Great Lakes Lighthouse Excursions
☐ Publishers of **The Beacon**, a quarterly magazine of Great Lakes lighthouse news and history

PO Box 219
Mackinaw City, MI 49701
(231) 436-5580   www.gllka.com
Visit our gift shop at 707 North Huron Ave. right across the street from Old Mackinac Point lighthouse in Mackinaw City, Mich.

Great Laker
Lighthouses, Lake Boats, Travel & Leisure

Great Laker is a quarterly magazine that covers the maritime history and culture of the Great Lakes region This beautiful, full-color, glossy magazine displays the Great Lakes in all their splendor. Each issue includes articles on: Lighthouse features, Laker Library (books/movies/video reviews), On the Radar (calendar of events), Meet the Fleet (Laker Profile) Laker & Lighthouse News, Meet the Crew (personality profile), *Great Lakes/Seaway Review*

SUBSCRIBE ON-LINE
WWW.GREATLAKER.COM

221 Water Street, Boyne City, MI 49712 USA
(800) 491-1760   FAX: (866) 906-3392
harbor@harborhouse.com   www.greatlaker.com

SEAWAY TURNS 50

The opening of the St. Lawrence Seaway in 1959 brought ships of all nations deep into America's heartland. A series of locks, canals, and waterways, the Seaway provides a link between the Great Lakes and the Atlantic Ocean.

The present-day Seaway's origins can be traced back to the 17th century, when the French tried building a canal to bypass the Lachine Rapids, near Montreal. While the effort was unsuccessful, the effort was based on the same ideas that would drive future projects – producing power and improving navigation.

The beginnings of the current waterway date to 1954, when the St. Lawrence Seaway Authority was established with the mandate to acquire lands to construct, operate and maintain a deep draft waterway between the port of Montreal and Lake Erie, along with the international bridges that cross it and other lands and structures.

That same year, the United States joined Canada on the development of the Seaway with the passage of the Wiley-Dondero (or Seaway) Act; the U.S. Saint Lawrence Seaway Development Corporation was also created by the law.

(Continued on Page 8)

Two views of the Eisenhower Lock, at Massena, N.Y.

Seaway facts

One 1000-foot-long Great Lakes vessel carries enough iron ore to operate a steel mill for more than four days. A similar vessel carries enough coal to power greater Detroit for one day.

A Seaway-size vessel moves enough wheat to make bread for every resident of New York City for nearly a month.

Since 1959, more than two billion tons of cargo, valued at $300 billion, have moved to and from Canada, the United States, and nearly 50 other nations.

Almost 50 percent of Seaway traffic travels to and from overseas ports.

Each lock is 766 feet (233.5 meters) long, 80 feet (24.4 meters wide) and 30 feet (9.1 meters) deep over the sill. A lock fills with approximately 24 million gallons (91 million liters) of water in just 7-10 minutes. Getting through a lock takes about 45 minutes.

Year by year

1954: Constructions begins

1958: The new Iroquois Lock is in regular use by May. On July 4, the Snell and Eisenhower locks, built by the U.S. at Massena, N.Y., are opened, and the power is switched on at the Moses-Saunders generating station.

1959: On April 25, the icebreaker *D'Iberville* begins the first through transit of the St. Lawrence Seaway. The Canada Steamship Lines' canaller *Simcoe* is the first commercial transit. Official opening ceremonies are June 26.

1966: The first Welland Canal traffic control center enters service.

After opening the Seaway, Queen Elizabeth toured the Great Lakes aboard the royal yacht *Britannia*, shown here at the Soo Locks. *(Tom Manse Coll.)* **Below, the Snell Lock under construction.**

An agreement was also reached between the U.S. and Canada concerning construction of the Seaway. The cost of the navigation project was $470.3 million, of which Canada paid $336.5 million and the U.S. $133.8 million.

Work on the Seaway began in September 1954. Four Montreal-area bridges were modified, new channels were dug and existing ones dredged. The related power development flooded 100 square miles (259 square km); land was expropriated and entire towns resettled. In addition to improved navigation, the Seaway allowed Ontario Hydro and the New York State Power Authority to develop new hydroelectric facilities

The new Seaway would replace a waterway with a depth of 14 feet with one that ran 27 feet deep and reduce the number of locks from 30 to 15.

On April 25, 1959, the St. Lawrence Seaway opened for business with the passage of the Canadian Coast Guard icebreaker *D'Iberville*, followed by the Dutch freighter *Prins Willem George Frederick**, captained by T. Aaldijk, whose

Seaway Queen, **built in 1959, was named in honor of the new waterway.** *(Bob Campbell)*

nickname was "the Flying Dutchman."

It was an exciting event. One newspaper, The Chicago American, reported "Seaway open to Chicago, 50 ships in flotilla. The race is on!"

Official opening ceremonies were on June 26, 1959, when Queen Elizabeth II and President Dwight D. Eisenhower met at the St. Lambert Lock. Dedication ceremonies were also held June 27 in Massena, N.Y., and involved the queen and U.S. Vice-President Richard M. Nixon.

Simcoe **made the Seaway's first commercial passage.** *(John Bascom)*

Following the ceremonies, Queen Elizabeth II cruised the Great Lakes aboard the royal yacht *Britannia,* escorted by a 28-ship detachment of the U.S. Atlantic Fleet.

Construction of the 189-mile (306 km) stretch of the Seaway between Montreal and Lake Ontario was a challenging engineering feat. Seven locks were built in the Montreal-Lake Ontario section of the Seaway – five Canadian and two U.S. – in order to lift vessels to 246 feet (75 meters) above sea level.

The 28-mile (44 km) Welland Canal was the fourth version of a waterway link between Lake Ontario and Lake Erie, first built in 1829. The present canal was completed in 1932, deepened in the 1950s as part of the Seaway project and further straightened in 1973. Today, its eight locks lift ships 326 feet (100 meters) over the Niagara Escarpment.

The Soo Locks, at Sault Ste. Marie, Mich., linking Lake Huron to Lake Superior, are also part of the St. Lawrence Seaway system, making Duluth, Minn., deep in America's interior, a busy port for oceangoing freighters.

* Prins Willem George Frederik was scrapped in Piraeus, Greece, in 1978 under the name Alimos.

1973: The Welland Canal realignment to bypass the city of Welland opens to navigation.

1978: Canadian Seaway operations become self-sufficient, depending on revenue from tolls and investments. The federal government still contributes to major capital works.

1983: The Seaway carries its billionth ton of cargo.

1984: The Seaway celebrates its 25th anniversary.

1993: The Seaway's draft is increased from 26 feet to 26 feet, 3 inches, enabling ships to carry more cargo per voyage, and wide-beam ships, exceeding the 76 foot limit by up to 2 feet, are first admitted through the locks.

1996: May 10 marks the passage through the Seaway system of two billion tons of cargo, valued at more than $400 billion.

1999: 40th anniversary of the opening of the St. Lawrence Seaway.

2004: 175th anniversary of the first Welland Canal. The Seaway's draft is increased from 26 feet, 3 inches, to 26 feet, 6 inches, enabling ships to carry up to 300 tons of additional cargo per voyage. The Great Lakes St. Lawrence Seaway is now branded as HwyH2O.

2007: 75th anniversary of the fourth Welland Canal.

Source: St. Lawrence Seaway Authority and St. Lawrence Seaway Development Corp.

9

TRADING & PROMOTIONS

"Whatever It Takes!"

anythingPROMO

Logo-shirts Caps and Jackets...

...for Fashionable Boatwatchers

WE SPECIALILZE IN MARITIME ITEMS!

www.force5-trading.com

Logo-wear from...

Paul R. Tregurtha
James R. Barker
Elton Hoyt II
Kaye E. Barker
Mesabi Miner
Lee A. Tregurtha
Stewart J. Cort
Herbert C. Jackson
Charles M. Beeghly
Dorothy Ann/Pathfinder
Moran Towing
BoatNerd.com

330-703-8789 • Fax: 330-467-7038 • Email: vp@anythingpromo.com

Sleep through the sunrise.

There'll be another one tomorrow.

The INN ON LAKE SUPERIOR

350 CANAL PARK DRIVE • DULUTH, MN 55802
218-726-1111 888-ON-THE-LAKE
INNONLAKESUPERIOR.COM

J.W. Shelley enters the Welland Canal with her first cargo. *(John C. Knecht)*

PASSAGES

Changes in the shipping scene since our last edition

Fleets & Vessels

The big news as the 2009 shipping season opened was the economy. After a strong performance for most of 2008, the shipping industry took a nosedive in the fall when steel mills around the Great Lakes cut back as demand for their products fell. Many U.S.-flagged vessels entered winter lay-up early, and projections for the 2009 season continue to be gloomy.

The bulk carrier *Algocen*, sold to a U.S. East Coast company in 2005 for use as a spoils barge, was bought, refurbished and brought back to the lakes for further service in 2008. Under the name *J.W. Shelley*, the 1969-built motorship was back sailing last September, painted a bright blue and owned by Vanguard Shipping (Great Lakes). The vessel is named in honor of John Shelley Sr., for many years a principal of Sarnia's Shelley Marine.

On June 3, 2008, Algoma Central's bulk carrier *Algoville* was renamed *Tim S. Dool,* in honor of the firm's retiring president and CEO. The company turned to saltwater in 2008 to expand its

Scrapping of the 1929-built *Calumet,* underway at Port Colborne, Ont., in 2008. *(Jeff Cameron)*

(Continued on Page 12)

fleet, puchasing three vessels from Norway's Viken Shipping AS. The *Daviken* is now *Algoma Discovery*, *Sandviken* is *Algoma Spirit*, and *Goviken* now carries the name *Algoma Guardian*.

Hopes were dashed in late 2008 when the Interlake Steamship Co. pulled the plug – at least for now – on the complete refurbishment and return to service of the 1958-built bulk carrier *John Sherwin*, which has been laid up since 1981. The bad economy was blamed for the decision. The *Sherwin* was towed to Bay Ship Building in Sturgeon Bay, Wis., in August and, after repowering and conversion to a self-unloader, had been expected back in service in early 2010. However, Interlake did decide to go ahead with a conversion to diesel power of the steamer *Charles M. Beeghly*.

Canada Steamship Lines also added four former saltwater vessels to its fleet last year, acquiring the 730-foot vessels *Lake Erie* (now *Richelieu*), *Lake Michigan* (now *Mapleglen*), *Lake Superior* (now *Saguenay*) and *Lake Ontario* (now *Oakglen*) from Fednav Ltd.

(Continued on Page 14)

John Sherwin on the drydock. Note the workman sandblasting the hull. *(Chris Winters)*

Tim S. Dool, the former *Algoville*, on its first trip under her new name. *(Paul Beesley)*

The former Oglebay Norton Co. motor vessel *Wolverine* was rechristened *Robert S. Pierson* for Lower Lakes Towing at Sarnia, Ont., on March 22, 2008.

(Marc Dease; champagne bottle, Fred Miller)

The steamer *E. M. Ford*, the oldest freighter on the Great Lakes, arrived in Sault Ste. Marie, Ont., in November 2008 for eventual scrapping by Purvis Marine. The *Ford*, with its magnificent, 1,500-horsepower, quadruple-expansion steam engine, built in 1898 as the bulk carrier *Presque Isle*, was converted to haul cement in 1956. In recent years, she was used as a cement storage barge at Saginaw, Mich. It is expected her former fleetmate, *J.B. Ford*, dating from 1904, will follow her to the boneyard in 2009.

The cement carrier *J.A.W. Iglehart* continued its role as a storage hull at Superior, Wis., in 2008, while the *S.T. Crapo* at Green Bay, Wis., and *Paul H. Townsend* at Muskegon, Mich., were also used in a similar fashion. Other vessels remain in limbo at various Great Lakes ports, including *Windoc* (Port Weller, Ont.), the car ferry *Viking* (Marinette, Wis.) and the former Lake Michigan ferry *Spartan* (Ludington, Mich.). *Canadian Miner* and *Halifax*, which reportedly need repair, may stay laid up this year as well.

50
1959-2009

James L. Kuber, the former *Reserve*, at Marquette. *(Rod Burdick)*

The new tanker *Algonova* on her first Seaway trip.
(Alain Gindroz)

The 111-year old *E.M. Ford*, under tow of the tug *Avenger IV* on the Saginaw River, headed for eventual scraping at Sault Ste. Marie, Ont. *(Mike Koprowicz)*

ROBERT McGREEVY

Mystery steamer *Keystone State*, disappeared in Lake Huron with her entire crew and has never been found

Prints available
at galleries
or from
the artist

(989) 479-9592

www.mcgreevy.com
robertmcgreevy1@aol.com

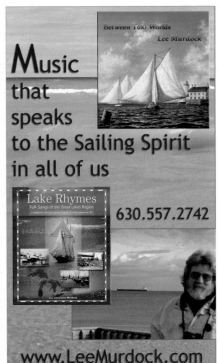

Between Two Worlds

Lee Murdock

Music
that
speaks
to the Sailing Spirit
in all of us

630.557.2742

Lake Rhymes
Folk Songs of the Great Lakes Region

www.LeeMurdock.com

Diamond Jack's
River Tours

Enjoy 16 miles of Detroit River cruising

JOHN G. MUNSON
USS GREAT LAKES FLEET

Ken Borg

DETROIT'S BEST FAMILY RIVERBOAT VALUE
Two Hour Detroit River Tours
From Hart Plaza in Detroit or Bishop Park in Wyandotte
www.diamondjack.com -- 313-843-9376

Vessel Index

Canadian Provider on the open lake. *(Mike Sipper)*

Vessel Name	Fleet #

A

Vessel Name	Fleet #
A-390	A-10
A-397	A-10
A-410	A-10
Aachen	II-2
Abaco	R-3
Abegweit	C-17
Acacia	A-6
Acquamarina	IF-4
Adamastos	IE-6
Adanac	P-11
Agawa Canyon	A-5
Agena	IR-4
Aggie C	I-2
Agios Minas	IH-2
AGS-359	M-14
Aird, John B.	A-5
Aivik	T-18
Alabama	G-16
Albert C	I-2
Alcona	R-10
Alder	U-3
Aldo H.	M-14
Aleksandrov, Grigoriy	IF-2
Alesia	IR-1
Alessandro DP	ID-1
Alexandria Belle	U-1
Alexis-Simard	A-4
Algobay	A-5
Algocanada	A-5
Algocape	A-5
Algoeast	A-5
Algoisle	A-5
Algolake	A-5
Algoma Discovery	A-5
Algoma Guardian	A-5
Algoma Spirit	A-5
Algomah	A-14
Algomarine	A-5
Algonorth	A-5
Algonova	A-5
Algontario	A-5
Algoport	A-5
Algorail	A-5
Algosar	A-5
Algoscotia	A-5
Algosea	A-5
Algosoo	A-5
Algosteel	A-5
Algoway	A-5
Algowood	A-5
Alice E	A-7, E-4
Alkyon	II-4
Alouette Spirit	M-14
Alpena	I-3
Altman, Anna Marie	Z-1
Altman, Victor J.	Z-1

Vessel Name	Fleet #
Alton Andrew	M-10
Amalia	II-2
Amanda	II-2
Ambassador	IC-14
Amber Mae	R-10
Americaborg	IW-2
American Century	A-8
American Courage	A-8
American Fortitude	A-8
American Girl	S-21
American Integrity	A-8
American Mariner	A-8
American Republic	A-8
American Spirit	A-8
American Valor	A-8
American Victory	A-8
Amundsen	C-3
Anchor Bay	G-17
Anderson, Arthur M.	G-15
Andre H.	L-10
Andrea J.	E-3
Andrea Marie I	D-2
Andrew J.	E-3
Andrie, Barbara	A-10
Andrie, Karen	A-10
Andromeda	IB-1
Anglian Lady	P-11
Angus, D.J.	G-10
Anja	II-2
Ann Marie	L-16
Annalisa	II-2
Antalina	IT-1
Antikeri	IA-2
Apalachee	U-4
Apollon	IS-2
Appledore IV	B-5
Appledore V	B-5
Arabian Wind	IE-1
Arca	S-5
Arctic	F-1
Arizona	G-16
Arkansas	G-16
Asher, Chas.	R-5
Asher, John R.	R-5
Asher, Stephan M.	R-5
Ashland Bayfield Express	A-15
ASI Clipper	A-16
Asiaborg	IW-2
Atchafalaya	P-10
Atigamayg	O-3
Atkinson, Arthur K.	S-2
Atlantic Erie	C-2
Atlantic Huron	C-2
Atlantic Superior	C-2
Atwell, Idus	M-16
Aurora Borealis	C-15
Australiaborg	IW-2
Avantage	L-10
Avataq	T-16

Vessel Name	Fleet #
Avenger IV	P-11

B

Vessel Name	Fleet #
B.J. & C.J.	F-2
Badger	L-5
Bagotville	M-16
Baird, Spencer F.	U-6
Balticland	IE-4
Barbro	IF-8
Barker, James R.	I-6
Barker, Kaye E.	I-6
Barry J	K-7
Basse-Cote	L-10
Batchawana	G-2
Bavaria	IB-8
Bayfield	M-4
Bayridge Service	H-10
Bayship	B-4
BBC Asia	IB-8
BBC Atlantic	IB-8
BBC Australia	IB-8
BBC Campana	IW-1
BBC Delaware	IW-1
BBC Elbe	IB-8
BBC Ems	IB-8
BBC England	IJ-2
BBC Europe	IB-8
BBC Finland	IN-2
BBC France	IB-8
BBC Germany	IB-8
BBC Iceland	IB-8
BBC India	IB-2
BBC Italy	IW-1
BBC Maine	IW-1
BBC Mexico	IW-1
BBC Mississippi	IB-8
BBC Ontario	IK-3
BBC Peru	IW-1
BBC Plata	IW-1
BBC Rosario	IM-1
BBC Scandinavia	IB-8
BBC Scotland	IB-8
BBC Shanghai	IB-8
BBC Spain	IW-1
BBC Venezuela	IB-8
BBC Zarate	IW-1
Beaupre	Q-1
Beaver	A-14
Beaver D.	V-3
Beaver Delta II	M-16
Beaver Gamma	M-16
Beaver Islander	B-7
Beaver Kay	M-16
Beaver State	M-1
Bee Jay	G-3
Beeghly, Charles M.	I-6
Beluga Constellation	IB-2

Vessel Name	Fleet #	Vessel Name	Fleet #	Vessel Name	Fleet #
Beluga Constitution	IB-2	Birchglen	C-2	Bunyan, Paul	U-2
Beluga Efficiency	IB-2	Biscayne Bay	U-3	Burns Harbor	A-8
Beluga Elegance	IB-2	Black Carrier	M-14	Busch, Gregory J.	B-21
Beluga Emotion	IB-2	Black, Martha L.	C-3	Busse, Fred A.	D-7
Beluga Endurance	IB-2	Blacky	IN-1	Buxton II	K-7
Beluga Energy	IB-2	Block, Joseph L.	C-6		
Beluga Enterprise	IB-2	Blough, Roger	G-15		
Beluga Eternity	IB-2	Blue Heron	U-9		
Beluga Expectation	IB-2	Blue Heron V	B-11		
Beluga Federation	IB-2	Bluebill	IN-1		

C

Vessel Name	Fleet #	Vessel Name	Fleet #	Vessel Name	Fleet #
Beluga Fighter	IB-2	Bluewing	IN-1	C.T.C. No. 1	S-25
Beluga Flirtation	IB-2	Boatman No. 3	M-14	C.T.M.A. Vacancier	C-23
Beluga Formation	IB-2	Boatman No. 6	M-14	C.T.M.A. Voyageur	C-23
Beluga Fusion	IB-2	Boland, John J.	A-8	Cabot	IO-2
Beluga Indication	IB-2	Bonnie B. III	M-14	Cadillac	S-27
Beluga Recognition	IB-2	Bonnie G.	T-5	California	G-16
Beluga Recommendation	IB-2	Borkum	IB-8	Callaway, Cason J.	G-15
Beluga Resolution	IB-2	Bornholm	IH-7	Callie M.	M-10
Beluga Revolution	IB-2	Bowes, Bobby	D-3	Callitsis, Athanasios G.	IC-2
Berdyansk	IC-10	Boyd, David	G-21	Calumet	L-15
Bertina	IB-3	Boyer, Willis B.	M-27	Cameron O.	S-3
Betsiamites	L-10	Bramble	P-8	Canadian	M-16
Bide-A-Wee	S-13	Brandon E.	E-4	Canadian Argosy	M-16
Big 503	U-12	Breaker	S-28	Canadian Empress	S-22
Big 543	U-12	Brenda L.	F-3	Canadian Enterprise	U-12
Big 546	U-12	Bright Laker	ID-2	Canadian Jubilee	D-3
Big 548	U-12	Bristol Bay	U-3	Canadian Leader	U-12
Big 549	U-12	Brown, Prentiss	P-7	Canadian Miner	U-12
Big 551	U-12	Brutus I	T-12	Canadian Navigator	U-12
Big 9708 B	U-12	Buckley	K-6	Canadian Olympic	U-12
Big 9917 B	U-12	Buckthorn	U-3	Canadian Progress	U-12
Billmaier, D.L.	U-2	Buffalo	A-8	Canadian Prospector	U-12
				Canadian Provider	U-12

Great Lakes Fleet's *Arthur M. Anderson* in the Detroit River. *(Wade P. Streeter)*

Saginaw passes Herbert C. Jackson, unloading at Essar Steel Algoma in Sault Ste. Marie, Ont. (John C. Knecht)

Vessel Name	Fleet #
Canadian Ranger	U-12
Canadian Transfer	U-12
Canadian Transport	U-12
Cantankerus	E-9
Cap Charles	IE-8
Cap Diamant	IE-8
Cap Georges	IE-8
Cap Guillaume	IE-8
Cap Lara	IE-8
Cap Laurent	IE-8
Cap Leon	IE-8
Cap Philippe	IE-8
Cap Pierre	IE-8
Cap Streeter	S-11
Cape Discovery	C-3
Cape Dundas	C-3
Cape Hurd	C-3
Cape Storm	C-3
Capetan Michalis	IU-1
Capt. Shepler	S-7
Carey, Emmet J.	O-6
Cargo Master	M-16
Caribou Isle	C-3
Carina	R-3
Carl M.	M-16
Carlee Emily	K-3
Carleton, George N.	G-11
Carol Ann	K-7
Carola	II-2
Carrick, John J.	M-13
Carrol C. 1	M-14
Catharina-C	IC-4
Catherine-Legardeur	S-12
Cavalier des Mers	C-20
Cavalier Maxim	C-20
Cavalier Royal	C-20
Cedarglen	C-2
Celebreeze, Anthony J.	C-14
Celine	IE-7
Cemba	C-5
CFL Prospect	IC-1
CFL Prudence	IC-1
CGB-12000	U-3
CGB-12001	U-3
Challenge	G-19
Champion	C-7, D-12
Channahon	I-2
Channel Cat	M-19
Charlevoix	C-8
Charlie E.	I-7
Chemical Trader	IE-9
Cheraw	U-2
Chicago's First Lady	M-18
Chicago's Little Lady	M-18
Chi-Cheemaun	O-7
Chief Shingwauk	L-13
Chief Wawatam	P-11
Chippewa	A-14
Chippewa III	S-18

Vessel Name	Fleet #
Cinnamon	IN-1
Cisco	S-21
City of Algonac	D-1
City of Milwaukee	S-19
Clark, Wilbur R.	H-4
Clarke, Philip R.	G-15
Cleanshores	H-3
Clelia II	IL-7
Cleveland	L-7
Cleveland Rocks	L-7
Clipper Golfito	IC-8
Clipper Karen	IC-8
Clipper Katja	IC-8
Clipper Kira	IC-8
Clipper Klara	IC-8
Clipper Kristin	IC-8
Clipper Krystal	IC-8
Clipper Kylie	IC-8
Clipper Lancer	IC-8
Clipper Leader	IC-8
Clipper Leander	IC-8
Clipper Legacy	IC-8
Clipper Legend	IC-8
Clipper Loyalty	IC-8
Clipper Tasmania	IC-8
Clipper Tobago	IC-8
Clipper Trinidad	IC-8
Clipper Trojan	IC-8
Clyde	G-6
Coastal Cruiser	T-4
Cobia	W-8
Cod	U-14
Cohen, Wilfred M.	P-11
Colorado	G-16
Columbia	P-10, S-29
Columbia V (The)	A-9
Commodore Straits	U-12
Condarrell	M-14
Coo-Coo	L-10
Cooper, J.W.	C-18
Cooper, Wyn	F-2
Cornelius, Adam E.	A-8
Corsair	A-14
Cort, Stewart J.	I-6
Cotter, Edward M.	B-19
Coucoucache	L-10
Covadonga	IA-1
Cove Isle	C-3
Crapo, S.T.	I-3
Cresswell, Peter R	A-5
Croaker	B-16
Crystal Diamond	IC-13
Crystal Topaz	IC-13
CSL Assiniboine	C-2
CSL Laurentien	C-2
CSL Niagara	C-2
CSL Tadoussac	C-2
CT Cork	IY-2
Cuyahoga	L-14

D

Vessel Name	Fleet #
D.T. Derrick No. 2	M-14
Dagna	IW-2
Dahlke, Ronald J.	A-10
Daldean	B-13
Dalmig	H-7
Danicia	B-2
Daniel E.	E-4
Daniella	IJ-3
Dapper Dan	M-16
Darrell, William	H-11
Dauntless	A-7
David Allen	N-9
David E.	E-4, H-4
David T.D.	L-10
Dawn Light	T-6
de Champlain, Samuel	L-2
Dean, Annie M.	D-3
Debbie Lyn	M-3
Defiance	A-7
Delaware	G-16
Deltuva	IL-5
Demolen	U-2
Denis M	M-24
Denise E.	E-4
Derek E.	E-4
Des Groseilliers	C-3
Des Plaines	C-1
Deschenes, Jos.	S-12
Desgagnés, Amelia	T-15
Desgagnés, Anna	T-15
Desgagnés, Camilla	T-15
Desgagnés, Catherine	T-15
Desgagnés, Maria	T-15
Desgagnés, Melissa	T-15
Desgagnes, Petrolia	T-15
Desgagnés, Rosaire A.	T-15
Desgagnes, Sarah	T-15
Desgagnes, Thalassa	T-15
Desgagnes, Vega	T-15
Desgagnés, Zelada	T-15
Desjardins, Alphonse	S-12
Detroit Princess	D-5
Devine, Barney	W-7
Diamond Belle	D-6
Diamond Jack	D-6
Diamond Queen	D-6
Diamond Star	T-15
Diezeborg	IW-2
Dilly, William B.	M-16
Dintelborg	IW-2
Dobrush	IC-10
Doc Morin	U-12
Doggersbank	IP-4
Donald Bert	M-3
Donald Mac	G-11

Vessel Name	Fleet #	Vessel Name	Fleet #	Vessel Name	Fleet #
Dongeborg	IW-2	Experanza IV	R-7	Flinterduin	IF-6
Donner, William H.	K-9	Eyrarbakki	W-2	Flintereems	IF-6
Dool, Tim S.	A-5			Flinterland	IF-6
Dora	IT-2			Flintermaas	IF-6
Dorothy Ann	I-6	**F**		Flinterspirit	IF-6
Dover	M-3			Flo-Mac	M-14
Doyle	C-1	Fairchem Colt	IF-1	Florence M.	M-14
Dr. Bob	T-1	Fairlane	IJ-3	Florida	G-16
Drechtborg	IW-2	Fairlift	IJ-3	Fodas Pescadores	IS-4
Dredge Primrose	M-14	Fairload	IJ-3	Ford, E.M.	P-11
Drummond Islander II	M-1	Fairmast	IJ-3	Ford, J.B.	L-2
Drummond Islander III	E-1	Fairpartner	IJ-3	Forest City	W-4
Drummond Islander IV	E-1	Fairplayer	IJ-3	Frederick, Owen M.	U-2
Duc d'Orleans	F-5	Federal Agno	IF-3	Friendship	P-9
Duc d'Orleans II	D-10	Federal Asahi	IF-3	Frisian Spring	IB-7
Duga	L-10	Federal Danube	IA-5	Frontenac	C-2
Duluth	G-13	Federal Elbe	IA-5	Frontenac Howe Islander	O-4
Durocher, Ray	D-12	Federal Ems	IA-5	Frontenac II	O-4
Dutch Runner	IG-2	Federal Fuji	IV-2	Ft. Dearborn	C-10
Dzintari	IL-1	Federal Hudson	IF-3		
		Federal Hunter	IF-3		
		Federal Katsura	IF-3	**G**	
E		Federal Kivalina	IF-3		
		Federal Kumano	IF-10	G.L.B. No. 1	P-11
Eagle	S-10	Federal Kushiro	ID-2	G.L.B. No. 2	P-11
Ebn Al Waleed	IE-2	Federal Leda	IA-5	Gadwall	IP-1
Ecosse	N-1	Federal Maas	IF-3	Gardiner, Joyce B.	P-11
Edelweiss I	E-2	Federal Mackinac	IF-3	Garganey	IP-1
Edelweiss II	E-2	Federal Manitou	IS-11	Gaynor, William C.	M-1
Edisongracht	T-17	Federal Margaree	IF-3	General	D-12
Edith J.	E-3	Federal Matane	IS-11	General Brock III	T-3
Edna G.	L-3	Federal Mattawa	IR-2	General Chemical No. 37	M-14
Edward H.	H-9	Federal Miramichi	IS-11	Georgian Queen	A-13
Eider	IP-1	Federal Nakagawa	IF-3	Georgiev, Kapitan Georgi	IN-3
Eileen C	I-2	Federal Oshima	IF-3	Geraldine	S-6
Elikon	IH-5	Federal Patriot	II-3	Gillen III, Edward E.	E-3
Elpida	IS-8	Federal Patroller	IA-5	Glen	IE-3
Elsie D.	R-7	Federal Pendant	II-3	Glenada	T-4
Emerald Isle	B-7	Federal Pioneer	IA-5	Glenora	O-4
Emerald Star	T-15	Federal Polaris	IV-2	Global Carrier	II-5
Empire Sandy	N-3	Federal Power	IA-5	Glory	IC-5
Empire State	N-9	Federal Pride	IA-5	Glory	IH-1
Empress of Canada	E-5	Federal Progress	IF-3	Goldeneye	IS-2
Emsmoon	IO-6	Federal Rhine	IF-3	Goodtime I	G-7
Enchanter	IB-5	Federal Rideau	IF-3	Goodtime III	G-8
Endeavour	A-10	Federal Saguenay	IF-3	Gott, Edwin H.	G-15
Endurance	IH-1	Federal Sakura	IF-3	Gouin, Lomer	S-12
Energy 5501	H-10	Federal Schelde	IF-3	Graham, H.E.	L-10
Energy 6506	H-10	Federal Seto	IF-3	Graham, Sandy	B-6
English River	L-1	Federal Shimanto	IF-10	Grand Fleuve	C-20
Enterprise 2000	O-2	Federal St. Laurent	IF-3	Grand Island	P-3
Environaut	G-5	Federal Venture	IF-3	Grand Portal	P-3
Epinette II	E-7	Federal Welland	IF-3	Grande Baie	E-7
Erich	M-15	Federal Weser	IA-5	Grande Caribe	IA-3
Erie Explorer	O-3	Federal Yoshino	IF-10	Grande Mariner	IA-3
Erie-West	M-14	Federal Yukon	IF-3	Grant, R.F.	L-10
Escort	B-2	Felicity	S-7	Grayfox	U-8
Escorte	L-10	Fen	IE-3	Grayling	G-20
Evening Star	S-11	Finex	IF-9	Great Blue Heron	B-11
Everlast	M-13	Flinders, Capt. Matthew	M-11	Great Lakes	K-5

Vessel Name	Fleet #	Vessel Name	Fleet #	Vessel Name	Fleet #
Great Lakes Trader	V-1	Hannah 6301	H-4	Howe Islander	C-19
Green, Magdalena	IH-8	Hannah 7701	H-4	Huron	A-14, P-8
Green, Makiri	IH-8	Hannah, Daryl C.	H-4	Huron Belle	L-8
Green, Margaretha	IB-2	Hannah, Donald C.	H-4	Huron Lady II	B-12
Green, Marinus	IH-8	Hannah, Hannah D.	H-4	Huron Maid	L-8
Green, Marion	IB-2	Hannah, James A.	H-4		
Green, Marissa	IC-8	Hannah, Kristin Lee	H-4		
Green, Marlene	IH-8	Hannah, Mark	H-4		
Greenstone II	U-7	Hannah, Mary E.	H-4		
Greenwing	IN-1	Hannah, Mary Page	S-3	I.V. No. 10	D-9
Greta V	M-16	Hannah, Peggy D.	H-4	I.V. No. 11	D-9
Gretchen B.	L-16	Hannah, Susan W.	H-4	I.V. No. 13	D-9
Griffon	C-3	Happy Ranger	IB-5	I.V. No. 14	D-9
Grue-des-Iles	S-12	Harbour Star	B-20	I.V. No. 8	D-9
Gull Isle	C-3	Harvey	U-2	I.V. No. 9	D-9
Gulmar	IG-3	Hayden, Fischer	G-13	Ian Mac	M-3
		Helene	S-4	Ida M.	R-4
		Hennepin	I-2	Ida M. II	R-4
H		Henry, Alexander	M-9	Idaho	G-16
		Hiawatha	R-7, S-13	Iglehart, J.A.W.	I-3
Haida	H-6	Highlander Sea	A-3	Illinois	G-16
Halifax	C-2	Hoey, Carolyn	G-1	Imbeau, Armand	S-12
Hamilton Energy	U-12	Hoey, Patricia	G-1	Indian Maiden	B-6
Hamilton Harbour Queen	H-2	Hoey, William	G-1	Indiana	G-16
Hammond Bay	L-12, U-2	Hogan, Joseph J.	J-1	Indiana Harbor	A-8
Hamp Thomas	H-12	Holden, John	M-16	Inglis, William	T-11
Handy Andy	M-16	Holiday	S-13	Inland Seas	I-4
Hanlan, Ned II	T-13	Hollyhock	U-3	Innisfree	C-10
Hannah 3601	H-4	Hope (The)	S-7	Innovation	L-2
Hannah 5101	H-4	Houghton	K-2	Integrity	L-2
				Intrepid III	N-1

Algowood on the St. Marys River in 2008. *(Roger LeLievre)*

Vessel Name	Fleet #	Vessel Name	Fleet #	Vessel Name	Fleet #
Inviken	IV-2	Joliet	S-27	Krios	IS-1
Invincible	L-15	Jolliet, Louis	C-20	Krista S	C-1
Iowa	G-16	Joncaire, Daniel	S-28	Kristen D	P-5
Ira	IC-11	Josee H.	L-10	Kristin	I-7
Irma	IP-5	Joseph-Savard	S-12	Kristin J.	E-3
Iroquois	M-23	Joyce Marie	T-5	Kristina Theresa	IB-4
Irvin, William A.	D-11	Jubilee Queen	J-3	Kroonborg	IW-2
Iryda	IP-5	Judge McCombs	H-3	Krystal	B-2
Isa	IP-5	Judique Flyer	R-1	Kuber, James L.	K-9
Isadora	IP-5	Juleen 1	C-18	Kuber, Lewis J.	K-9
Isarstern	IR-3	Julia	II-2	Kwasind	R-7
Island Belle I	K-8	Julie Dee	K-7	Kwintebank	IP-4
Island Clipper	V-7	Julietta	II-2		
Island Duchess	U-1	Jullane J.	E-3		
Island Express	A-14	Jumbo Challenger	IJ-3		
Island Heritage	T-3	Jumbo Javelin	IJ-3	**L**	
Island Princess	A-11	Jumbo Jubilee	IJ-3		
Island Queen	M-4, T-20	Jumbo Spirit	IJ-3	La Croche	L-10
Island Queen III	K-8	Jumbo Vision	IJ-3	La Prairie	L-10
Island Skipper	IS-6			La Salle	S-27
Island Star	K-8			Lac Como	M-16
Island Triangle	IS-6	**K**		Lac Erie	V-3
Island Wanderer	U-1			Lac Manitoba	M-14
Islander	B-3, M-22, R-9	Kaho	G-20	Lac St. Jean	M-14
Islay	N-8	Kajama	G-19	Lac St-Francois	L-10
Isle Royale Queen III	S-17	Kamenitza	IN-3	Lac Vancouver	M-16
Isle Royale Queen IV	I-9	Kaministiqua	L-14	Lady Kate	B-8
Isolda	IP-5	Kane, M.R.	T-8	Lady Kim	C-18
Ivi	IC-11	Kansas	G-16	Laguna D	ID-1
		Kasteelborg	IW-2	Lake Char	M-19
J		Kastor P	IC-12	Lake Explorer	B-2
		Katanni	I-5	Lake Express	L-4
Jackman, Capt. Henry	A-5	Kathryn Spirit	M-14	Lake Superior	B-9, IC-15
Jackson, Herbert C.	I-6	Kathy Lynn	R-10	Lambert Spirit	M-14
Jackson, W.G.	G-10	Katja	II-2	Lapointe, Ernest	M-25
Jacquelyn Nicole	S-3	Katmai Bay	U-3	Lara	II-2
Jacques-Cartier	C-21	Kayla Marie	K-3	Last Chance	C-13
Jade Star	T-15	KCL Barracuda	IT-4	Laud, Sam	A-8
Jamie L.	M-16	Keenosay	O-3	Laurentian	G-14
Jana	II-2	Keewatin	P-2	LCU 1680	N-5
Jane Ann IV	T-2	Keizersborg	IW-2	Le Bateau-Mouche	L-9
Janice C. No. 1	C-18	Kendzora, Wally	F-3	Le Draveur	C-21
Jarco 1402	R-10	Kenosha	U-2	Le Phil D.	L-10
Jarrett M	M-14	Kent Timber	IK-1	Lee, Nancy A.,	L-12
Jeanette M	D-2	Kent Trader	IK-1	Lehmann, Hans	IL-4
Jean-Raymond	M-14	Kenteau	G-2	Leitch, Gordon C.	U-12
Jerry G.	L-10	Kentucky	G-16	Leitch, John D.	U-12
Jet Express	P-12	Keweenaw Star	K-4	Lemont Trader	I-2
Jet Express II	P-12	Khudozhnik Kraynev	IF-2	Leona B.	M-21
Jet Express III	P-12	Kim R.D.	L-10	LeVoyageur	S-13
Jiimaan	O-4	King Fish 1	H-7	Liamare	IL-6
Jill Marie	C-4	Kiyi	G-20	Lime Island	V-5
Jimmy L.	S-3	Knutsen, Ellen	IK-2	Limnos	C-3
Jo Spirit	IJ-1	Knutsen, Sidsel	IK-2	Linda Jean	N-9
Johanna-C	IC-4	Knutsen, Synnove	IK-2	Lisa E.	E-4
John Francis	G-6	Knutsen, Turid	IK-2	Lisbon Express	IH-1
John Henry	K-7	Kobasic, Erika	B-2	Little Rock	B-16
Johnson, Martin E.	P-11	Kom	IN-3	Lodestar Grace	IY-1
Johnson, Reuben	F-3	Koningsborg	IW-2	Loftus, K.H.	O-3
				Loireborg	IW-2

Canadian Transport loads at Quebec City. *(Chris Winters)*

USCG *Mackinaw* casts an early winter reflection. *(Roger LeLievre)*

Vessel Name	Fleet #	Vessel Name	Fleet #	Vessel Name	Fleet #
Nordik Express	T-15	Ocean Jupiter	L-10	Orsula	IA-6
Norgoma	S-26	Ocean K. Rusby	L-10	Osborne, F.M.	O-6
Norisle	F-4	Ocean Pride	IF-4	OSC Vlistdiep	IH-4
Norris, James	U-12	Ocean Raymond Lemay	L-10	Oshawa	M-16
North Carolina	G-16	Oceanex Avalon	IO-2	Osprey	P-11
North Channel	C-7	Oceanex Sanderling	IO-2	Ostrander, G.L.	L-2
North Dakota	G-16	Odra	IP-5	Ottawa	A-14
North Fighter	IE-3	Ohio	G-16	Ottawa Express	IH-1
Northern Spirit I	S-15	Oil Queen	S-21	Outer Island	E-8
Northwestern	G-17	Ojibway	L-14, M-1		
Noyes, Hack	W-7	Okapi	IF-5		
		Oklahoma	G-16		
		Old Mission	K-6		

Vessel Name	Fleet #	Vessel Name	Fleet #	Vessel Name	Fleet #
		Olympic Melody	IO-3	P.M.L. 2501	P-11
Oakglen	C-2	Olympic Mentor	IO-3	P.M.L. 357	P-11
Oatka	B-15	Olympic Merit	IO-3	P.M.L. 9000	P-11
Obsession III	C-22	Olympic Miracle	IO-3	P.M.L. Alton	P-11
OC 181	M-14	Omni St. Laurent	L-10	P.M.L. Tucci	P-11
Ocean Abys	L-10	Omni-Atlas	L-10	P.M.L. Tucker	P-11
Ocean Bertrand Jeansonne	L-10	Omni-Richelieu	L-10	Pacific Standard	M-14
Ocean Bravo	L-10	Onego Merchant	IO-5	Paddy Miles	H-12
Ocean Charlie	L-10	Onego Trader	IO-5	Palessa	IH-3
Ocean Delta	L-10	Onego Traveller	IO-5	Pan Voyager	IS-10
Ocean Echo II	L-10	Ongiara	T-11	Panam Atlantico	IC-8
Ocean Foxtrot	L-10	Ontamich	B-13	Panam Flota	IC-8
Ocean Golf	L-10	Orfea	IT-6	Panama	B-9
Ocean Henry Bain	L-10	Oriental Kerria	IS-3	Panos G	IG-1
Ocean Hercule	L-10	Oriole	S-15	Papoose III	K-8
Ocean Intrepide	L-10	Orla	IP-5	Pathfinder	I-6
		Orna	IS-2	Pathfinder	T-7

Tug *Missouri* assists *American Mariner* through spring ice.
(Eric Treece)

Vessel Name	Fleet #
Patronicola, Calliroe	IO-3
Paula M.	M-16
Peach State	M-1
Pearkes, George R.	C-3
Pearl Mist	IP-2
Pelee Islander	O-4
Peninsula	G-11
Pennsylvania	G-16
Pere Marquette 10	E-12
Pere Marquette 41	P-1
Perelik	IN-3
Performance	S-23
Perrin, J.V.	L-10
Persenk	IN-3
Pete, C. West	B-1
Peter Wise Lake Guardian	U-5
Petite Forte	S-25
Pictured Rocks	P-3
Pierson, Robert S.	L-14
Pilica	IP-5
Pineglen	C-2
Pioneer	IC-14
Pioneer Princess	T-10
Pioneer Queen	T-10
Pioneerland	G-6
Pitts Carillon	G-2
Pitts No. 3	G-2
Playfair	T-7
Pochard	IH-3
Point Valour	T-4
Point Viking	A-2
Polaris	I-8
Polydefkis	IS-2
Polydefkis P	IC-12
Pomorze Zachodnie	IP-5
Pontokratis	IO-1
Pontoporos	IO-1
Port City Princess	P-6
Port Mechins	D-9
Power	IH-1
Prairieland	G-6
Presque Isle	G-15
Pride	W-6
Pride of Michigan	U-8
Princess Wenonah	B-3
Prinsenborg	IW-2
Provmar Terminal	U-12
Provmar Terminal II	U-12
Puffin	IH-3
Purcell, Robert W.	A-10
Purha	IF-7
Purves, John	D-8
Purvis, Ivan W.J.	P-11
Purvis, W.I. Scott	P-11
Put-In-Bay	M-22
Pyrgos	IF-5

Q-R

Vessel Name	Fleet #
Quebecois	U-12
Quinte Loyalist	O-4
R.C.L. Tug II	M-16
Racine	U-2
Radisson	S-12, S-27
Radisson, Pierre	C-3
Radium Yellowknife	N-7
Raguva	IL-5
Randolph, Curtis	D-4
Ranger III	U-7
Rapide Blanc	L-10
Rebecca	II-2
Rebecca Lynn	A-10
Redhead	IP-1
Rega	IP-5
Reiss	N-8
Reliance	P-11
Rennie, Thomas	T-11
Rest, William	T-12
Rhode Island	G-16
Richelieu	C-2
Richter, Arni J.	W-2
Richter, C.G.	W-2
Risley, Samuel	C-3
Robert John	G-11
Robert W.	T-4
Robin E.	E-4
Robin Lynn	S-6
Robinson Bay	S-23
Rochelle Kaye	R-10
Rocket	P-11
Roman, Stephen B.	E-13
Rosaire	D-9
Rosalee D.	T-4
Rosemary	M-11
Rouble, J.R.	T-1
Roxane D.	L-10
Royal Pescadores	IS-4
Ryerson, Edward L.	C-6

S

Vessel Name	Fleet #
S Pacific	IJ-2
S/VM 86	M-14
Sabina	IE-7
Sacre Bleu	S-7
Saginaw	L-14
Sagittarius	II-1
Saguenay	C-2
Sakarya	IC-6
Salvage Monarch	H-8
Salvor	M-14
Sandpiper	H-5
Sandra Mary	M-16
Santiago	IB-8

Vessel Name	Fleet #
Sarah B	G-13
Sarah No. 1	T-1
Sault au Cochon	M-14
Sauniere	A-5
Savard, Felix Antoine	S-12
Scandrett, Fred	T-12
Schlaeger, Victor L.	C-9
Schwartz, H.J.	U-2
SCL Bern	IE-7
Sea Chief	B-2
Sea Eagle II	S-25
Sea Force	IP-3
Sea Fox II	T-3
Sea Prince II	R-4
Sea Service	H-10
Sea Veteran	IV-1
Seaguardian II	IT-3
Seahound	N-1
Sealink	IT-3
Segwun	M-28
Selvick, Bonnie G.	C-1
Selvick, Carla Anne	S-3
Selvick, John M.	C-1
Selvick, Kimberly	C-1
Selvick, Sharon M.	S-3
Selvick, Steven	C-1
Selvick, William C.	S-3
Senator (The)	R-8
Seneca	IA-2
Seram Wind	IE-1
Serena	II-2
Serendipity Princess	M-20
Service Boat No. 1	L-10
Service Boat No. 4	L-10
Seymour, Wilf	M-14
Shamrock	J-2
Shannon	G-1
Shark	B-20, C-3
Sheila Kaye	M-8
Sheila P.	P-11
Shelley, J.W.	V-2
Shelter Bay	U-7
Shenandoah	R-2
Shenehon	G-14
Sherwin, John	I-6
Shipsands	T-14
Shirley Irene	K-3
Shoreline (The)	S-9
Shoreline II	S-11
Showboat Royal Grace	M-11
Siam Star	IE-5
Sichem Aneline	IE-3
Sichem Beijing	IE-3
Sichem Challenge	IE-3
Sichem Defiance	IE-3
Sichem Eva	IE-3
Sichem Manila	IE-3
Sichem Melbourne	IE-3
Sichem Mumbai	IE-3

Vessel Name	Fleet #
Sichem New York	IE-3
Sichem Onomichi	IE-3
Sichem Padua	IE-3
Sichem Palace	IE-3
Sichem Paris	IE-3
Sichem Peace	IE-3
Sichem Princess Marie-Chantal	IE-3
Sichem Singapore	IE-3
Silver Wind	IE-1
Silversides	G-18
Simcoe Islander	C-19
Simonsen	U-2
Simpson, Miss Kim	T-14
Sioux	M-1, Z-1
Sir Walter	IH-6
Siscowet	B-2
Skaftafell	IB-8
Skyline Princess	M-18
Skyline Queen	M-18
Smith Jr., L.L.	U-11
Smith, Dean R.	M-10
Smith, F.C.G.	C-3
Snohomish	S-1
Sofia	II-2
Songa Crystal	IB-6
Songa Pearl	IB-6
Soo River Belle	S-14
Soulanges	E-6
South Bass	M-22
South Carolina	G-16
South Channel	C-7
Spar Garnet	IS-7
Spar Jade	IS-7
Spar Opal	IS-7
Spar Ruby	IS-7
Spartan	L-5
Speer, Edgar B.	G-15
Spence, John	M-14
Spencer, Sarah	T-2
Spirit of Chicago	S-16
Spirit of LaSalle	S-17
Spruceglen	C-2
Spuds	R-5
St. Clair	A-8
St. John, J.S.	E-11
St. Lawrence II	B-14
St. Marys Cement	S-25
St. Marys Cement II	S-25
St. Marys Challenger	S-25
St. Marys Conquest	S-25
Stacey Dawn	C-18
Star of Chicago	S-11
Staris	IL-5
Starlight	IO-4
State of Michigan	G-17
STC 2004	B-21
Ste. Claire	M-12
Ste. Claire V (The)	A-9
Steelhead	M-19

Vessel Name	Fleet #
Stefania I	IF-8
Stella Borealis	C-15
Stellanova	IJ-3
Stellaprima	IJ-3
Stolt Kite	IS-9
Stormont	M-14
Straits Express	A-14
Straits of Mackinac II	A-14
Strekalovskiy, Mikhail	IM-2
Sturgeon	G-20
Sugar Islander II	E-1
Sullivan, Denis	P-4
Sundew	D-11
Sundstraum	IA-4
Sunliner	W-3
Superior	G-16
Susan L.	S-3
Susan Michelle	D-2
Suvorov, Aleksandr	IM-2
Swan Lake	IL-3
Sykes, Wilfred	C-6

T

Vessel Name	Fleet #
Tanker II	J-2
Tanner	K-6
Tatjana	II-2
TCCA 1	T-12
Tecumseh II	P-11
Tenacious	R-10
Tennessee	G-16
Texas	G-16
The Sullivans	B-16
Thekla	II-2
Thompson Jr., Joseph H.	U-13
Thompson, Joseph H.	U-13
Thompson, Maxine	F-3
Thousand Islander	G-4
Thousand Islander II	G-4
Thousand Islander III	G-4
Thousand Islander IV	G-4
Thousand Islander V	G-4
Thunder Cape	C-3
Timberland	G-6
Timesaver II	T-1
Timmy A.	R-5
Togue	B-2
Toni D	V-3
Toronto Express	IH-1
Torontonian	M-11
Townsend, Paul H.	I-3
Tracer	IB-5
Tracy	C-3
Tradewind Service	H-10
Tradewind Union	IT-5
Tramper	IB-5
Transit	C-20, N-4
Transporter	IB-5

Vessel Name	Fleet #
Traveller	IB-5
Tregurtha, Lee A.	I-6
Tregurtha, Paul R.	I-6
Trillium	T-11
Triumph	IH-1
Turchese	IF-4
Tuscarora	IA-2
Tuvaq	IC-9
Twolan, W.N.	A-1

U-V

Vessel Name	Fleet #
Umiak I	F-1
Umiavut	T-17
Uncle Sam 7	U-1
Undaunted	P-1
Upper Canada	L-6
Uta	II-2
Utviken	IV-2
Vaasaborg	IW-2
Vac	N-1
Valencia Express	IH-1
Valerie B.	D-12
Valley Camp	L-11
Van, Joe	D-12
Vancouverborg	IW-2
VanEnkevort, Joyce L.	V-1
Vanessa-C	IC-4
Varnebank	IP-4
Vechtborg	IW-2
Veerseborg	IF-9
Veler	U-2
Vermont	G-16
Versluis, James J.	C-11
Viateur's Spirit	M-14
Victoria	II-2
Victoriaborg	IW-2
Victorian Princess	V-4
Victorious	M-13
Victory	IH-1, K-9
Vida C.	C-16
Vigilant 1	N-1
Viking I	K-9
Vindemia	IS-5
Virginia	G-16
Virginiaborg	IW-2
Vista King	V-6
Vista Queen	V-6
Vista Star	V-6
Vlistborg	IW-2
VM/S Hercules	S-24
VM/S Maisonneuve	S-24
VM/S St. Lambert	S-24
VM/S St. Louis III	S-24
Voorneborg	IW-2
Voosborg	IW-2
Vossborg	IF-9
Voyager	S-11

Vessel Name	Fleet #	Vessel Name	Fleet #	Vessel Name	Fleet #
Voyageur	M-23	William C	I-2	Yosemite	IE-1
Voyageur II	G-9	Willmac	M-16	Yucatan	IE-1
Vysotskiy, Vladimir	IN-4	Windmill Point	T-12		

W

		Windoc	A-5		
		Windy	W-6		
		Windy II	W-6	# Z	
		Windy City	I-2		
Wagenborg, Egbert	IW-2	Winnebago	J-4	Zanis Griva	IL-1
Walpole Islander	D-1	Winona	II-2	Zeus	IW-3
Wanda III	M-28	Wisconsin	G-16	Zeynep A	IC-6
Warner, William L.	W-1	W-O Topa	IW-4	Ziemia Chelminska	IP-5
Warta	IP-5	Wolf River	G-11	Ziemia Cieszynska	IP-5
Washington	G-16, W-2	Wolfe Islander III	O-4	Ziemia Gnieznienska	IP-5
Wayward Princess	N-3	Wolverine	T-5	Ziemia Gornoslaska	IP-5
Welcome (The)	S-7	Woody	IS-2	Ziemia Lodzka	IP-5
Welland	D-2	Wyandot	S-7	Ziemia Suwalska	IP-5
Wendella	W-3	Wyatt M.	M-14	Ziemia Tarnowska	IP-5
Wendella LTD	W-3	Wyoming	G-16	Ziemia Zamojska	IP-5
Wendy Anne	A-12			Zuccolo	C-1
Wenonah	G-9				
Wenonah II	M-28	# X–Y			
Weserstern	IR-3				
West Shore	B-3	Xenia	II-2		
West Wind	B-18	Yamaska	IE-1		
Westcott II, J.W.	J-1	Yankcanuck	P-11		
Whistler	IP-1	Yankee Clipper	V-7		
Whitby	M-16	Yarmouth	IE-1		
White, H. Lee	A-8	Yellowknife	IE-1		
Whitefish Bay	U-2	Yick Hua	IC-7		
Wigeon	IP-1	YM Jupiter	IY-3		

Car ferry *Badger*, the last coal-fired steamer on the Great Lakes.
(Nathan Nieterling)

1959-2009

AV
MARITIME
DVD COLLECTION

Acheson Ventures of Port Huron, Michigan,
offers you these exciting Great Lakes Maritime DVDs
with this special *KNOW YOUR SHIPS 2009* offer!

PORT HURON TO MACKINAC RACE SERIES

BREAKING ICE: USCGC MACKINAW
OLD MACKINAW'S LAST MISSION /
NEW MACKINAW'S ICE TRIALS

FRESHWATER FOCUS:
UNDERWATER LIFE
DOCUMENTARY

Please visit our website for complete details and video summaries!

ONLY
$19.95 ea.
WITH FREE SHIPPING!

ORDER BY PHONE:
810.966.3488

ORDER ONLINE:
www.AchesonVentures.com

Fleet Listings

Charles M. Beeghly on the
St. Marys River. *(Roger LeLievre)*

GREAT LAKES / SEAWAY FLEETS

Listed after each vessel in order are: Type of Vessel, Year Built, Type of Engine, Maximum Cargo Capacity (at midsummer draft in long tons) or Gross Tonnage*, Overall Length, Breadth and Depth (from the top of the keel to the top of the upper deck beam) or Draft*. Only commercial vessels over 30 feet long are included. The figures given are as accurate as possible and are given for informational purposes only. Vessels and owners are listed alphabetically as per American Bureau of Shipping and Lloyd's Register formats. Builder yard and location, as well as other pertinent information, are listed for major vessels; former names of vessels and years of operation under the former names appear in parentheses. A number in brackets following a vessel's name indicates how many vessels, including the one listed, have carried that name.

KEY TO TYPE OF VESSEL

2B	Brigantine	**DS**	Spud Barge	**PB**	Pilot Boat
2S	2-Masted Schooner	**DV**	Drilling Vessel	**PF**	Passenger Ferry
3S	3-Masted Schooner	**DW**	Scow	**PK**	Package Freighter
4S	4-Masted Schooner	**ES**	Excursion Ship	**RR**	Roll On/Roll Off
AC	Auto Carrier	**EV**	Environmental Response	**RT**	Refueling Tanker
AT	Articulated Tug	**FB**	Fireboat	**RV**	Research Vessel
ATB	Articulated Tug/Barge	**FD**	Floating Dry Dock	**SB**	Supply Boat
BC	Bulk Carrier	**FT**	Fishing Tug	**SC**	Sand Carrier
BK	Bulk Carrier/Tanker	**GC**	General Cargo	**SR**	Search and Rescue
BT	Buoy Tender	**GL**	Gate Lifter	**SU**	Self-Unloader
CA	Catamaran	**GU**	Grain Self-Unloader	**SV**	Survey Vessel
CC	Cement Carrier	**HL**	Heavy Lift Vessel	**TB**	Tugboat
CF	Car Ferry	**IB**	Ice Breaker	**TF**	Train Ferry
CO	Container Vessel	**IT**	Integrated Tug	**TK**	Tanker
CS	Crane Ship	**ITB**	Integrated Tug/Barge	**TW**	Towboat
DB	Deck Barge	**MB**	Mailboat	**TT**	Tractor Tugboat
DH	Hopper Barge	**MU**	Museum Vessel	**TV**	Training Vessel
DR	Dredge	**PA**	Passenger Vessel		

KEY TO PROPULSION

B	Barge	**R**	Steam - Triple Exp. Compound Engine
D	Diesel	**S**	Steam - Skinner "Uniflow" Engine
DE	Diesel Electric	**T**	Steam - Turbine Engine
Q	Steam - Quad Exp. Compound Engine	**W**	Sailing Vessel (Wind)

Fleet # Fleet Name Vessel Name	Type of Vessel	Year Built	Type of Engine	Cargo Cap. or Gross*	Overall Length	Breadth	Depth or Draft*
A-1 **A. B. M. MARINE, THUNDER BAY, ON**							
McAllister 132	DB	1954	B	7,000	343' 00"	63' 00"	19' 00"
Built: Burrard Dry Dock, N. Vancouver, BC (Powell No. 1 '54-'61, Alberni Carrier '61-'77, Genmar 132 '77-'79)							
W. N. Twolan	TB	1962	D	299*	106' 00"	29' 05"	15' 00"
Built: George T. Davie & Sons, Lauzon, QC							
A-2 **ABITIBI-CONSOLIDATED INC., MONTREAL, QC**							
Point Viking	TB	1962	D	207*	98' 05"	27' 10"	13' 05"
Built: Davie Shipbuilding Co., Lauzon, QC (Foundation Viking '62-'75)							
A-3 **ACHESON VENTURES LLC, PORT HURON, MI** *(achesonventures.com)*							
Highlander Sea	ES/2S	1927	W/D	140*	154' 00"	25' 06"	14' 00"
Built: A.D. Story Shipyard, Essex, MA (Pilot '27-'76, Star Pilot '76-'98, Caledonia '98-'98)							
A-4 **ALCAN INC., MONTREAL, QC** *(alcan.com)*							
Alexis-Simard	TT	1980	D	286*	92' 00"	34' 00"	13' 07"
Built: Georgetown Shipyards Ltd., Georgetown, PEI							

ALGOMA CENTRAL CORP., ST. CATHARINES, ON *(www.algonet.com)*

*** VESSELS OPERATED & MANAGED BY SEAWAY MARINE TRANSPORT, ST. CATHARINES, ON,
A PARTNERSHIP BETWEEN ALGOMA CENTRAL AND UPPER LAKES GROUP INC.**

Agawa Canyon*   SU   1970   D   23,400   647' 00"   72' 00"   40' 00"
Built: Collingwood Shipyards, Collingwood, ON

Algobay*   SU   1978   D   34,900   730' 00"   75' 10"   46' 06"
*Built: Collingwood Shipyards, Collingwood, ON; last operated in 2002; expected to re-enter service in
December 2009 with a new forebody (Algobay '78-'94, Atlantic Trader '94-'97)*

Algocape* {2}   BC   1967   D   29,950   729' 09"   75' 04"   39' 08"
Built: Davie Shipbuilding Co., Lauzon, QC (Richelieu {3} '67-'94)

Algoisle*   BC   1963   D   26,700   730' 00"   75' 05"   39' 03"
Built: Verolme Cork Shipyard, Ltd., Cork, Ireland (Silver Isle '63-'94)

Algolake*   SU   1977   D   32,150   730' 00"   75' 06"   46' 06"
Built: Collingwood Shipyards, Collingwood, ON

Algomarine*   SU   1968   D   27,000   729' 10"   75' 04"   39' 08"
*Built: Davie Shipbuilding Co., Lauzon, QC; converted to a self-unloader by Port Weller Dry Docks, St.
Catharines, ON, in '89 (Lake Manitoba '68-'87)*

Algonorth*   BC   1971   D   28,000   729' 11"   75' 02"   42' 11"
*Built: Upper Clyde Shipbuilders, Govan, Scotland
(Temple Bar '71-'76, Lake Nipigon '76-'84, Laketon {2} '84-'86, Lake Nipigon '86-'87)*

Algontario*   BC   1960   D   29,100   730' 00"   75' 09"   40' 02"
*Built: Schlieker-Werft, Hamburg, West Germany; rebuilt and lengthened with new forebody at Davie Shipyard,
Lauzon, QC, in '77 ([**Fore Section**] Cartiercliffe Hall '76-'88, Winnipeg {2} '88-'94 [**Stern Section**] Ruhr Ore '60-'76)*

Algoport*   SU   1979   D   32,000   658' 00"   75' 10"   46' 06"
Built: Collingwood Shipyards, Collingwood, ON; scheduled for forebody replacement in 2010

Algorail* {2}   SU   1968   D   23,750   640' 05"   72' 03"   40' 00"
Built: Collingwood Shipyards, Collingwood, ON

Algosoo* {2}   SU   1974   D   31,300   730' 00"   75' 05"   44' 06"
Built: Collingwood Shipyards, Collingwood, ON; last Great Lakes vessel built with cabins at the bow

Algosteel* {2}   SU   1966   D   27,000   729' 11"   75' 04"   39' 08"
*Built: Davie Shipbuilding Co., Lauzon, QC; converted to a self-unloader by Port Weller Dry Docks, St. Catharines,
ON, in '89 (A. S. Glossbrenner '66-'87, Algogulf {1} '87-'90)*

Algoway* {2}   SU   1972   D   24,000   650' 00"   72' 00"   40' 00"
Built: Collingwood Shipyards, Collingwood, ON

Algowood*   SU   1981   D   31,750   740' 00"   76' 01"   46' 06"
Built: Collingwood Shipyards, Collingwood, ON; lengthened 10' in '00 at Port Weller Dry Docks, St. Catharines, ON

Capt. Henry Jackman*   SU   1981   D   30,550   730' 00"   76' 01"   42' 00"
*Built: Collingwood Shipyards, Collingwood, ON; converted to a self-unloader by Port Weller Dry Docks, St.
Catharines, ON, in '96 (Lake Wabush '81-'87)*

John B. Aird*   SU   1983   D   31,300   730' 00"   76' 01"   46' 06"
Built: Collingwood Shipyards, Collingwood, ON

Peter R. Cresswell*   SU   1982   D   31,700   730' 00"   76' 01"   42' 00"
*Built: Collingwood Shipyards, Collingwood, ON; converted to a self-unloader by Port Weller Dry Docks,
St. Catharines, ON, in '98 (Algowest '82-'01)*

Tim S. Dool*   SU   1967   D   31,250   730' 00"   77' 11"   39' 08"
*Built: St. John Shipbuilding & Drydock Co., St. John, NB; widened by 3' at Port Weller Dry Docks, St. Catharines,
ON, in '96 (Senneville '67-'94, Algoville '94-'08)*

ALGOMA SHIPPING LTD., ST. CATHARINES, ON – DIVISION OF ALGOMA CENTRAL CORP.

Algoma Discovery   BC   1987   D   35,532   729' 00"   75' 09"   48' 05"
Built: 3 Maj Brodogradiliste d.d., Rijeka, Croatia (Malinska '87-'97, Daviken '97-'08)

Algoma Guardian   BC   1987   D   35,532   729' 00"   75' 09"   48' 05"
Built: 3 Maj Brodogradiliste d.d., Rijeka, Croatia (Omisalj '87-'97, Goviken '97-'08)

Algoma Spirit   BC   1986   D   35,532   729' 00"   75' 09"   48' 05"
Built: 3 Maj Brodogradiliste d.d., Rijeka, Croatia (Petka '86-'00, Sandviken '00-'08)

ALGOMA TANKERS LTD., ST. CATHARINES, ON – DIVISION OF ALGOMA CENTRAL CORP.

Algocanada   TK   2008   D   11,062   426' 00"   65' 00"   32' 08"
Built: Eregli Shipyard, Zonguldak, Turkey

Algoeast   TK   1977   D   9,750   431' 05"   65' 07"   35' 05"
*Built: Mitsubishi Heavy Industries Ltd., Shimonoseki, Japan; converted from single to double hull by Port Weller
Dry Docks, St. Catharines, ON, in '00 (Texaco Brave {2} '77-'86, Le Brave '86-'97, Imperial St. Lawrence {2} '97-'97)*

Manitowoc is the former *Earl W. Oglebay*. She was renamed in 2008. *(Roger LeLievre)*

| Algonova {2} | TK | 2008 | D | 11,062 | 426' 00" | 65' 00" | 32' 08" |

Built: Eregli Shipyard, Zonguldak, Turkey (Eregli 04 '07-'08)

| Algosar {2} | TK | 1978 | D | 10,099 | 432' 06" | 65' 00" | 29' 04" |

Built: Levingston Shipbuilding Co., Orange, TX (Gemini '78-'05)

| Algoscotia | TK | 2004 | D | 18,010 | 488' 01" | 78' 00" | 42' 00" |

Built: Jiangnan Shipyard (Group) Co. Ltd., Shangahi, Peoples Republic of China

| Algosea | TK | 1998 | D | 16,775 | 472' 04" | 75' 04" | 41'09" |

Built: Alabama Shipyard Inc., Mobile, Ala. (Aggersborg '98-'05)

SOCIÉTÉ QUÉBECOISE D' EXPLORATION MINIÈRE, SAINTE-FOY, QC – CHARTERER

| Sauniere | SU | 1970 | D | 23,900 | 642' 10" | 74' 10" | 42' 00" |

Built: Lithgows Ltd., East Yard, Glasgow, Scotland; lengthened 122' by Swan Hunter Ship Repairers, North Shields, UK, in '75; converted to a self-unloader by Herb Fraser & Associates, Port Colborne, ON, in '76
(Bulknes '70-'70, Brookknes '70-'76, Algosea {1} '76-'82)

VESSEL JOINTLY OWNED BY ALGOMA CENTRAL MARINE AND UPPER LAKES SHIPPING LTD.

| Windoc {2} | BC | 1959 | B | 29,100 | 730' 00" | 75' 09" | 40' 02" |

Built: Schlicting-Werft Willy H. Schlieker, East Germany; rebuilt and lengthened with new forebody at Davie Shipbuilding Co., Lauzon, QC, in '78; damaged by fire in 2001; laid up and awaiting a decision on its future at Port Weller, ON ([Stern Section] Rhine Ore '59-'76, [Fore Section] Steelcliffe Hall '76-'88)

A-6   **AMERICAN ACADEMY OF INDUSTRY, CHICAGO, IL** (aai-acacia.org)

| Acacia | MU | 1944 | DE | 1,025* | 180' 00" | 37' 00" | 17' 04" |

Built: Marine Ironworks and Shipbuilding Corp., Duluth, MN; former U.S. Coast Guard bouy tender/ icebreaker was decommissioned in '06; scheduled to become a museum near Chicago, IL
(Launched as USCGC Thistle [WAGL-406])

A-7   **AMERICAN MARINE CONSTRUCTORS INC., BENTON HARBOR, MI** (americanmarineconstructors.com)

| Alice E | TB | 1944 | T | 146* | 81' 01" | 24' 00" | 9' 10" |

Built: George Lawley & Son Corp., Neponset, MA

| Defiance | TW | 1966 | D | 26* | 44' 08" | 18' 00" | 6' 00" |

A-8   **AMERICAN STEAMSHIP CO., WILLIAMSVILLE, NY** (americansteamship.com)

| Adam E. Cornelius {4} | SU | 1973 | D | 28,200 | 680' 00" | 78' 00" | 42' 00" |

Built: American Shipbuilding Co., Toledo, OH (Roger M. Kyes '73-'89)

| American Century | SU | 1981 | D | 78,850 | 1,000' 00" | 105' 00" | 56' 00" |

Built: Bay Shipbuilding Co., Sturgeon Bay, WI (Columbia Star '81-'06)

| American Courage | SU | 1979 | D | 23,800 | 636' 00" | 68' 00" | 40' 00" |

Built: Bay Shipbuilding Co., Sturgeon Bay, WI (Fred R. White Jr. '79-'06)

| American Fortitude | SU | 1953 | T | 22,300 | 690' 00" | 70' 00" | 37' 00" |

Built: American Shipbuilding Co., Lorain, OH; converted to a self-unloader by Bay Shipbuilding, Sturgeon Bay, WI, in '81 (Ernest T. Weir {2} '53-'78, Courtney Burton '78-'06)

| American Integrity | SU | 1978 | D | 78,850 | 1,000' 00" | 105' 00" | 56' 00" |

Built: Bay Shipbuilding Co., Sturgeon Bay, WI (Lewis Wilson Foy '78-'91, Oglebay Norton '91-'06)

| American Mariner | SU | 1980 | D | 37,200 | 730' 00" | 78' 00" | 45' 00" |

Built: Bay Shipbuilding Co., Sturgeon Bay, WI (Laid down as Chicago {3})

| American Republic | SU | 1981 | D | 24,800 | 634' 10" | 68' 00" | 40' 00" |

Built: Bay Shipbuilding Co., Sturgeon Bay, WI

| American Spirit | SU | 1978 | D | 59,700 | 1,004' 00" | 105' 00" | 50' 00" |

Built: American Shipbuilding Co., Lorain, OH (George A. Stinson '78-'04)

| American Valor | SU | 1953 | T | 25,500 | 767' 00" | 70' 00" | 36' 00" |

Built: American Shipbuilding Co., Lorain, OH; lengthened 120' by Fraser Shipyard, Superior, WI, in '74, converted to a self-unloader in '82 (Armco '53-'06)

| American Victory | SU | 1942 | T | 26,300 | 730' 00" | 75' 00" | 39' 03" |

Built: Bethlehem Shipbuilding and Drydock Co., Sparrows Point, MD; converted from saltwater tanker to a Great Lakes bulk carrier by Maryland Shipbuilding in '61; converted to a self-unloader by Bay Shipbuilding Co., Sturgeon Bay, WI, in '82 (Laid down as Marquette. USS Neshanic [AO-71] '42-'47, Gulfoil '47-'61, Pioneer Challenger '61-'62, Middletown '62-'06)

| Buffalo {3} | SU | 1978 | D | 23,800 | 634' 10" | 68' 00" | 40' 00" |

Built: Bay Shipbuilding Co., Sturgeon Bay, WI

| Burns Harbor {2} | SU | 1980 | D | 78,850 | 1,000' 00" | 105' 00" | 56' 00" |

Built: Bay Shipbuilding Co., Sturgeon Bay, WI

H. Lee White {2}	SU	1974	D	35,200	704' 00"	78' 00"	45' 00"

Built: Bay Shipbuilding Co., Sturgeon Bay, WI

Indiana Harbor	SU	1979	D	78,850	1,000' 00"	105' 00"	56' 00"

Built: Bay Shipbuilding Co., Sturgeon Bay, WI

John J. Boland {4}	SU	1973	D	33,800	680' 00"	78' 00"	45' 00"

Built: Bay Shipbuilding Co., Sturgeon Bay, WI (Charles E. Wilson '73-'00)

Sam Laud	SU	1975	D	23,800	634' 10"	68' 00"	40' 00"

Built: Bay Shipbuilding Co., Sturgeon Bay, WI

St. Clair {3}	SU	1976	D	44,000	770' 00"	92' 00"	52' 00"

Built: Bay Shipbuilding Co., Sturgeon Bay, WI

Walter J. McCarthy Jr.	SU	1977	D	78,850	1,000' 00"	105' 00"	56' 00"

Built: Bay Shipbuilding Co., Sturgeon Bay, WI (Belle River '77-'90)

A-9   AMHERSTBURG FERRY CO. INC, AMHERSTBURG, ON

Columbia V (The)	PA/CF	1946	D	65*	65' 00"	28' 10"	8' 06"

Built: Champion Auto Ferries, Algonac, MI (Crystal O, St. Clair Flats)

Ste. Claire V (The)	PA/CF	1997	D	82*	86' 06"	32' 00"	6' 00"

Built: Les Ateliers Maurice Bourbonnais Ltée, Gatineau, QC (Courtney O., M. Bourbonnais)

A-10   ANDRIE INC., MUSKEGON, MI *(andrie.com)*

A-390	TK	1982	B	2,346*	310' 00"	60' 00"	19' 03"

Built: St. Louis Shipbuilding & Steel Co., St. Louis, MO (Canonie 40 '82-'92)

A-397	TK	1962	B	2,928*	270' 00"	60' 00"	25' 00"

Built: Dravo Corp., Pittsburgh, PA (Auntie Mame '62-'91, Iron Mike '91-'93)

A-410	TK	1955	B	3,793*	335' 00"	54' 00"	26' 06"

Built: Ingalls Shipbuilding Corp., Birmingham, AL (Methane '55-'63, B-6400 '63-'71, Kelly '71-'86, Canonie 50 '86-'93)

Barbara Andrie	TB	1940	D	298*	121' 10"	29' 06"	16' 00"

Built: Pennsylvania Shipyards Inc., Beaumont, TX (Edmond J. Moran '40-'76)

Endeavour	TK	2009	B		360' 00"	60' 00"	24' 00"

Built: Jeffboat LLC, Jeffersonville, IN

Karen Andrie {2}	TB	1965	D	433*	120' 00"	31' 06"	16' 00"

Built: Gulfport Shipbuilding, Port Arthur, TX (Sarah Hays '65-'93)

Rebecca Lynn	TB	1964	D	433*	120' 00"	31' 08"	18' 09"

Built: Gulfport Shipbuilding, Port Arthur, TX (Kathrine Clewis '64-'96)

Robert W. Purcell	TB	1943	D	29*	45' 02"	12' 08"	7' 09"

Built: Sturgeon Bay Shipbuilding, Sturgeon Bay, WI

Ronald J. Dahlke	TB	1903	D	58*	63' 03"	17' 05"	9' 03"

Built: Johnston Bros., Ferrysburg, MI (Bonita '03-'14, Chicago Harbor No. 4 '14-'60, Eddie B. '60-'69, Seneca Queen '69-'70, Ludington '70-'96, Seneca Queen '96-'04)

A-11   APOSTLE ISLANDS CRUISE SERVICE, BAYFIELD, WI *(apostleisland.com)*

Island Princess {2}	ES	1973	D	63*	65' 07"	20' 05"	7' 03"

Built: Defoe Shipbuilding Co., Bay City, MI

A-12   AQUA BLUE MARINE LLC, BEAVER ISLAND, MI

Wendy Anne	TB	1955	D	89*	71' 00"	19' 05"	9' 07"

(Fort Point)

A-13   ARGEE BOAT CRUISES LTD., PENETANGUISHENE, ON *(georgianbaycruises.com)*

Georgian Queen	ES	1918	D	249*	119' 00"	36' 00"	16' 06"

Built: Port Arthur Shipbuilding, Port Arthur, ON (Victoria '18-'18, Murray Stewart '18-'48, David Richard '48-'79)

A-14   ARNOLD TRANSIT CO., MACKINAC ISLAND, MI *(arnoldline.com)*

Algomah	PF/PK	1961	D	81*	93' 00"	31' 00"	8' 00"

Built: Paasch Marine Services Inc., Erie, PA

Beaver	CF	1952	D	83*	64' 09"	30' 02"	8' 00"

Built: Lock City Machine/Marine, Sault Ste. Marie, MI

Chippewa {6}	PF/PK	1962	D	81*	93' 00"	31' 00"	8' 00"

Built: Paasch Marine Services Inc., Erie, PA

Corsair	CF	1955	D	98*	94' 06"	33' 00"	8' 06"

Built: Blount Marine Corp., Warren, RI

Huron {5}	PF/PK	1955	D	99*	91' 06"	25' 00"	10' 01"

Built: Paasch Marine Services Inc., Erie, PA

Fleet #	Fleet Name / Vessel Name	Type of Vessel	Year Built	Type of Engine	Cargo Cap. or Gross*	Overall Length	Breadth	Depth or Draft*
	Island Express	PF/CA	1988	D	90*	82' 07"	28' 06"	8' 05"
	Built: Gladding-Hearn Shipbuilding, Somerset, MA							
	Mackinac Express	PF/CA	1987	D	90*	82' 07"	28' 06"	8' 05"
	Built: Gladding-Hearn Shipbuilding, Somerset, MA							
	Mackinac Islander	CF	1947	D	99*	84' 00"	30' 00"	8' 03"
	Built: Sturgeon Bay Shipbuilding, Sturgeon Bay, WI (Drummond Islander '47-'02)							
	Ottawa {2}	PF/PK	1959	D	81*	93' 00"	31' 00"	8' 00"
	Built: Paasch Marine Services Inc., Erie, PA							
	Straits Express	PF/CA	1995	D	99*	101' 00"	29' 11"	6' 08"
	Built: Marinette Marine Corp., Marinette, WI							
	Straits of Mackinac II	PF/PK	1969	D	89*	89' 11"	27' 00"	8' 08"
	Built: Blount Marine Corp., Warren, RI							
A-15	**ASHLAND BAYFIELD CRUISE LINE INC., WASHBURN, WI**							
	Ashland Bayfield Express	PA	1995	D	13*	49' 00"	18' 05"	5' 00"
	Built: Bellecraft Industries, Naples, FL (Sea Ventue II)							
A-16	**ASI GROUP LTD., ST. CATHARINES, ON** *(asi-group.com)*							
	ASI Clipper	SV	1939	D	64*	70' 00"	23' 00"	6' 06"
	Built: Port Colborne Iron Works, Port Colborne, ON (Stanley Clipper '39-'94, Nadro Clipper '94-'08)							
B-1	**B & L TUG SERVICE, THESSALON, ON**							
	C. West Pete	TB	1958	D	29*	65' 00"	17' 05"	6' 00"
	Built: Erieau Shipbuilding & Drydock Co. Ltd., Erieau, ON							
B-2	**BASIC TOWING INC., ESCANABA, MI** *(basicmarine.com)*							
	Danicia	TB	1944	DE	382*	110' 02"	27' 03"	15' 07"
	Built: Ira S. Bushy and Sons Inc., Brooklyn, NY (USCGC Chinook [WYT / WYTM-96] '44-'86, Tracie B '86-'98)							
	Erika Kobasic	TB	1939	DE	226*	110' 00"	26' 05"	15' 01"
	Built: Gulfport Shipbuilding, Port Arthur, TX (USCGC Arundel [WYT / WYTM-90] '39-'84, Karen Andrie {1} '84-'90)							
	Escort	TB	1969	D	26*	50' 00"	13' 00"	7' 00"
	Built: Jakobson Shipyard, Oyster Bay, NY							
	Krystal	TB	1954	D	23*	45' 02"	12' 08"	6' 00"
	Built: Roamer Boat Co., Holland, MI (ST-2168 '54-'62, Thunder Bay '62-'02)							
	Lake Explorer	RV	1962	D	69*	82' 10"	17' 07"	5' 11"
	Former EPA research vessel; inactive at Escanaba, MI (USCGC Point Roberts [WPB-82332] '62-'92)							
	Nickelena	TB	1973	D	356*	109' 00"	30' 06"	16' 03"
	Built: Marinette Marine Corp., Marinette, WI (USS Chetek [YTB-827] '73-'96, Chetek '96-'00, Koziol '00-'08)							
	Sea Chief	TB	1952	D	390*	107' 00"	26' 06"	14' 10"
	Built: Avondale Marine Ways Inc., Westwego, LA; (U. S. Army LT-1944 '52-'62, USCOE Washington '62-'00)							
	Siscowet	RV	1946	D	54*	57' 00"	14' 06"	7' 00"
	Former U.S. Department of the Interior research vessel; inactive at Escanaba, MI							
	Togue	RV	1975	D	95*	73' 00"	22' 00"	10' 00"
B-3	**BAY CITY BOAT LINES LLC, BAY CITY, MI** *(baycityboatlines.com)*							
	Islander {1}	ES	1946	D	39*	53' 04"	21' 00"	5' 05"
	Built: Knudsen Brothers Shipbuilding Co., Superior, WI							
	Princess Wenonah	ES	1954	D	96*	64' 09"	32' 09"	9' 09"
	Built: Sturgeon Bay Shipbuilding Co., Sturgeon Bay, WI (William M. Miller '54-'98)							
	West Shore {2}	ES	1947	D	94*	64' 10"	30' 00"	9' 03"
	Built: Sturgeon Bay Shipbuilding Co., Sturgeon Bay, WI; inactive at Bay City, MI							
B-4	**BAY SHIPBUILDING CO., STURGEON BAY, WI** *(manitowocmarine.com)*							
	Bayship	TB	1943	D	19*	45' 00"	12' 06"	6' 00"
	Built: Sturgeon Bay Shipbuilding Co., Sturgeon Bay, WI (Sturshipco)							
B-5	**BAYSAIL, BAY CITY, MI** *(baysailbaycity.org)*							
	Appledore IV	2S/ES	1989	W/D	48*	85' 00"	19' 00"	9' 06"
	Built: Trewogy Yachts, Palm Coast, FL							
	Appledore V	2S/ES	1992	W/D	34*	65' 00"	16' 00"	8' 06"
	Built: Trewogy Yachts, Palm Coast, FL							

SALUTING THE RYERSON

Edward L. Ryerson in the Rock Cut on her first trip of 2008. *(Chris Winters)*

The steamer *Edward L. Ryerson* holds the record for the most appearance in these pages over 50 years. With her sleek lines, it's easy to see why. In keeping with tradition, here are a few new and old images to enjoy.

Ryerson in the 1960s (left), and last summer.
(Tom Manse, Roger LeLievre)

Edward L. Ryerson upbound under a beautiful summer sky. (Roger LeLievre)

B-6   BEAUSOLEIL FIRST NATION TRANSPORTATION, CHRISTIAN ISLAND, ON *(chimnissing.ca)*

Indian Maiden	PA/CF	1987	D	91.5*	73' 06"	23' 00"	8' 00"

Built: Duratug Shipyard & Fabricating Ltd., Port Dover, ON

Sandy Graham	PA/CF	1957	D	212*	125' 07"	39' 09"	8' 00"

Built: Barbour Boat Works Inc., New Bern, NC

B-7   BEAVER ISLAND BOAT CO., CHARLEVOIX, MI *(www.bibco.com)*

Beaver Islander	PF/CF	1963	D	95*	96' 03"	27' 05"	9' 09"

Built: Sturgeon Bay Shipbuilding, Sturgeon Bay, WI

Emerald Isle {2}	PF/CF	1997	D	95*	130' 00"	38' 08"	12' 00"

Built: Washburn & Doughty Associates Inc., East Boothbay, ME

B-8   BEST OF ALL TOURS LTD., ERIE, PA *(piboattours.com)*

Lady Kate {2}	ES	1952	D	11*	59' 03"	15' 00"	4' 00"

Built: J. W. Nolan & Sons, Erie, PA (G. A. Boeckling II, Cedar Point III, Island Trader '89-'97)

B-9   BILLINGTON CONTRACTING INC., DULUTH, MN

Lake Superior	TB	1943	D	248*	114' 00"	26' 00"	13' 08"

Built: Tampa Marine Corp., Tampa, FL (Major Emil H. Block '43-'47, U. S. Army LT-18 '47-'50)

Panama	DS	1942	B		210' 01"	44' 01"	10' 01"

B-10   BLACK CREEK CONSTRUCTION CO., NANTICOKE, ON

H. H. Misner	TB	1946	D	28*	66' 09"	16' 04"	4' 05"

Built: George Gamble, Port Dover, ON

B-11   BLUE HERON CO., TOBERMORY, ON *(blueheronco.com)*

Blue Heron V	ES	1983	D	24*	54' 06"	17' 05"	7' 02"

Built: Kanter Yacht Corp., St. Thomas, ON

Great Blue Heron	ES	1994	D	112*	79' 00"	22' 00"	6' 05"

Built: Hike Metal Products, Wheatley, ON

B-12   BLUEWATER EXCURSIONS INC., FORT GRATIOT, MI *(huronlady.com)*

Huron Lady II	ES	1993	D	82*	65' 00"	19' 00"	10' 00"

Built: Navigator Boat Works (Lady Lumina '93-'99)

B-13   BLUE WATER FERRY CO., SOMBRA, ON *(bluewaterferry.com)*

Daldean	CF	1951	D	145*	75' 00"	35' 00"	7' 00"

Built: Erieau Shipbuilding & Drydock Co. Ltd., Erieau, ON

Ontamich	CF	1939	D	55*	65' 00"	28' 10"	8' 06"

Built: Champion Auto Ferries, Harsens Island, MI (Harsens Island '39-'73)

B-14   BRIGANTINE INC., KINGSTON, ON *(brigantine.ca)*

St. Lawrence II	TV	1954	W/D	34*	72' 00"	15' 00"	8' 06"

Built: Kingston Shipyards, Kingston, ON

B-15   BRUCE VON RIEDEL, KNIFE RIVER, MN

Oatka	TB	1935	D	10*	40' 00"	10' 00"	4' 06"

Built: Marine Iron & Shipbuilding Co., Duluth, MN

B-16   BUFFALO AND ERIE COUNTY NAVAL & MILITARY PARK, BUFFALO, NY *(buffalonavalpark.org)*

Croaker	MU	1944	D	1,526*	311' 07"	27' 02"	33' 09"

Former U. S. Navy "Gato" class submarine IXSS-246; open to the public at Buffalo, NY

Little Rock	MU	1945	T	10,670*	610' 01"	66' 04"	25' 00"

Former U. S. Navy "Cleveland / Little Rock" class guided missile cruiser; open to the public at Buffalo, NY

The Sullivans	MU	1943	T	2,500*	376' 06"	39' 08"	22' 08"

Former U. S. Navy "Fletcher" class destroyer; open to the public at Buffalo, NY (Launched as USS Putnam)

B-17   BUFFALO CHARTERS INC. , BUFFALO, NY *(missbuffalo.com)*

Miss Buffalo II	ES	1972	D	88*	81' 09"	24' 00"	6' 00"

B-18   BUFFALO INDUSTRIAL DIVING CO. (BIDCO), BUFFALO, NY *(bidcomarine.com)*

West Wind	TB	1941	D	54*	60' 04"	17' 01"	7' 07"

Built: Lester F. Alexander Co., New Orleans, LA (West Wind '41-'46, Russell 2 '61-'97)

B-19   BUFFALO DEPARTMENT OF PUBLIC WORKS, BUFFALO, NY

	Edward M. Cotter	FB	1900	D	208*	118' 00"	24' 00"	11' 06"

Built: Crescent Shipbuilding, Elizabeth, NJ (W. S. Grattan 1900-'53, Firefighter '53-'54)

B-20   BUS & BOAT COMPANY, TORONTO, ON *(thebusandboatcompany.com)*

	Harbour Star	ES	1978	D	45*	63' 06"	15' 09"	3' 09"

Built: Eastern Equipment Ltd., LaSalle, QC (K. Wayne Simpson '78-'95)

	Shark	ES	2003	Gas	10*	39' 05"	14' 09"	36' 00"

B-21   BUSCH MARINE INC., CARROLLTON, MI

	Gregory J. Busch	TB	1919	D	299*	151' 00"	28' 00"	16' 09"

Built: Whitney Bros. Co., Superior, WI (Humaconna '19-'77)

	STC 2004	TK	1986	B	2,364	240' 00"	50' 00"	9' 05"

Built: St. Louis Shipbuilding & Steel Co., St. Louis, MO

C-1   CALUMET RIVER FLEETING INC., CHICAGO, IL

	Bonnie G. Selvick	TB	1981	D	45*	51' 09"	17' 00"	6' 01"

(Captain Robbie '81-'90, Philip M. Pearse '90-'97, Chris Ann '97-'09)

	Des Plaines	TW	1956	D	175*	98' 00"	28' 00"	8' 04"

Built: St. Louis Shipbuilding & Steel Co., St. Louis, MO

	Doyle	TB	1932	D	36*	62' 00"	16' 01"	8' 00"

Built: Hans Hansen Welding Co., Toledo, OH (G. F. Becker, Baldy B. ?-'08)

	John M. Selvick	TB	1898	D	256*	118' 00"	24' 00"	12' 07"

Built: Chicago Shipbuilding Co., Chicago, IL (Illinois {1} 1898-'41, John Roen III '41-'74)

	Kimberly Selvick	TW	1975	D	93*	51' 10"	28' 00"	10' 00"

Built: Grafton Boat Co., Grafton, IL (Scout '75-'02)

	Krista S	TB	1954	D	95*	72' 00"	22' 00"	8' 00"

Built: Pascagoula, MS (Sea Wolf '54-'01, Jimmy Wray '01-'08)

	Nathan S	TB	1951	D	144*	90' 00"	24' 00"	12' 00"

Built: Ira S. Bushey & Sons Inc., Brooklyn, NY (Huntington '51-'05, Spartacus '05-'06, Huntington '06-'08)

	Niki S	TW	1971	D	39*	42' 00"	18' 00"	6' 00"

Built: Scully Bros. Boat Builders, Morgan City LA (Miss Josie '71-'79, Matador VI '79-'08))

	Steven Selvick	TB	1954	D	120*	82' 00"	24' 06"	11' 06"

Built: Defoe Shipbuilding Co., Bay City, MI (John A. McGuire '54-'87, William Hoey {1} '87-'94, Margaret Ann '94-'08)

	Zuccolo	TB	1954	D	76*	66' 00"	19' 00"	9' 00"

(Sanita '54-'77, Soo Chief '77-'81, Susan M. Selvick '81-'96, Nathan S. '96-'02, John M. Perry '02-'08)

C-2   CANADA STEAMSHIP LINES INC., MONTREAL, QC *(csl.ca)*
       (VESSELS MANAGED BY V.SHIPS CANADA INC., MONTREAL, QC)

	Atlantic Erie	SU	1985	D	37,411	736' 07"	75' 10"	50' 00"

Built: Collingwood Shipyards, Collingwood, ON (Hon. Paul Martin '85-'88)

	Atlantic Huron {2}	SU	1984	D	34,800	736' 07"	78' 01"	46' 06"

*Built: Collingwood Shipyards, Collingwood, ON; converted to a self-unloader in '89 and widened 3' in '03 at Port
Weller Dry Docks, St. Catharines, ON (Prairie Harvest '84-'89, Atlantic Huron {2} '89-'94, Melvin H. Baker II {2} '94-'97)*

	Atlantic Superior	SU	1982	D	36,219	730' 00"	75' 10"	50' 00"

Built: Collingwood Shipyards, Collingwood, ON (Atlantic Superior '82-'97, M. H. Baker III '97-'03)

	Birchglen {2}	BC	1983	D	33,824	730' 01"	75' 09"	48' 00"

*Built: Govan Shipyards, Glasgow, Scotland
(Canada Marquis '83-'91, Federal Richelieu '91-'91, Federal MacKenzie '91-'01, MacKenzie '01-'02)*

	Cedarglen {2}	BC	1959	D	29,510	730' 00"	75' 09"	40' 02"

*Built: Schlieker-Werft, Hamburg, West Germany; rebuilt, lengthened with a new forebody at Davie Shipbuilding
Co., Lauzon, QC, in '77 ([**Stern Section**] Ems Ore '59-'76, [**Fore Section**] Montcliffe Hall '76-'88, Cartierdoc '88-'02)*

	CSL Assiniboine	SU	1977	D	36,768	739' 10"	78' 01"	48' 05"

*Built: Davie Shipbuilding Co., Lauzon, QC; rebuilt with a new forebody at Port Weller Dry Docks, St.
Catharines, ON, in '05 (Jean Parisien '77-'05)*

	CSL Laurentien	SU	1977	D	37,795	739' 10"	78' 01"	48' 05"

*Built: Collingwood Shipyards, Collingwood, ON; rebuilt with new forebody in '01 at Port Weller Dry Docks,
St. Catharines, ON (Stern section: Louis R. Desmarais '77-'01)*

	CSL Niagara	SU	1972	D	37, 694	739' 10"	78' 01"	48' 05"

*Built: Collingwood Shipyards, Collingwood, ON; rebuilt with a new forebody in '99 at Port Weller Dry Docks,
St. Catharines, ON (Stern section: J. W. McGiffin '72-'99)*

	CSL Tadoussac	SU	1969	D	30,051	730' 00"	78' 00"	42' 00"

Built: Collingwood Shipyards, Collingwood, ON; rebuilt with new midbody, widened 3' at Port Weller Dry Docks, St. Catharines, ON, in '01 (Tadoussac {2} '69-'01)

	Frontenac {5}	SU	1968	D	26,822	729' 07"	75' 03"	39' 08"

Built: Davie Shipbuilding Co., Lauzon, QC; converted to a self-unloader by Collingwood Shipyards, Collingwood, ON, in '73

	Halifax	SU	1963	T	29,283	730' 02"	75' 00"	39' 03"

Built: Davie Shipbuilding Co., Lauzon, QC; converted to a self-unloader, deepened 6' at Port Arthur Shipbuilding, Thunder Bay, ON, in '80 (Frankcliffe Hall {2} '63-'88)

	Mapleglen {3}	BC	1981	D	38,294	730' 00"	76' 01"	47' 03"

Built: N.V. Cockerill Yards, Hoboken, Belgium (Federal Maas {1} '81-'95, Lake Michigan '95-'09)

	Nanticoke	SU	1980	D	35,123	729' 10"	75' 08"	46' 06"

Built: Collingwood Shipyards, Collingwood, ON

	Oakglen {3}	BC	1980	D	38,294	730' 00"	76' 01"	47' 03"

Built: Boelwerf Vlaanderen Shipbuilding N.V., Temse, Belgium (Federal Danube '80-'95, Lake Ontario '95-'09)

	Pineglen {2}	BC	1985	D	33,197	736' 07"	75' 10"	42' 00"

Built: Collingwood Shipyards, Collingwood, ON (Paterson '85-'02)

	Richelieu {3}	BC	1981	D	38,294	730' 00"	76' 01"	47' 03"

Built: Boelwerf Vlaanderen Shipbuilding N.V., Temse, Belgium (Federal Ottawa '80-'95, Lake Erie '95-'09)

	Rt. Hon. Paul J. Martin	SU	1973	D	37,694	739' 10"	78' 01"	48' 05"

Built: Collingwood Shipyards, Collingwood, ON; rebuilt with a new forebody in '00 at Port Weller Dry Docks, St. Catharines, ON (Stern section: H. M. Griffith '73-'00)

	Saguenay {3}	BC	1981	D	38,294	730' 00"	76' 01"	47' 03"

Built: Boelwerf Vlaanderen Shipbuilding N.V., Temse, Belgium Federal Thames '81-'95, Lake Superior '95-'09)

	Spruceglen {2}	BC	1983	D	33,824	730' 01"	75' 09"	48' 00"

Built: Govan Shipyards, Glasgow, Scotland
(Selkirk Settler '83-'91, Federal St. Louis '91-'91, Federal Fraser {2} '91-2001, Fraser '01-'02)

C-3 CANADIAN COAST GUARD (FISHERIES AND OCEANS CANADA), OTTAWA, ON

(www.ccg-gcc.gc.ca) ***CENTRAL AND ARCTIC REGION, SARNIA, ON***

	Cape Discovery	SR	2004	D	34*	47' 09"	14' 00"	4' 05"
	Cape Hurd	SR	1982	D	55*	70' 10"	18' 00"	8' 09"

(CG 126 '82-'85)

***Lee A. Tregurtha* at sunset.** *(Roger LeLievre)*

Fleet #	Fleet Name / Vessel Name	Type of Vessel	Year Built	Type of Engine	Cargo Cap. or Gross*	Overall Length	Breadth	Depth or Draft*
	Caribou Isle	BT	1985	D	92*	75' 06"	19' 08"	7' 04"
	Cape Dundas	SR	2004	D	39*	47' 09"	14' 00"	4' 05"
	Cape Storm	SR	1999	D	34*	47' 09"	14' 00"	4' 05"
	Cove Isle	BT	1980	D	92*	65' 07"	19' 08"	7' 04"
	Griffon	IB	1970	D	2,212*	234' 00"	49' 00"	21' 06"
	Built: Davie Shipbuilding Co., Lauzon, QC							
	Gull Isle	BT	1980	D	80*	65' 07"	19' 08"	7' 04"
	Limnos	RV	1968	D	460*	147' 00"	32' 00"	12' 00"
	Built: Port Weller Dry Docks, St. Catharines, ON							
	Samuel Risley	IB	1985	D	1,988*	228' 09"	47' 01"	21' 09"
	Built: Vito Steel Boat & Barge Construction Ltd., Delta, BC							
	Shark	RV	1971	D	30*	52' 06"	14' 09"	7' 03"
	Thunder Cape	SR	2000	D	34*	47' 09"	14' 00"	4' 05"
	LAURENTIAN REGION, QUÉBEC, QC *(Vessels over 100' only have been listed)*							
	Amundsen	RV	1978	D	5,910*	295' 09"	63' 09"	31' 04"
	Built: Burrard Dry Dock Co., N. Vancouver, BC (Sir John Franklin '78-'03)							
	Des Groseilliers	IB	1983	D	5,910*	322' 07"	64' 00"	35' 06"
	Built: Port Weller Dry Docks, St. Catharines, ON							
	F. C. G. Smith	SV	1985	D	439*	114' 02"	45' 11"	11' 02"
	Built: Georgetown Shipyard, Georgetown, PEI							
	George R. Pearkes	IB	1986	D	3,809*	272' 04"	53' 02"	25' 02"
	Built: Versatile Pacific Shipyards, Victoria, BC							
	Martha L. Black	IB	1986	D	3,818*	272' 04"	53' 02"	25' 02"
	Built: Versatile Pacific Shipyards, Victoria, BC							
	Pierre Radisson	IB	1978	D	5,910*	322' 00"	62' 10"	35' 06"
	Built: Burrard Dry Dock Co., N. Vancouver, BC							
	Tracy	BT	1968	D	963*	181' 01"	38' 00"	16' 00"
	Built: Port Weller Dry Docks, St. Catharines, ON							
C-4	**CAUSLEY CONTRACTING, BAY CITY, MI**							
	Jill Marie	TB	1891	D	24*	60' 00"	12' 06"	6' 00"
	Built: Cleveland Shipbuilding Co., Cleveland, OH (Cisco 1891-'1952, Capama-S '52-'07)							
C-5	**CEMBA MOTOR SHIPS LTD., PELEE ISLAND, ON**							
	Cemba	TK	1960	D	17*	50' 00"	15' 06"	7' 06"
	Built: Elmer Haikala, Wheatley, ON							
C-6	**CENTRAL MARINE LOGISTICS INC., GRIFFITH, IN** *(centralmarinelogistics.com)*							
	Edward L. Ryerson	BC	1960	T	27,500	730' 00"	75' 00"	39' 00"
	Built: Manitowoc Shipbuilding Co., Manitowoc, WI; last U.S.-flagged non-self-unloader built on the lakes							
	Joseph L. Block	SU	1976	D	37,200	728' 00"	78' 00"	45' 00"
	Built: Bay Shipbuilding Co., Sturgeon Bay, WI							
	Wilfred Sykes	SU	1949	T	21,500	678' 00"	70' 00"	37' 00"
	Built: American Shipbuilding Co., Lorain, OH; converted to a self-unloader by Fraser Shipyards, Superior, WI, in '75							
C-7	**CHAMPION'S AUTO FERRY INC., ALGONAC, MI**							
	Champion {1}	CF	1941	D	65*	65' 00"	29' 00"	8' 06"
	Built: Arthur R. Champion, Algonac, MI							
	Middle Channel	CF	1997	D	97*	79' 00"	31' 00"	8' 03"
	Built: T.D. Vinette Co., Escanaba, MI							
	North Channel	CF	1967	D	67*	75' 00"	30' 00"	8' 00"
	Built: Blount Marine Corp., Warren, RI							
	South Channel	CF	1973	D	94*	79' 00"	31' 00"	8' 03"
	Built: Blount Marine Corp., Warren, RI							
C-8	**CHARLEVOIX COUNTY TRANSPORTATION AUTHORITY, CHARLEVOIX, MI**							
	Charlevoix {1}	CF	1926	D	43*	50' 00"	32' 00"	3' 09"
C-9	**CHICAGO FIRE DEPARTMENT, CHICAGO, IL**							
	Victor L. Schlaeger	FB	1949	D	350*	92' 06"	24' 00"	11' 00"

Canadian Miner passing the Sisters Island Lighthouse in the St. Lawrence River, near Alexandria Bay, N.Y. *(Eric Treece)*

C-10 CHICAGO LINE CRUISES LLC, CHICAGO, IL (chicagoline.com)

Ft. Dearborn	ES	1985	D	72*	64' 10"	22' 00"	7' 04"
Built: Blount Marine Corp., Warren, RI							
Innisfree	ES	1980	D	35*	61' 09"	15' 06"	5' 07"
Built: Blount Marine Corp., Warren, RI							
Marquette {6}	ES	1957	D	39*	50' 07"	15' 00"	4' 00"
Built: Burger Boat Co., Manitowoc, WI							

C-11 CHICAGO WATER PUMPING STATION, CHICAGO, IL

James J. Versluis	TB	1957	D	126*	83' 00"	22' 00"	11' 02"
Built: Sturgeon Bay Shipbuilding Co., Sturgeon Bay, WI							

C-12 CITY OF KEWAUNEE, KEWAUNEE, WI (cityofkewaunee.org)

Ludington	MU	1943	D	249*	115' 00"	26' 00"	13' 08"
Built: Jacobson Shipyard, Oyster Bay, NY; former U.S. Army Corps of Engineers tug is open to the public as a marine museum at Kewaunee, WI (Major Wilbur F. Browder [LT-4] '43-'47)							

C-13 CLAYTON FIRE DEPARTMENT, CLAYTON, NY

Last Chance	FB	2003	D		36' 00"	13' 00"	2' 04"

C-14 CLEVELAND FIRE DEPARTMENT, CLEVELAND, OH

Anthony J. Celebrezze	FB	1961	D	42*	66' 00"	17' 00"	5' 00"
Built: Paasch Marine Services Inc., Erie, PA							

C-15 CLUB CANAMAC CRUISES, TORONTO, ON (canamac.com)

Aurora Borealis	ES	1983	D	277*	101' 00"	24' 00"	6' 00"
Built: Ralph Hurley, Port Burwell, ON							
Stella Borealis	ES	1989	D	356*	118 '00"	26' 00"	7' 00"
Built: Duratug Shipyard & Fabricating Ltd., Port Dover, ON							

C-16 COBBY MARINE (1985) INC., KINGSVILLE, ON

Vida C.	TB	1960	D	17*	46 '03"	15' 05"	3' 02"

C-17 COLUMBIA YACHT CLUB, CHICAGO, IL (columbiayachtclub.com)

Abegweit	CF	1947	D	6,694*	372' 06"	61' 00"	24' 09"
Built: Marine Industries Ltd., Sorel, QC; former CN Marine Inc. vessel last operated in 1981; in use as a private, floating clubhouse in Chicago, IL (Abegweit '47- 81, Abby '81- '97)							

C-18 COOPER MARINE LTD., SELKIRK, ON

J. W. Cooper	PB	1984	D	25*	48' 00"	14' 07"	5' 00"
Janice C. No. 1	TB	1980	D	33*	56' 10"	20' 02"	5' 07"
Built: James O. Case, Lowbanks, ON							
Juleen I	PB	1972	D	23*	46' 00"	14' 01"	4' 05"
Lady Kim	PB	1974	D	20*	44' 00"	13' 00"	4' 00"
Mrs. C.	PB	2006	D	26*	50' 00"	14' 05"	4' 05"
Stacey Dawn	TB	1993	D	14*	35' 09"	17' 04"	3' 05"

C-19 CORPORATION OF THE TOWNSHIP OF FRONTENAC ISLANDS, WOLFE ISLAND, ON

Howe Islander	CF	1946	D	13*	53' 00"	12' 00"	3' 00"
Built: Canadian Dredge & Dock Co. Ltd., Kingston, ON							
Simcoe Islander	PF	1964	D	24*	47' 09"	18' 00"	3' 06"
Built: Canadian Dredge & Dock Co. Ltd., Kingston, ON							

C-20 CROISIÈRES AML INC., QUÉBEC, QC (croisieresaml.com)

Cavalier des Mers	ES	1974	D	161*	91' 08"	21' 03"	8' 05"
Built: Camcraft Inc., Crown Point, LA (Marine Sprinter '74-'84)							
Cavalier Maxim	ES	1962	D	752*	191' 02"	42' 00"	11' 07"
Built: John I. Thornycroft & Co., Wollston, Southampton, England (Osborne Castle '62-'78, Le Gobelet D' Argent '78-'88, Gobelet D' Argent '88-'89, Le Maxim '89-'93)							
Cavalier Royal	ES	1971	D	283*	125' 00"	24' 00"	5' 00"
Built: Beaux's Bay Craft, Loreauville, LA							
Grand Fleuve	ES	1987	D	499*	145' 00"	30' 00"	5' 06"
Built: Kanter Yacht Co., St. Thomas, ON							

Louis Jolliet	ES	1938	R	2,436*	170' 01"	70' 00"	17' 00"

Built: Davie Shipbuilding Co., Lauzon, QC

Transit	ES	1992	D	102*	66' 00"	22' 00"	2' 08"

Built: Chantier AML Inc., Ile-Aux-Coudres, QC

C-21 CROISIERES M/S JACQUES-CARTIER, TROIS-RIVIERES, QC (croisieres.qc.ca)

Jacques-Cartier	ES	1924	D	457*	135' 00"	35' 00"	10' 00"

Built: Davie Shipbuilding Co., Lauzon, QC

Le Draveur	ES	1992	D	79*	58' 07"	22' 00"	5' 24"

Built: Chantier Naval Matane Inc., Matane, QC

C-22 CRUISE TORONTO INC., TORONTO ON (cruisetoronto.com)

Obsession III	ES	1967	D	160*	66' 00"	25' 00"	6' 01"

Built: Halter Marine Services, New Orleans, LA (Mystique)

C-23 CTMA GROUP, CAP-AUX-MEULES, QC (ctma.ca)

C.T.M.A. Vacancier	PA/RR	1973	D	11,481*	388' 04"	70' 02"	43' 06"

*Built: J.J. Sietas KG Schiffswerft, Hamburg, Germany (Aurella '80-'82, Saint Patrick II '82-'98,
Egnatia II '98-'00, Ville de Sete '00-'01, City of Cork '01-'02)*

C.T.M.A. Voyageur	PA/RR	1972	D	4,526*	327' 09"	52' 06"	31' 07"

Built: Trosvik Versted A/S, Brevik, Norway (Anderida)

Madeleine	PA	1981	D	10,024*	381' 04"	60' 06"	41' 00"

Built: Verolme Cork Dockyard Ltd., Cobh, Ireland (Isle of Inishturk)

D-1 DALE T. DEAN / WALPOLE-ALGONAC FERRY LINE, PORT LAMBTON, ON (walpolealgonacferry.com)

City of Algonac	CF	1990	D	82*	62' 06"	27' 09"	5' 09"

Built: Duratug Shipyard & Fabricating Ltd., Port Dover, ON

Walpole Islander	CF	1986	D	72*	54' 05"	27' 09"	6' 03"

Built: Hike Metal Products, Wheatley, ON

D-2 DAN MINOR & SONS INC., PORT COLBORNE, ON

Andrea Marie I	TB	1963	D	87*	75' 02"	24' 07"	7' 03"

Built: Dan Minor & Sons Inc., Port Colborne, ON

Jeanette M	TB	1981	D	31*	62' 09"	20 01"	4' 05"

Built: Hike Metal Products, Wheatley, ON

Susan Michelle	TB	1995	D	89*	79' 10"	20' 11"	6' 02"

Built: Vic Powell Welding Ltd., Dunnville, ON

Welland	TB	1954	D	94*	86' 00"	20' 00"	8' 00"

Built: Russel-Hipwell Engines, Owen Sound, ON

D-3 DEAN CONSTRUCTION CO. LTD., BELLE RIVER, ON (deanconstructioncompany.com)

Annie M. Dean	TB	1981	D	58*	50' 00"	19' 00"	5' 00"

Built: Dean Construction Co. Ltd., Tecumseh, ON

Bobby Bowes	TB	1944	D	11*	37' 04"	10' 02"	3' 06"

Built: Russel Brothers, Owen Sound, ON (La Praxis)

Canadian Jubilee	DR	1978	B	896*	149' 09"	56' 01"	11' 01"

Built: Omnimar Inc., Sorel, QC

Neptune III	TB	1939	D	23*	53' 10"	15' 06"	5' 00"

Built: Harold Cromwell, London, ON

D-4 DETROIT CITY FIRE DEPARTMENT, DETROIT, MI

Curtis Randolph	FB	1979	D	85*	77' 10"	21' 06"	9' 03"

Built: Peterson Builders Inc., Sturgeon Bay, WI

D-5 DETROIT PRINCESS LLC, DETROIT, MI (detroitprincess.com)

Detroit Princess	PA	1993	D	1,430*	190' 09"	60' 00"	11' 01"

Built: Leevac Shipyards Inc., Jennings, LA (Players Riverboat Casino II '93-'04)

D-6 DIAMOND JACK'S RIVER TOURS, DETROIT, MI (diamondjack.com)

Diamond Belle	ES	1958	D	93*	93' 06"	25' 10"	10' 01"

Built: Hans Hansen Welding Co., Toledo, OH (Mackinac Islander {2} '58-'90, Sir Richard '90-'91)

Diamond Jack	ES	1955	D	82*	72' 00"	25' 00"	8' 00"

Built: Christy Corp., Sturgeon Bay, WI (Emerald Isle {1} '55-'91)

BIGGEST: PAUL R. TREGURTHA

There's big, then there's *Paul R. Tregurtha* big. The longest laker, at over 1,013 feet in length, *Tregurtha* is the reigning "Queen of the Lakes," an honorary title which automatically passed to the large self-unloader upon her launching in 1981. At 29 years and counting, "Big Paul" has held this title longer than any other laker since the honor was first bestowed upon the 302-foot *Onoko* in 1882.

Constructed in two sections, the *Tregurtha*'s keel was laid July 12, 1979. The bow and part of the cargo section were built at American Ship Building Co., Toledo, Ohio, and towed upon completion to American Ship Building's Lorain, Ohio, yard where they were mated with the stern portion and launched Feb. 4, 1981. The vessel was christened April 25, 1981, as *William J. De Lancey* for the Interlake Steamship Co., Richfield, Ohio.

Built at an approximate cost of $60 million, the *William J. De Lancey* became the flagship of the Interlake fleet. Included in her construction were luxurious passenger accommodations to be used by Interlake's most important business customers. For her crew, the vessel's construction included air conditioning throughout, elevators and luxurious décor in the dining and mess rooms and crew's quarters, earning her the nickname "Fancy *De Lancey*." The *De Lancey* was the last 1,000-footer to enter service and was also the last Great Lakes vessel built at American Ship Building's Lorain yard.

Paul R. Tregurtha loads at the SMET dock in Superior, Wis. *(Brian Kimball)*

The *William J. De Lancey* departed Lorain on her maiden voyage May 10, 1981, sailing in ballast to Silver Bay, Minn., for a load of 55,944 tons of iron ore pellets for a return trip back to Lorain. She was rechristened *Paul R. Tregurtha* on May 23, 1990, in honor of Mr. Paul Richard Tregurtha, at the time vice chairman of Interlake Steamship Co. Iron ore and coal have been the main cargos carried, with coal being the dominant commodity carried in recent years. – George Wharton

"Big Paul" upbound at Port Huron after delivering a coal cargo. *(Roger LeLievre)*

| | Diamond Queen | ES | 1956 | D | 94* | 92' 00" | 25' 00" | 10' 00" |

Built: Marinette Marine Corp., Marinette, WI (Mohawk '56-'96)

D-7 **DOOR COUNTY CRUISES LLC, STURGEON BAY, WI** *(doorcountyfireboatcruises.com)*

| | Fred A. Busse | ES | 1937 | D | 99* | 92' 00" | 22' 04" | 11' 00" |

Built: Defoe Boat & Motor Works, Bay City, MI; former Chicago fireboat offers cruises at Sturgeon Bay, WI

D-8 **DOOR COUNTY MARITIME MUSEUM & LIGHTHOUSE PRESERVATION SOCIETY INC., STURGEON BAY, WI** *(dcmm.org)*

| | John Purves | MU | 1919 | D | 436* | 150' 00" | 27' 06" | 16' 08" |

Built: Bethlehem Steel Co., Elizabeth, NJ; former Roen/Andrie Inc. tug has been refurbished as a museum display at Sturgeon Bay, WI (Butterfield '19-'42, LT-145 '42-'57)

D-9 **DRAGAGE VERREAULT INC., LES MÉCHINS, QC** *(dragageverreault.com)*

| | I.V. No. 8 | DR | 1967 | B | 348* | 96' 03" | 36' 00" | 8' 05" |

Built: Verreault Navigation Inc., Les Méchins, QC

| | I.V. No. 9 | GC | 1936 | D | 148* | 106' 08" | 23' 10" | 8' 05" |

Built: Geo. T. Davie & Sons, Lauzon, QC (A.C.D. '36-'69)

| | I.V. No. 10 | GC | 1936 | D | 320* | 110' 00" | 23' 10" | 8' 05" |

Built: Geo. T. Davie & Sons, Lauzon, QC (G.T.D. '36-'69)

| | I.V. No. 11 | GC | 1935 | D | 144* | 106' 08" | 24' 00" | 8' 00" |

Built: Geo. T. Davie & Sons, Lauzon, QC (Donpaco '35-'72)

| | I.V. No. 13 | GC | 1936 | D | 148* | 106' 08" | 24' 00" | 8' 00" |

Built: Geo. T. Davie & Sons, Lauzon, QC (Newscarrier '36-'72)

| | I.V. No. 14 | GC | 1937 | D | 229* | 113' 00" | 22' 05" | 8' 06" |

Built: Geo. T. Davie & Sons, Lauzon, QC (Kermic '37-'74)

| | Port Méchins | DR | 1949 | R | 1,321* | 200' 00" | 40' 02" | 18' 00" |

Built: Lobnitz & Co., Renfrew, Scotland (Haffar '49-'88, Lockeport '88-'92)

| | Rosaire | DR | 1952 | B | 714* | 137' 07" | 44' 06" | 9' 01" |

Built: Saint John Drydock Co., Saint John, NB

D-10 **DUC D' ORLEANS CRUISE BOAT, CORUNNA, ON** *(ducdorleans.com)*

| | Duc d' Orleans II | ES | 1987 | D | 120* | 71' 03 | | 7' 07" |

Built: Blount Marine Corp., Warren, RI (Spirit of Newport '87-'06)

D-11 **DULUTH ENTERTAINMENT CONVENTION CENTER, DULUTH, MN** *(decc.org/attractions/irvin)*

| | Sundew | MU | 1944 | DE | 1,025* | 180' 00" | 37' 00" | 17' 04" |

Built: Marine Ironworks and Shipbuilding Corp., Duluth, MN; former U.S. Coast Guard cutter WLB-404 was decommissioned in 2004; open to the public at Duluth, MN

| | William A. Irvin | MU | 1938 | T | 14,050 | 610' 09" | 60' 00" | 32' 06" |

Built: American Shipbuilding Co., Lorain, OH; former United States Steel Corp. bulk carrier last operated Dec. 16, 1978; open to the public at Duluth, MN

D-12 **DUROCHER MARINE, DIV. OF KOKOSING CONSTRUCTION CO., CHEBOYGAN, MI** *(durocher.biz)*

| | Champion {3} | TB | 1974 | D | 125* | 75' 00" | 24' 00" | 9' 06" |

Built: Service Machine & Shipbuilding Co., Amelia, LA

| | General {2} | TB | 1954 | D | 119* | 71' 00" | 19' 06" | 9' 06" |

Built: Missouri Valley Bridge & Iron Works, Leavenworth, KS (U. S. Army ST-1999 '54-'61, USCOE Au Sable '61-'84, Challenger {3} '84-'87)

| | Joe Van | TB | 1955 | D | 32* | 57' 09" | 16' 06" | 9' 00" |

Built: W.J. Hingston, Buffalo, NY

| | Nancy Anne | TB | 1969 | D | 73* | 60' 00" | 20' 00" | 6' 00" |

Built: Houma Shipbuilding Co., Houma, LA

| | Ray Durocher | TB | 1943 | D | 20* | 45' 06" | 12' 05" | 7' 06" |
| | Valerie B. | TB | 1981 | D | 101* | 65' 00" | 24' 06" | 10' 00" |

Built: Rayco Shipbuilders & Repairers, Bourg, LA (Mr. Joshua, Michael Van -'03)

E-1 **EASTERN UPPER PENINSULA TRANSPORTATION AUTHORITY, SAULT STE. MARIE, MI** *(http://eupta.net)*

| | Drummond Islander III | CF | 1989 | D | 96* | 108' 00" | 37' 00" | 12' 03" |

Built: Moss Point Marine Inc., Escatawpa, MS

| | Drummond Islander IV | CF | 2000 | D | 377* | 148' 00" | 40' 00" | 12' 00" |

Built: Basic Marine Inc., Escanaba, MI

Neebish Islander II   CF   1946   D   90*   89' 00"   29' 06"   6' 09"
Built: Lock City Machine/Marine, Sault Ste. Marie, MI (Sugar Islander '46-'95)

Sugar Islander II   CF   1995   D   223*   114' 00"   40' 00"   10' 00"
Built: Basic Marine Inc., Escanaba, MI

E-2   EDELWEISS CRUISE DINING, MILWAUKEE, WI *(edelweissboats.com)*

Edelweiss I   ES   1988   D   87*   64' 08"   18' 00"   6' 00"
Edelweiss II   ES   1989   D   89*   73' 08"   20' 00"   7' 00"

E-3   EDWARD E. GILLEN CO., MILWAUKEE, WI *(gillenco.com)*

Andrea J.   PA   1958   D   24*   39' 00"   11' 00"   6' 05"
   (Kayla D. Kadinger '58-'06)

Andrew J.   TB   1950   D   25*   47' 00"   15' 07"   8' 00"
Edith J.   TB   1962   D   19*   45' 03"   13' 00"   8' 00"
Edward E. Gillen III   TB   1988   D   95*   75' 00"   26' 00"   9' 06"
Built: Terrebonne Shipbuilders Inc., Houma, LA

Jullane J.   TB   1969   D   98*   65' 06"   22' 00"   8' 06
Built: Bollinger Shipyards, Lockport, LA (N. F. Candies, Connie Guidry, David J. Kadinger '89-'06)

Kristin J.   TB   1963   D   60*   52' 06"   19' 01"   7' 04"
Built: St. Charles Steel Works, Thibodaux, LA (Jason A. Kadinger '63-'06)

E-4   EGAN MARINE CORP., LEMONT, IL

Alice E.   TB   1950   D   183*   100' 00"   26' 00"   9' 00"
Built: St. Louis Shipbuilding, St. Louis, MO (L. L. Wright '50-'55, Martin '55-'74, Mary Ann '74-'77, Judi C. '77-'94)

Brandon E.   TB   1945   D   21*   45' 00"   12' 08"   6' 00"
Built: Sturgeon Bay Shipbuilding & Drydock Co., Sturgeon Bay, WI (ST-929 '45-'45, Heron '46-'62, Heidi '62-'64, James Edward '64-?, David E. ?-'96)

Daniel E.   TW   1967   D   70*   70' 00"   18' 06"   6' 08"
Built: River Enterprises Inc., Morris, IL (Foster M. Ford '67-'84)

David E.   TW   1952   D   236*   95' 00"   30' 00"   8' 06"
Built: Sturgeon Bay Shipbuilding & Drydock Co., Sturgeon Bay, WI (Irving Crown '52-'01)

Denise E.   TB   1889   D   123*   84' 09"   19' 00"   9' 00"
Built: Dialogue & Son, Camden, NJ (Asa W. Hughes 1889-'1913, Triton {1} '13-'81, Navajo {2} '81-'92, Robin E. '92-'06)

Derek E.   TB   1907   D   85*   72' 06"   20' 01"   10' 06"
Built: Benjamin T. Cowles, Buffalo, NY (John Kelderhouse '07-'13, Sachem '13-'90)

Lisa E.   TB   1963   D   75*   65' 06"   20' 00"   8' 06"
Built: Main Iron Works Inc., Houma, LA (Dixie Scout '63-'90)

Robin E.   TB   1912   D   138*   80' 07"   21' 06"   10' 03"
Built: Dialogue & Son, Camden, NJ (Caspian '12-'48, Trojan '48-'81, Cherokee {1} '81-'93, Denise E. '93-'06)

E-5   EMPRESS OF CANADA ENTERPRISES LTD., TORONTO, ON *(empressofcanada.com)*

Empress of Canada   ES   1980   D   399*   116' 00"   28' 00"   6' 06"
Built: Hike Metal Products, Wheatley, ON (Island Queen V {2} '80-'89)

E-6   ENTREPRISE MARISSA INC., BEAUPORT, QC

Soulanges   TB   1905   D   72*   77' 00"   17' 00"   8' 00"
Built: Cie Pontbriand Ltee., Sorel, QC (Dandy '05-'39)

E-7   EQUIPMENTS VERREAULT INC., LES MÉCHINS, QC

Epinette II   TB   1965   D   75*   61' 03"   20' 01"   8' 05"
Grande Baie   TT   1972   D   194*   86' 06"   30' 00"   12' 00"
Built: Prince Edward Island Lending Authority, Chalottetown, PEI

E-8   ERICKSON MARINE FREIGHT INC., BAYFIELD, WI

Outer Island   PK   1942   D   136*   103' 05"   32' 00"   5' 00"
   (LCT 203 '42-'46, Pluswood '46-'53)

E-9   ERIE ISLANDS PETROLEUM INC., PUT-IN-BAY, OH

Cantankerus   TK   1955   D   43*   53' 02"   14' 00"   7' 00"
Built: Marinette Marine Corp., Marinette, WI

E-10   ERIE MARITIME MUSEUM, ERIE, PA *(brigniagara.org)*

Niagara   MU/2B   1988   W   295*   198' 00"   32' 00"   10' 06"
Reconstruction of Oliver Hazard Perry's U. S. Navy brigantine from the War of 1812

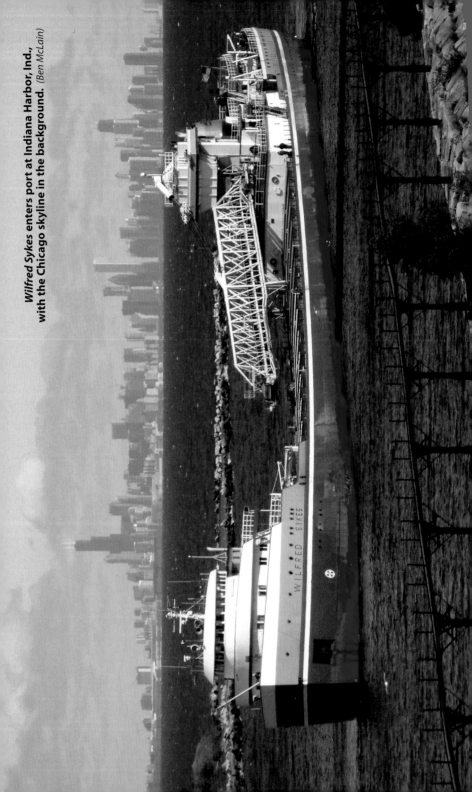

Wilfred Sykes enters port at Indiana Harbor, Ind., with the Chicago skyline in the background. *(Ben McLain)*

E-11 ERIE SAND AND GRAVEL CO., ERIE, PA

Vessel	Type	Year	Engine	Cap.	Length	Beam	Depth
J. S. St. John	SC	1945	D	680	174' 00"	32' 02"	15' 00"

Built: Smith Shipyards & Engineering Corp., Pensacola, FL (USS YO-178 '45-'51, Lake Edward '51-'67)

E-12 ESCANABA & LAKE SUPERIOR RAILROAD, WELLS, MI *(elsrr.com)*

Vessel	Type	Year	Engine	Cap.	Length	Beam	Depth
Pere Marquette 10	TF	1945	B	27 rail cars	400' 00"	53' 00"	22' 00"

Built: Manitowoc Shipbuilding Co., Manitowoc, WI; last operated Oct. 7, 1994; laid up at Toledo, OH

E-13 ESSROC CANADA INC., NORTH YORK, ON *(essroc.com)*
(VESSELS MANAGED BY UPPER LAKES GROUP INC.)

Vessel	Type	Year	Engine	Cap.	Length	Beam	Depth
Metis	CC	1956	B	5,800	331' 00"	43' 09"	26' 00"

Built: Davie Shipbuilding Co., Lauzon, QC; lengthened 72', deepened 3'06" in '59 and converted to a self-unloading cement barge in '91 by Kingston Ship Building & Dry Dock Co., Kingston, ON

Vessel	Type	Year	Engine	Cap.	Length	Beam	Depth
Stephen B. Roman	CC	1965	D	7,600	488' 09"	56' 00"	35' 06"

Built: Davie Shipbuilding Co., Lauzon, QC; converted to a self-unloading cement carrier by Collingwood Shipyards, Collingwood, ON, in '83 (Fort William '65-'83)

F-1 FEDNAV LTD., MONTREAL, QC *(www.fednav.com)*
CANARCTIC SHIPPING CO. LTD. - DIVISION OF FEDNAV LTD. (SEE ALSO SALTWATER FLEET IF-3)

Vessel	Type	Year	Engine	Cap.	Length	Beam	Depth
Arctic	GC	1978	D	26,440	692' 04"	75' 05"	49' 05"

Built: Port Weller Dry Docks, Port Weller, ON

Vessel	Type	Year	Engine	Cap.	Length	Beam	Depth
Umiak I	BC	2006	D	31,992	619' 04"	87' 02"	51' 50"

Built: Universal Shipbuilding Corp., Kawasaki, Japan

F-2 FITZ SUSTAINABLE FORESTRY MANAGEMENT LTD., MANITOWANING, ON

Vessel	Type	Year	Engine	Cap.	Length	Beam	Depth
B.J. & C.J.	TB	1952	D	12*	44' 04"	12' 00"	3' 05"
Wyn Cooper	TB	1973	D	25*	48' 00"	13' 00"	4' 00"

F-3 FRASER SHIPYARDS INC., SUPERIOR, WI *(frasershipyards.com)*

Vessel	Type	Year	Engine	Cap.	Length	Beam	Depth
Brenda L.	TB	1941	D	11*	36' 00"	10' 00"	3' 08"

(Harbour I '41-'58, Su-Joy III '58 -'78)

Vessel	Type	Year	Engine	Cap.	Length	Beam	Depth
Maxine Thompson	TB	1959	D	30*	47' 04"	13' 00"	6' 06"

(Susan A. Fraser '59-'78)

Vessel	Type	Year	Engine	Cap.	Length	Beam	Depth
Reuben Johnson	TB	1912	D	71*	78' 00"	17' 00"	11' 00"

Built: Great Lakes Towing Co., Cleveland, OH (Buffalo '12-'28, Churchill '28-'48, Buffalo '48-'74, Todd Fraser '74-'78)

Vessel	Type	Year	Engine	Cap.	Length	Beam	Depth
Wally Kendzora	TB	1956	D	24*	43' 00"	12' 00"	5' 00"

F-4 FRIENDS OF THE NORISLE, MANITOWANING, ON *(norisle.com)*

Vessel	Type	Year	Engine	Cap.	Length	Beam	Depth
Norisle	MU	1946	R	1,668*	215' 09"	36' 03"	16' 00"

Built: Collingwood Shipyards, Collingwood, ON; former Ontario Northland Transportation Commission passenger vessel last operated in 1974; open to the public at Manitowaning, Manitoulin Island, ON

F-5 FRIENDS OF THE Q105, SARNIA, ON

Vessel	Type	Year	Engine	Cap.	Length	Beam	Depth
Duc d' Orleans	ES	1943	D	112*	112' 00"	17' 10"	6' 03"

Former World War II sub chaser is undergoing restoration at Sarnia, ON (HMCS ML-105 '43-'48)

G-1 GAELIC TUGBOAT CO., DETROIT, MI *(gaelictugboat.com)*

Vessel	Type	Year	Engine	Cap.	Length	Beam	Depth
Carolyn Hoey	TB	1951	D	146*	88' 06"	25' 06"	11' 00"

Built: Alexander Shipyard Inc., New Orleans, LA (Atlas '51-'84, Susan Hoey {1} '84-'85, Atlas '85-'87)

Vessel	Type	Year	Engine	Cap.	Length	Beam	Depth
LSC 236	TK	1943	B	584*	195' 06"	35' 01"	10' 01
Marysville	TK	1973	B	1,136*	200' 00"	50' 00"	12' 06"

(N.M.S. No. 102 '73-'81)

Vessel	Type	Year	Engine	Cap.	Length	Beam	Depth
Patricia Hoey {2}	TB	1949	D	146*	88' 06"	25' 06"	11' 00"

Built: Alexander Shipyard, Inc., New Orleans, LA (Propeller '49-'82, Bantry Bay '82-'91)

Vessel	Type	Year	Engine	Cap.	Length	Beam	Depth
Shannon	TB	1944	D	145*	101' 00"	28' 00"	13' 00"

Built: Consolidated Shipbuilding Corp., Morris Heights, NY (USS Connewango [YT / YTB / YTM-388] '44-'77)

Vessel	Type	Year	Engine	Cap.	Length	Beam	Depth
William Hoey {2}	TB	1924	D	99*	85' 00"	21' 06"	10' 09"

Built: Manitowoc Shipbuilding Co., Manitowoc, WI (Martha C. '24-'52, Langdon C. Hardwicke '52-'82, Wabash {2} '82-'93, Katie Ann {1} '93-'99)

G-2 GALCON MARINE LTD., TORONTO, ON

Vessel	Type	Year	Engine	Cap.	Length	Beam	Depth
Batchawana	TB	1912	D	40*	49' 00"	13' 00"	7' 08"

Kenteau	TB	1937	D	15*	54' 07"	16' 04"	4' 02"
Built: George Gamble, Port Dover, ON							
Pitts Carillon	DB	1959	B	260*	91' 08"	39' 00"	8' 01"
Pitts No. 3	DB	1961	B	107*	78' 02"	32' 00"	5' 05"

G-3   GALLAGHER MARINE CONSTRUCTION CO. INC., ESCANABA, MI

Bee Jay	TB	1939	D	19*	45' 00"	13' 00"	7' 00"

G-4   GANANOQUE BOAT LINE, GANANOQUE, ON *(ganboatline.com)*

Thousand Islander	ES	1972	D	200*	96' 11"	22' 01"	5' 05"
Thousand Islander II	ES	1973	D	200*	99' 00"	22' 01"	5' 00"
Thousand Islander III	ES	1975	D	376*	118' 00"	28' 00"	6' 00"
Thousand Islander IV	ES	1976	D	347*	110' 09"	28' 04"	10' 08"
Thousand Islander V	ES	1979	D	246*	88' 00"	24' 00"	5' 00"
(Concordia '79-'97)							

G-5   GANNON UNIVERSITY, ERIE, PA *(www.gannon.edu)*

Environaut	RV	1950	D	13*	36' 05"	12' 00"	5' 00"
Built: Paasch Marine Services Inc., Erie, PA							

G-6   GEO. GRADEL CO., TOLEDO, OH *(georgegradelco.tripod.com)*

Clyde	DB	1922	B	704*	134' 00"	41' 00"	12' 00"
John Francis	TB	1965	D	99*	75' 00"	22' 00"	9' 00"
Built: Bollinger Shipbuilding Inc., Lockport, LA (Dad '65-'98, Creole Eagle '98-'03)							
Mighty Jake	TB	1969	D	15*	36' 00"	12' 03"	7' 03"
Mighty Jessie	TB	1954	D	57*	61' 02"	18' 00"	7' 03"
Mighty Jimmy	TB	1945	D	27*	56' 00"	15' 10"	7' 00"
Mighty John III	TB	1962	D	24*	45' 00"	15' 00"	5' 10"
(Niagara Queen '62-'99)							
Moby Dick	DB	1952	B	835	121' 00"	33' 02"	10' 06"
Pioneerland	TB	1943	D	53*	58' 00"	16' 08"	8' 00"
Prairieland	TB	1955	D	35*	49' 02"	15' 02"	6' 00"
Timberland	TB	1946	D	20*	41' 03"	13' 01"	7' 00"

G-7   GOODTIME LAKE ERIE ISLAND CRUISES LLC, SANDUSKY, OH *(goodtimeboat.com)*

Goodtime I	ES	1960	D	81*	111' 00"	29' 08"	9' 05"
Built: Blount Marine Corp., Warren, RI							

G-8   GOODTIME TRANSIT BOATS INC., CLEVELAND, OH *(goodtimeiii.com)*

Goodtime III	ES	1990	D	95*	161' 00"	40' 00"	11' 00"
Bulit: Leevac Shipyards Inc., Jennings, LA							

G-9   GRAND PORTAGE / ISLE ROYALE TRANSPORTATION LINE, SUPERIOR, WI *(isleroyaleboats.com)*

Voyageur II	ES	1970	D	40*	63' 00"	18' 00"	5' 00"
Wenonah	ES	1960	D	91*	70' 07"	19' 04"	9' 07"
Built: Dubuque Boat & Boiler Works, Dubuque, IA (Jamaica '60-'64)							

G-10   GRAND VALLEY STATE UNIVERSITY, ANNIS WATER RESOURCES, MUSKEGON, MI *(gvsu.edu/wri)*

D. J. Angus	RV	1986	D	16*	45' 00"	14' 00"	4' 00"
W. G. Jackson	RV	1996	D	80*	64' 10"	20' 00"	5' 00"

G-11   GRAVEL AND LAKE SERVICES LTD., THUNDER BAY, ON

Donald Mac	TB	1914	D	69*	71' 00"	17' 00"	10' 00"
Built: Thor Iron Works Ltd., Toronto, ON							
George N. Carleton	TB	1943	D	97*	82' 00"	21' 00"	11' 00"
Built: Russel Brothers, Owen Sound, ON (HMCS Glenlea [W-25] '43-'45, Bansaga '45-'64)							
Peninsula	TB	1944	D	261*	111' 00"	27' 00"	13' 00"
Built: Montreal Drydock Ltd., Montreal, QC (HMCS Norton [W-31] '44-'45, W.A.C. 1 '45-'46)							
Robert John	TB	1945	D	98*	82' 00"	20' 01"	11' 00"
Built: Canadian Dredge & Dock Co., Kingston, ON (HMCS Gleneagle [W-40] '45-'46, Bansturdy '46-'65)							
Wolf River	BC	1956	D	5,880	349' 02"	43' 07"	25' 04"
Built: Port Weller Dry Docks, Port Weller, ON; last operated in 1998; laid up at Thunder Bay, ON							
(Tecumseh {2} '56-'67, New York News {3} '67-'86, Stella Desgagnés '86-'93, Beam Beginner '93-'95)							

G-12   **GREAT LAKES CLIPPER PRESERVATION ASSOCIATION, MUSKEGON, MI** *(milwaukeeclipper.com)*
Milwaukee Clipper   MU   1904   Q   4,272   361' 00"   45' 00"   28' 00"
    Built: American Shipbuilding Co., Cleveland, OH; rebuilt in '40 at Manitowoc Shipbuilding Co., Manitowoc,
    WI; former Wisconsin & Michigan Steamship Co. passenger/auto carrier last operated in 1970; undergoing
    restoration and open to the public at Muskegon, MI (Juniata '04–'41)

G-13   **GREAT LAKES DOCK & MATERIALS LLC, MUSKEGON, MI** *(greatlakesdock.com)*
Duluth   TB   1954   D   87*   70' 01"   19' 05"   9' 08"
    Built: Missouri Valley Bridge & Iron Works, Leavenworth, KS (U. S. Army ST-2015 '54–'62)
Fischer Hayden   TB   1967   D   64*   54' 00"   22' 1"   7' 1"
    Built: Main Iron Works Inc., Houma, LA (Gloria G. Cheramie, Joyce P. Crosby)
Sarah B   TB   1953   D   23*   45' 00"   13' 00"   7' 00"
    Built: Nashville Bridge Co., Nashville, TN (ST-2161 '53–'63, Tawas Bay '63–'03)

G-14   **GREAT LAKES ENVIRONMENTAL RESEARCH LABORATORY, MUSKEGON, MI** *(www.glerl.noaa.gov)*
Laurentian   RV   1974   D   129*   80' 00"   21' 06"   11' 00"
Shenehon   SV   1953   D   90*   65' 00"   17' 00"   6' 00"

G-15   **GREAT LAKES FLEET INC./KEY LAKES INC., DULUTH, MN (MANAGER)** *(www.keyship.com)*
    CANADIAN NATIONAL RAILWAY, MONTREAL, QC – OWNER *(www.cn.ca)*
Arthur M. Anderson   SU   1952   T   25,300   767' 00"   70' 00"   36' 00"
    Built: American Shipbuilding Co., Lorain, OH; lengthened 120' in '75 and converted to a self-unloader in
    '82 at Fraser Shipyards, Superior, WI
Cason J. Callaway   SU   1952   T   25,300   767' 00"   70' 00"   36' 00"
    Built: Great Lakes Engineering Works, River Rouge, MI; lengthened 120' in '74 and converted to a self-unloader in
    '82 at Fraser Shipyards, Superior, WI

***Maritime Trader* heading for a lower lakes port in 2008.** *(Roger LeLievre)*

Edgar B. Speer	SU	1980	D	73,700	1,004' 00"	105' 00"	56' 00"

Built: American Shipbuilding Co., Lorain, OH

| Edwin H. Gott | SU | 1979 | D | 74,100 | 1,004' 00" | 105' 00" | 56' 00" |

Built: Bay Shipbuilding Co., Sturgeon Bay, WI; converted from shuttle self-unloader to deck-mounted self-unloader at Bay Shipbuilding, Sturgeon Bay, WI, in '96

| John G. Munson {2} | SU | 1952 | T | 25,550 | 768' 03" | 72' 00" | 36' 00" |

Built: Manitowoc Shipbuilding Co., Manitowoc, WI; lengthened 102' at Fraser Shipyards, Superior, WI, in '76

| Philip R. Clarke | SU | 1952 | T | 25,300 | 767' 00" | 70' 00" | 36' 00" |

Built: American Shipbuilding Co., Lorain, OH; lengthened 120' in '74 and converted to a self-unloader in '82 at Fraser Shipyards, Superior, WI

| Presque Isle {2} | IT | 1973 | D | 1,578* | 153' 03" | 54' 00" | 31' 03" |

Built: Halter Marine Services, New Orleans, LA

| Presque Isle {2} | SU | 1973 | B | 57,500 | 974' 06" | 104' 07" | 46' 06" |

Built: Erie Marine Inc., Erie, PA

| **[ITB Presque Isle OA dimensions together]** | | | | | 1,000' 00" | 104' 07" | 46' 06" |

| Roger Blough | SU | 1972 | D | 43,900 | 858' 00" | 105' 00" | 41' 06" |

Built: American Shipbuilding Co., Lorain, OH

G-16   **THE GREAT LAKES GROUP, CLEVELAND, OH** (thegreatlakesgroup.com)

THE GREAT LAKES TOWING CO., CLEVELAND, OH – DIVISION OF THE GREAT LAKES GROUP

Alabama {2}	TB	1916	DE	98*	81' 00"	21' 03"	12' 05"
Arizona	TB	1931	D	98*	84' 04"	20' 00"	12' 06"
Arkansas {2}	TB	1909	D	98*	81' 00"	21' 03"	12' 05"

(Yale '09-'48)

California	TB	1926	DE	98*	81' 00"	20' 00"	12' 06"
Colorado	TB	1928	D	98*	84' 04"	20' 00"	12' 06"
Delaware {4}	TB	1924	DE	98*	81' 00"	20' 00"	12' 06"
Florida	TB	1926	D	99*	81' 00"	20' 00"	12' 06"

(Florida '26-'83, Pinellas '83-'84)

Idaho	TB	1931	DE	98*	84' 00"	20' 00"	12' 06"
Illinois {2}	TB	1914	D	99*	81' 00"	20' 00"	12' 06"
Indiana	TB	1911	DE	97*	81' 00"	20' 00"	12' 06"
Iowa	TB	1915	D	98*	81' 00"	20' 00"	12' 06"
Kansas	TB	1927	D	98*	81' 00"	20' 00"	12' 06"
Kentucky {2}	TB	1929	D	98*	84' 04"	20' 00"	12' 06"
Louisiana	TB	1917	D	98*	81' 00"	20' 00"	12' 06"
Maine {1}	TB	1921	D	96*	81' 00"	20' 00"	12' 06"

(Maine {1} '21-'82, Saipan '82-'83, Hillsboro '83-'84)

| Massachusetts | TB | 1928 | D | 98* | 84' 04" | 20' 00" | 12' 06" |
| Milwaukee | DB | 1924 | B | 1,095 | 172' 00" | 40' 00" | 11' 06" |

Built: Bay Shipbuildng Co., Sturgeon Bay, WI

Minnesota {1}	TB	1911	D	98*	81' 00"	20' 00"	12' 06"
Mississippi	TB	1916	DE	98*	81' 00"	20' 00"	12' 06"
Missouri {2}	TB	1927	D	149*	88' 04"	24' 06"	12' 03"

(Rogers City {1} '27-'56, Dolomite {1} '56-'81, Chippewa {7} '81-'90)

Montana	TB	1929	DE	98*	84' 04"	20' 00"	12' 06"
Nebraska	TB	1929	D	98*	84' 04"	20' 00"	12' 06"
New Jersey	TB	1924	D	98*	81' 00"	20' 00"	12' 06"

(New Jersey '24-'52, Petco-21 '52-'53)

| New York | TB | 1913 | D | 98* | 81' 00" | 20' 00" | 12' 06" |
| North Carolina {2} | TB | 1952 | DE | 145* | 87' 09" | 24' 01" | 10' 07" |

(Limestone '52-'83, Wicklow '83-'90)

| North Dakota | TB | 1910 | D | 97* | 81' 00" | 20' 00" | 12' 06" |

(John M. Truby '10-'38)

| Ohio {3} | TB | 1903 | D | 194* | 118' 00" | 24' 00" | 13' 06" |

Built: Great Lakes Towing Co., Chicago, IL (M.F.D. No. 15 '03-'52, Laurence C. Turner '52-'73)

| Oklahoma | TB | 1913 | DE | 97* | 81' 00" | 20' 00" | 12' 06" |

(T. C. Lutz {2} '13-'34)

Pennsylvania {3}	TB	1911	D	98*	81' 00"	20' 00"	12' 06"
Rhode Island	TB	1930	D	98*	84' 04"	20' 00"	12' 06"
South Carolina	TB	1925	D	102*	86' 00"	21' 00"	11' 00"

(Welcome {2} '25-'53, Joseph H. Callan '53-'72, South Carolina '72-'82, Tulagi '82-'83)

Fleet #	Fleet Name / Vessel Name	Type of Vessel	Year Built	Type of Engine	Cargo Cap. or Gross*	Overall Length	Breadth	Depth or Draft*
	Superior {3}	TB	1912	D	147*	97' 00"	22' 00"	12' 00"
	(Richard Fitzgerald '12-'46)							
	Tennessee	TB	1917	D	98*	81' 00"	20' 00"	12' 06"
	Texas	TB	1916	DE	97*	81' 00"	20' 00"	12' 06"
	Vermont	TB	1914	D	98*	81' 00"	20' 00"	12' 06"
	Virginia {2}	TB	1914	DE	97*	81' 00"	20' 00"	12' 06"
	Washington {1}	TB	1925	DE	97*	81' 00"	20' 00"	12' 06"
	Wisconsin {4}	TB	1897	D	105*	90' 03"	21' 00"	12' 03"
	(America {3}, Midway)							
	Wyoming	TB	1929	D	104*	84' 04"	20' 00"	12' 06"

G-17   GREAT LAKES MARITIME ACADEMY – NORTHWESTERN MICHIGAN COLLEGE, TRAVERSE CITY, MI
(nmc.edu/maritime)

	Anchor Bay	TV	1953	D	23*	45' 00"	13' 00"	7' 00"
	Built: Roamer Boat Co., Holland, MI (ST-2158 '53-'62)							
	Northwestern {2}	TV	1969	D	12*	55' 00"	15' 00"	6' 06"
	Built: Paasch Marine Services Inc., Erie, PA (USCOE North Central '69-'98)							
	State of Michigan	TV	1986	D	1,914*	224' 00"	43' 00"	20' 00"
	(USS Persistent '86-'98, USCG Persistent '98-'02)							

G-18   GREAT LAKES NAVAL MEMORIAL & MUSEUM, MUSKEGON, MI *(silversides.org)*

	LST-393	MU	1942	D	2,100	328' 00"	50' 00"	25' 00"
	Built: Newport News Shipbuilding and Dry Dock Co., Newport News, VA; former U.S. Navy / Wisconsin &							
	Michigan Steamship Co. vessel last operated July 31, 1973; on display at Muskegon, MI							
	(USS LST-393 '42-'47, Highway 16 '47-'99)							
	McLane	MU	1927	D	289*	125' 00"	24' 00"	12' 06"
	Built: American Brown Boveri Electric Co., Camden, NJ; former U.S. Coast Guard Buck & A Quarter class							
	medium endurance cutter; on display at Muskegon, MI							
	(USCGC McLane [WSC / WMEC-146] '27-'70, Manatra II '70-'93)							
	Silversides	MU	1941	D/V	1,526*	311' 08"	27' 03"	33' 09"
	Built: Mare Island Naval Yard, Vallejo, CA; former U.S. Navy Albacore (Gato) class submarine AGSS-236;							
	open to the public at Muskegon, MI							

G-19   GREAT LAKES SCHOONER CO., TORONTO, ON *(greatlakesschooner.com)*

	Challenge	ES	1980	W/D	76*	96' 00"	16' 06"	8' 00"
	Built: Kanter Yachts Company, Port Stanley, ON							
	Kajama	ES	1930	W/D	263*	128' 09"	22' 09"	11' 08"
	Built: Nobis Krug, Rensburg, West Germany							

G-20   GREAT LAKES SCIENCE CENTER, ANN ARBOR, MI *(www.glsc.usgs.gov)*

	Grayling	RV	1977	D	198*	75' 00"	22' 00"	9' 10"
	Kaho	RV	1961	D	83*	64' 10"	17' 10"	9' 00"
	Kiyi	RV	1999	D	290*	107' 00"	27' 00"	12' 02"
	Musky II	RV	1960	D	25*	45' 00"	14' 04"	5' 00"
	Sturgeon	RV	1977	D	325*	100' 00"	25' 05"	10' 00"

G-21   GREAT LAKES SHIPWRECK HISTORICAL SOCIETY, SAULT STE. MARIE, MI *(shipwreckmuseum.com)*

	David Boyd	RV	1982	D	26*	47' 00"	17' 00"	3' 00"*

H-1   H. LEE WHITE MARINE MUSEUM, OSWEGO, NY *(hleewhitemarinemuseum.com)*

	LT-5	MU	1943	D	305*	115' 00"	28' 00"	14' 00"
	Built: Jakobson Shipyard, Oyster Bay, NY; former U.S. Army Corps of Engineers tug last operated in 1989;							
	open to the public at Oswego, NY (Major Elisha K. Henson '43-'47, U.S. Army LT-5 '47-'47, Nash '47-'95)							

H-2   HAMILTON HARBOUR QUEEN CRUISES, HAMILTON, ON *(hamiltonwaterfront.com)*

	Hamilton Harbour Queen	ES	1956	D	252*	100' 00"	22' 00"	4' 05"
	Built: Russel-Hipwell Engines, Owen Sound, ON (Johnny B. '56-'89, Garden City '89-'00, Harbour Princess '00-'05)							

H-3   HAMILTON PORT AUTHORITY, HAMILTON, ON *(hamiltonport.ca)*

	Cleanshores	TB	1979	D	10*	33' 08"	11' 03"	4' 05"
	Judge McCombs	TB	1948	D	10*	36' 00"	10' 03"	4' 00"
	Built: Northern Shipbuilding & Repair Co. Ltd., Bronte, ON (Bronte Sue '48-'50)							

Fleet #	Fleet Name / Vessel Name	Type of Vessel	Year Built	Type of Engine	Cargo Cap. or Gross*	Overall Length	Breadth	Depth or Draft*
H-4	**HANNAH MARINE CORP., LEMONT, IL** *(hannahmarine.com)*							
	Daryl C. Hannah {2}	TW	1956	D	268*	102' 00"	28' 00"	8' 00"
	Built: Calumet Shipyard & Drydock Co., Chicago, IL (Cindy Jo '56-'66, Katherine L. '66-'93)							
	David E.	TB	1944	D	602*	149' 00"	33' 00"	16' 00"
	Built: Marietta Manufacturing, Marietta, GA (LT 815 '44-'64, Henry Foss '64-'84, Kristin Lee '84-'93, Kristin Lee Hannah' 93-'00)							
	Donald C. Hannah	TB	1962	D	191*	91' 00"	29' 00"	11' 06"
	Built: Main Iron Works Inc., Houma, LA							
	Hannah 3601	TK	1972	B	5,035	290' 00"	60' 00"	18' 03"
	Hannah 5101	TK	1978	B	8,050	360' 00"	60' 00"	22' 06"
	Hannah 6301	TK	1980	B	8,050	407' 01"	60' 00"	21' 00"
	Hannah 7701	DB	1981	B	7,143	340' 00"	64' 00"	21' 02"
	Hannah D. Hannah	TB	1955	D	134*	86' 00"	24' 00"	10' 00"
	Built: Sturgeon Bay Shipbuilding, Sturgeon Bay, WI (Harbor Ace '55-'61, Gopher State '61-'71, Betty Gale '71-'93)							
	James A. Hannah	TB	1945	D	593*	149' 00"	33' 00"	16' 00"
	Built: Marietta Manufacturing, Marietta, GA (U. S. Army LT-820 '45-'65, Muskegon {1} '65-'71)							
	Kristin Lee Hannah	TW	1953	D	397*	111' 10"	35' 00"	8' 04"
	Built: Sturgeon Bay Shipbuilding, Sturgeon Bay, WI (Inwaco '53-'61, Carrie S. '61-'68, Clark Frame '68-'96, Cheri Conway '96-'96, David E '96-'00)							
	Margaret M.	TB	1956	D	167*	89' 06"	24' 00"	10' 00"
	Built: Sturgeon Bay Shipbuilding, Sturgeon Bay, WI (Shuttler '56-'60, Margaret M. Hannah '60-'84)							
	Mark Hannah	ATB	1969	D	191*	127' 05"	32' 01"	14' 03"
	Built: Burton Shipyard, Bridge City, TX (Lead Horse '69-'73, Gulf Challenger '73-'80, Challenger {2} '80-'93)							
	Mary E. Hannah	TB	1945	D	612*	149' 00"	33' 00"	16' 00"
	Built: Marietta Manufacturing, Marietta, GA (U. S. Army LT-821 '45-'47, Brooklyn '47-'66, Lee Reuben '66-'75)							
	Peggy D. Hannah	TB	1920	D	145*	108' 00"	25' 00"	14' 00"
	Built: Whitney Brothers Co., Superior, WI (William A. Whitney '20-'92)							
	Susan W. Hannah	ATB	1977	D	174*	121' 06"	34' 06"	18' 02"
	Built: Toche Enterprises Inc., Ocean Springs, MS (Lady Elda '77-'78, Kings Challenger '78-'78, ITM No. 1 '78-'81, Kings Challenger '81-'86)							
	Wilbur R. Clark	TB	1945	D	275*	151' 05"	33' 00"	18' 08"
	Built: Marietta Manufacturing, Marietta, GA (LT-789, Polar Challenger, Marine Challenger, Petro Challenger, Pacific Victory)							

***James Norris* in lower Lake Huron.** *(George Wharton)*

H-5   HARBOR LIGHT CRUISE LINES INC., TOLEDO, OH *(sandpiperboat.com)*

Name	Type	Year		Tonnage	Length	Beam	Depth
Sandpiper	ES	1984	D	21*	65' 00"	16' 00"	3' 00"

H-6   HCMS HAIDA NATIONAL HISTORICAL SITE, HAMILTON, ON *(hmcshaida.ca)*

Name	Type	Year		Tonnage	Length	Beam	Depth
Haida	MU	1943	T	2,744*	377' 00"	37' 06"	15' 02"

Former Royal Canadian Navy Tribal-class destroyer G-63 / DDE-215; open to the public at Hamilton, ON

H-7   HEDDLE MARINE SERVICE INC., HAMILTON, ON *(heddlemarine.com)*

Name	Type	Year		Tonnage	Length	Beam	Depth
Dalmig	CF	1957	D	538*	175' 10"	40' 01"	11' 10"

Built: Marine Industries Inc., Sorel, QC; vessel laid up at Hamilton, ON (Pierre de Saurel '57-'87)

Name	Type	Year		Tonnage	Length	Beam	Depth
King Fish 1	TB	1955	D	24*	47' 09"	12' 09"	5' 03"
Wyatt McKeil	TB	1950	D	237*	102' 06"	26' 00"	13' 06"

Built: Davie Shipbuilding Co., Lauzon, QC; vessel laid up at Hamilton, ON (Otis Wack '50-'97)

H-8   HERITAGE HARBOR MARINE LTD., LONDON, ON

Name	Type	Year		Tonnage	Length	Beam	Depth
Salvage Monarch	TB	1959	D	219*	97' 09"	28' 00"	14' 06"

Built: P.K. Harris Ltd., Appledore, England

H-9   HERITAGE MARINE, KNIFE RIVER, MN

Name	Type	Year		Tonnage	Length	Beam	Depth
Edward H.	TB	1944	D	142*	86' 00"	23' 00"	10' 04"

Built: Equitable Equipment Co., Madisonville, LA (ST-707 '44-'60, Forney '60-'07)

H-10   HORNBECK OFFSHORE SERVICES, COVINGTON, LA *(hornbeckoffshore.com)*

Name	Type	Year		Tonnage	Length	Beam	Depth
Bayridge Service	TB	1981	D	194*	100' 00"	30' 00"	14' 05"

Built: Bollinger Shipyard Inc., Lockport, LA

Name	Type	Year		Tonnage	Length	Beam	Depth
Energy 5501	TK	1969	B	2,878*	341' 00"	54' 00"	17' 09"
Energy 6506	TK	2007	B	5,778*	362' 00"	60' 00"	23' 07"
Sea Service	TB	1975	D	173*	109' 00"	31' 00"	16' 05"

Built: Halter Marine, New Orleans, LA

Name	Type	Year		Tonnage	Length	Beam	Depth
Tradewind Service	TB	1975	D	183*	104' 07"	30' 00"	12' 08"

Built: Bollinger Shipyard Inc., Lockport, LA

H-11   HORNE TRANSPORTATION LTD., WOLFE ISLAND, ON *(wolfeisland.com)*

Name	Type	Year		Tonnage	Length	Beam	Depth
William Darrell	CF	1952	D	66*	66' 00"	28' 00"	6' 00"

Built: Harry Gamble, Port Dover, ON

H-12   HUFFMAN EQUIPMENT RENTAL INC., EASTLAKE, OH

Name	Type	Year		Tonnage	Length	Beam	Depth
Hamp Thomas	TB	1968	D	22*	43' 00"	13' 00"	4' 00"
Paddy Miles	TB	1934	D	16*	45' 04"	12' 04"	4' 07"

I-1   ICEBREAKER MACKINAW MARITIME MUSEUM INC., MACKINAW CITY, MI

(icebreakermackinawmuseum.org)

Name	Type	Year		Tonnage	Length	Beam	Depth
Mackinaw **[WAGB-83]**	MU	1944	D	5,252*	290' 00"	74' 00"	29' 00"

Built: Toledo Shipbuilding Co., Toledo, OH; former U.S. Coast Guard icebreaker was decommissioned in 2006; open to the public at Mackinaw City, MI (Launched as USCGC Manitowoc [WAG-83])

I-2   ILLINOIS MARINE TOWING INC., LEMONT, IL *(imtowing.com)*

Name	Type	Year		Tonnage	Length	Beam	Depth
Aggie C	TW	1977	D	134*	81' 00"	26' 00"	9' 00"
Albert C	TW	1971	D	65*	61' 02"	18' 00"	5' 07"
Channahon	TW	2001	D	67*	52' 00"	22' 00"	7' 00"
Eileen C	TW	1982	D	145*	75' 00"	26' 00"	9' 00"
Hennepin	TW	1957	D	48*	48' 03"	16' 00"	5' 00"
Lemont Trader	TW	1974	D	319*	85' 05"	30' 00"	9' 05"
William C	TW	1968	D	143*	76' 06"	24' 00"	8' 00"
Windy City	TW	1979	D	141*	61' 03"	26' 00"	9' 02"

I-3   INLAND LAKES MANAGEMENT INC., ALPENA, MI

Name	Type	Year		Tonnage	Length	Beam	Depth
Alpena {2}	CC	1942	T	15,550	519' 06"	67' 00"	35' 00"

Built: Great Lakes Engineering Works, River Rouge, MI; shortened by 120' and converted to a self-unloading cement carrier at Fraser Shipyards, Superior, WI, in '91 (Leon Fraser '42-'91)

Name	Type	Year		Tonnage	Length	Beam	Depth
J. A. W. Iglehart	CC	1936	T	12,500	501' 06"	68' 03"	37' 00"

Built: Sun Shipbuilding and Drydock Co., Chester, PA; converted from a saltwater tanker to a self-unloading cement carrier at American Ship Building Co., South Chicago, IL , in '65; last operated Oct. 29, 2006; in use as a cement storage/transfer vessel at Superior, WI (Pan Amoco '36-'55, Amoco '55-'60, H. R. Schemm '60-'65)

Fleet #	Fleet Name / Vessel Name					Overall Length	Breadth	Depth or Draft*
	Paul H. Townsend	CC	1945	D	7,850	447' 00"	50' 00"	29' 00"

Built: Consolidated Steel Corp., Wilmington, DE; converted from a saltwater cargo vessel to a self-unloading cement carrier at Bethlehem Steel Co., Shipbuilding Div., Hoboken, NJ, & Calumet Shipyard, Chicago, IL, in '52 / '53; lengthened at Great Lakes Engineering Works, Ashtabula, OH, in '58; last operated Dec. 5, 2005; in use as a cement storage/transfer vessel at Muskegon, MI (USNS Hickory Coll '45-'46, USNS Coastal Delegate '46-'52)

| | S. T. Crapo | CC | 1927 | B | 8,900 | 402' 06" | 60' 03" | 29' 00" |

Built: Great Lakes Engineering Works, River Rouge, MI; last operated Sept. 4, 1996; in use as a cement storage and transfer vessel at Green Bay, WI

I-4 INLAND SEAS EDUCATION ASSOCIATION, SUTTONS BAY, MI (schoolship.org)

| | Inland Seas | RV | 1994 | W | 41* | 61' 06" | 17' 00" | 7' 00" |

Built: Treworgy Yachts, Palm Coast, FL

I-5 INLAND TUG & BARGE LTD., BROCKVILLE, ON

| | Katanni | TB | 1991 | D | 19* | 34' 08" | 14' 05" | 5' 05" |

I-6 INTERLAKE STEAMSHIP CO., RICHFIELD, OH (interlakesteamship.com)

| | Charles M. Beeghly | SU | 1959 | D | 31,000 | 806' 00" | 75' 00" | 37' 06" |

Built: American Shipbuilding Co., Lorain, OH; lengthened 96' in '72; converted to a self-unloader in '81 at Fraser Shipyards, Superior, WI (Shenango II '59-'67)

| | Herbert C. Jackson | SU | 1959 | T | 24,800 | 690' 00" | 75' 00" | 37' 06" |

Built: Great Lakes Engineering Works, River Rouge, MI; converted to a self-unloader at Defoe Shipbuilding Co., Bay City, MI, in '75

| | James R. Barker | SU | 1976 | D | 63,300 | 1,004' 00" | 105' 00" | 50' 00" |

Built: American Shipbuilding Co., Lorain, OH

| | Mesabi Miner | SU | 1977 | D | 63,300 | 1,004' 00" | 105' 00" | 50' 00" |

Built: American Shipbuilding Co., Lorain, OH

| | Paul R. Tregurtha | SU | 1981 | D | 68,000 | 1,013' 06" | 105' 00" | 56' 00" |

Built: American Shipbuilding Co., Lorain, OH (William J. DeLancey '81-'90)

| | Stewart J. Cort | SU | 1972 | D | 58,000 | 1,000' 00" | 105' 00" | 49' 00" |

Built: Erie Marine Inc., Erie, PA; the Cort was the first 1,000-footer to enter Great Lakes service

INTERLAKE TRANSPORTATION INC., RICHFIELD, OH – DIVISION OF INTERLAKE STEAMSHIP CO.

| | Dorothy Ann | AT/TT | 1999 | D | 1,600* | 124' 03" | 44' 00" | 24' 00" |

Built: Bay Shipbuilding Co., Sturgeon Bay, WI

| | Pathfinder {3} | SU | 1953 | B | 26,700 | 606' 02" | 70' 00" | 36' 00" |

Built: Great Lakes Engineering Works, River Rouge, MI; converted from a powered vessel to a self-unloading barge at Bay Shipbuilding, Sturgeon Bay, WI, in '98 (J. L. Mauthe '53-'98)

| | [ATB Dorothy Ann / Pathfinder {3} OA dimensions together] | | | | | 700' 00" | 70' 00" | 36' 00" |

LAKES SHIPPING CO. INC., RICHFIELD, OH – DIVISION OF INTERLAKE STEAMSHIP CO.

| | John Sherwin {2} | BC | 1958 | T | 31,500 | 806' 00" | 75' 00" | 37' 06" |

Built: American Steamship Co., Lorain, OH; lengthened 96' at Fraser Shipyards, Superior, WI, in '73; last operated Nov. 16, 1981; repowering and conversion to a self-unloader was begun at Bay Shipbuilding Co., Sturgeon Bay, WI, in 2008 but is now on hold pending an improvement in the economy

| | Kaye E. Barker | SU | 1952 | T | 25,900 | 767' 00" | 70' 00" | 36' 00" |

Built: American Shipbuilding Co., Toledo, OH; lengthened 120' at Fraser Shipyards, Superior, WI, in '76; converted to a self-unloader at American Shipbuilding Co., Toledo, OH, in '81 (Edward B. Greene '52-'85, Benson Ford {3} '85-'89)

| | Lee A. Tregurtha | SU | 1942 | D | 29,360 | 826' 00" | 75' 00" | 39' 00" |

Built: Bethlehem Shipbuilding and Drydock Co., Sparrows Point, MD; converted from a saltwater tanker to a Great Lakes bulk carrier in '61; lengthened 96' in '76 and converted to a self-unloader in '78, all at American Shipbuilding Co., Lorain, OH; repowered in '06 (Laid down as Mobiloil; launched as Samoset. USS Chiwawa [AO-68] '42-'46, Chiwawa '46-'61, Walter A. Sterling '61-'85, William Clay Ford {2} '85-'89)

I-7 INTERNATIONAL MARINE SALVAGE INC., PORT COLBORNE, ON (rawmaterials.com)

| | Kristin | TB | 1944 | D | 261* | 111' 00" | 27' 00" | 13' 00" |

Awaiting scrapping at Port Colborne, ON (HMCS Riverton [W-47 / ATA-528] '44-'79, Techno St-Laurent '79-'02)

| | Charlie E. | TB | 1943 | D | 32* | 63' 00" | 16' 06" | 7' 06" |

Built: W.F. Kolbe & Co. Ltd., Port Dover, ON (Kolbe '43-'86, Lois T. '86-'02)

I-8 ISLAND FERRY SERVICES CORP., CHEBOYGAN, MI

| | Polaris | PF | 1952 | D | 99* | 60' 02" | 36' 00" | 8' 06" |

Built: Weldship Corp., Bethlehem, PA

I-9   **ISLE ROYALE LINE INC., COPPER HARBOR, MI** *(isleroyale.com)*

Isle Royale Queen IV	PA/PK	1980	D	93*	98 09″	22′ 01″	7′ 00″

Built: Neuville Boat Works Inc., New Iberia, LA (American Freedom, John Jay, Shuttle V, Danielle G, Harbor Commuter V)

J-1   **J. W. WESTCOTT CO., DETROIT, MI** *(jwwestcott.com)*

J. W. Westcott II	MB	1949	D	11*	46′ 01″	13′ 04″	4′ 06″

Built: Paasch Marine Service, Erie, PA; floating post office has its own U.S. zip code, 48222

Joseph J. Hogan	MB	1957	D	16*	40′ 00″	12′ 06″	5′ 00″

Backup mailboat and water taxi for vessels docked at Great Lakes Steel / Zug Island (USCOE Ottawa '57-'95)

J-2   **JOSEPH B. MARTIN, BEAVER ISLAND, MI**

Shamrock {1}	TB	1933	D	60*	64′ 00″	18′ 00″	7′ 03″

Built: Pennsylvania Shipyard Inc., Beaumont, TX

Tanker II	TK	1964	B	60*	64′ 00″	18′ 00″	6′ 00″

Built: Christy Corp, Sturgeon Bay, WI

J-3   **JUBILEE QUEEN CRUISES, TORONTO, ON** *(jubileequeencruises.ca)*

Jubilee Queen	ES	1986	D	269*	122′ 00″	23′ 09″	5′ 05″

Built: Robin Lane Hanson, Oromocto, NB (Pioneer Princess III '86-'89)

J-4   **JULIO CONTRACTING CO., HANCOCK, MI**

Winnebago	TW	1945	D	14*	40′ 00″	10′ 02″	4′ 06″

K-1   **K-SEA CANADA CORP., HALIFAX, NS** *(k-sea.com)*
      VESSELS CHARTERED TO PETRO-NAV INC., MONTREAL, QC

McCleary's Spirit	TK	1969	B	6,888*	379′ 09″	63′ 03″	33′ 08″

Built: Boelwerf, Belgium (LeVent '69-'02)

William J. Moore	TB	1970	D	564*	135′ 00″	34′ 09″	19′ 04″

Built: Adelaide Ship Construction Pty. Ltd., Port Adelaide, S. Australia (Warrawee '70-'76, Seaspan Raider '76-'87, Raider '87-'87, Raider IV '87-'88, Alice A. '88-'02)

K-2   **KEHOE MARINE CONSTRUCTION CO., LANSDOWNE, ON**

Houghton	TB	1944	D	15*	45′ 00″	13′ 00″	6′ 00″

Built: Port Houston Iron Works, Houston, TX

K-3   **KELLEYS ISLAND BOAT LINES, MARBLEHEAD, OH** *(kelleysislandferry.com)*

Carlee Emily	PA/CF	1987	D	98*	101′ 00″	34′ 06″	10′ 00″

Built: Blount Marine Corp., Warren, RI (Endeavor '87-'02)

Kayla Marie	PA/CF	1975	D	93*	122′ 00″	40′ 00″	8′ 00″

Built: New Bern Shipyard, New Bern, NC (R. Bruce Etherige '75-'97)

Shirley Irene	PA/CF	1991	D	68*	160′ 00″	46′ 00″	9′ 00″

K-4   **KEWEENAW EXCURSIONS INC., HOUGHTON, MI** *(keweenawexcursions.com)*

Keweenaw Star	ES	1981	D	97*	110′ 00″	23′ 04″	6′ 03″

Built: Camcraft Inc., Crown Point, LA (Atlantic Star, Privateer, De De Bruce)

K-5   **KEYSTONE GREAT LAKES INC., BALA CYNWYD, PA** *(www.keyship.com)*

Great Lakes {2}	TK	1982	B	5,024*	414′ 00″	60′ 00″	30′ 00″

Built: Bay Shipbuilding Co., Sturgeon Bay, WI (Amoco Great Lakes '82-'85)

Michigan {10}	AT	1982	D	293*	107′ 08″	34′ 00″	16′ 00″

Built: Bay Shipbuilding Co., Sturgeon Bay, WI (Amoco Michigan '82-'85)
    [ATB Michigan / Great Lakes {2} OA dimensions together]   454′ 00″   60′ 00″   30′ 00″

K-6   **KINDRA LAKE TOWING LP, DOWNERS GROVE, IL** *(kindralake.com)*

Buckley	TW	1958	D	94*	95′ 00″	26′ 00″	11′ 00″

Built: Parker Bros. Shipyard, Houston, TX (Linda Brooks '58-'67, Eddie B. {2} '67-'95)

Morgan	TB	1974	D	134*	90′ 00″	30′ 00″	10′ 06″

Built: Peterson Builders Inc., Sturgeon Bay, WI (Donald O'Toole '74-'86, Bonesey B. '86-'95)

Old Mission	TB	1945	D	94*	85′ 00″	23′ 00″	10′ 04″

Built: Sturgeon Bay Shipbuilding, Sturgeon Bay, WI (U. S. Army ST-880 '45-'47, USCOE Avondale '47-'64, Adrienne B. '64-'95)

Tanner	TB	1976	D	62*	56′ 06″	22′ 00″	7′ 05″

Cement carrier *Alpena* on a fall day on the St. Marys River. *(Roger LeLievre)*

Fleet #	Fleet Name / Vessel Name	Type of Vessel	Year Built	Type of Engine	Cargo Cap. or Gross*	Overall Length	Breadth	Depth or Draft*
K-7	**KING CO. INC., HOLLAND, MI**							
	Barry J	TB	1943	D	26*	46' 00"	13' 00"	7' 00"
	Built: Sturgeon Bay Shipbuilding & Dry Dock Co., Sturgeon Bay, WI							
	Buxton II	DR	1976	B	147*	130' 02"	28' 01"	7' 00"
	Built: Barbour Boat Works Inc., Holland, MI							
	Carol Ann	TB	1981	D	86*	61' 05"	24' 00"	8' 07"
	Built: Rodriguez Boat Builders, Bayou La Batre, AL							
	John Henry	TB	1954	D	66*	65' 04"	19' 04"	9' 06"
	Built: Missouri Valley Steel, Leavenworth, KS (U. S. Army ST-2013 '54-'80)							
	Julie Dee	TB	1937	D	64*	68' 08"	18' 01"	7' 06"
	Built: Herbert Slade, Beaumont, TX (Dernier, Jerry O'Day, Cindy B)							
	Matt Allen	TB	1961	D	146*	80' 04"	24' 00"	11' 03"
	Built: Nolty Theriot Inc., Golden Meadow, LA (Gladys Bea '61-'73, American Viking '73-'83, Maribeth Andrie '83-'05)							
	Miss Edna	TB	1935	D	13*	36' 08"	11' 02"	4' 08"
	Built: Levingston Shipbuilding, Orange, TX							
K-8	**KINGSTON & THE ISLANDS BOAT LINES LTD., KINGSTON, ON** *(1000islandscruises.on.ca)*							
	Island Belle I	ES	1988	D	150*	65' 00"	22' 00"	8' 00"
	(Spirit of Brockville '88-'91)							
	Island Queen III	ES	1975	D	300*	96' 00"	26' 00"	11' 00"
	Island Star	ES	1994	D	220*	97' 00"	30' 00"	10' 00"
	(Le Bateau-Mouche II '94-'98)							
	Papoose III	ES	1968	D	110*	64' 08"	23' 03"	7' 03"
	(Peche Island II)							
K-9	**KK INTEGRATED LOGISTICS, MENOMINEE, MI** *(kkwarehousing.com)*							
	William H. Donner	CS	1914	B	9,400	524' 00"	54' 00"	30' 00"
	Built: Great Lakes Engineering Works, Ashtabula, OH; last operated in 1969; in use as a cargo transfer vessel at Marinette, WI							
	KK INTEGRATED SHIPPING LLC, MENOMINEE, MI							
	James L. Kuber	SU	1953	B	25,500	703' 08"	70' 00"	36' 00"
	Built: Great Lakes Engineering Works, River Rouge, MI; lengthened 120' by Fraser Shipyards, Superior, WI, in '75; converted to a self-unloader by Bay Shipbuilding, Sturgeon Bay, WI, in '83; converted to a barge by the owners in '07 (Reserve '53-'08)							
	Lewis J. Kuber	SU	1952	B	22,300	616' 10"	70' 00"	37' 00"
	Built: Bethlehem Steel Corp., Sparrows Point, MD; lengthened 72' by American Shipbuilding, South Chicago, IL, in '58; converted to a self-unloader by Fraser Shipyards, Superior, WI, in '80; converted to a barge by Erie Shipbuilding, Erie, PA, in '06; operated by VanEnkevort Tug & Barge Inc. (Sparrows Point '52-'90, Buckeye {3} '90-'06)							
	Manitowoc	DB	1926	B	3,080*	371' 03"	67' 03"	22' 06"
	Built: Manitowoc Shipbuilding Co., Manitowoc, WI; laid up at Marinette, WI							
	Olive L. Moore	AT	1928	D	301*	125' 00"	27' 01"	13' 09"
	Built: Manitowoc Shipbuilding Co., Manitowoc, WI (John F. Cushing '28-'66, James E. Skelly '66-'66)							
	Victory	TB	1980	D	194*	129' 00"	43' 01"	18' 00"
	Built: McDermott Shipyard Inc., Amelia, LA							
	Viking I	CF	1925	D	2,713*	360' 00"	56' 03"	21' 06"
	Built: Manitowoc Shipbuilding Co., Manitowoc, WI; laid up at Marinette, WI (Ann Arbor No. 7 '25-'64, Viking {2} '64-'96)							
L-1	**LAFARGE CANADA INC., MONTREAL, QC**							
	THE FOLLOWING VESSEL MANAGED BY CANADA STEAMSHIP LINES INC.							
	English River	CC	1961	D	7,450	404' 03"	60' 00"	36' 06"
	Built: Canadian Shipbuilding and Engineering Ltd., Collingwood, ON; converted to a self-unloading cement carrier by Port Arthur Shipbuilding, Port Arthur (now Thunder Bay), ON, in '74							
L-2	**LAFARGE NORTH AMERICA INC., SOUTHFIELD, MI** *(lafargenorthamerica.com)*							
	J. B. Ford	CC	1904	R	8,000	440' 00"	50' 00"	28' 00"
	Built: American Ship Building Co., Lorain, OH; converted to a self-unloading cement carrier in '59; last operated Nov. 15, 1985; most recently used as a cement storage and transfer vessel at Superior, WI, and now laid up at that port (Edwin F. Holmes '04-'16, E. C. Collins '16-'59)							
	THE FOLLOWING VESSELS MANAGED BY ANDRIE INC., MUSKEGON, MI *(andrie.com)*							
	G. L. Ostrander	AT	1976	D	198*	140' 02"	40' 01"	22' 03"
	Built: Halter Marine, New Orleans, LA (Andrew Martin '76-'90, Robert L. Torres '90-'94, Jacklyn M '94-'04)							

Fleet #	Fleet Name / Vessel Name	Type of Vessel	Year Built	Type of Engine	Cargo Cap. or Gross*	Overall Length	Breadth	Depth or Draft*
	Integrity	CC	1996	B	14,000	460' 00"	70' 00"	37' 00"
	Built: Bay Shipbuilding Co., Sturgeon Bay, WI							
	[ATB G.L. Ostrander / Integrity OA dimensions together]					543' 00"	70' 00"	37' 00"
	Innovation	CC	2006	B	7,320*	460' 00"	70' 00"	37' 00"
	Built: Bay Shipbuilding Co., Sturgeon Bay, WI							
	Samuel de Champlain	AT	1975	D	299*	140' 02"	39' 02"	20' 00"
	Built: Mangone Shipbuilding, Houston, TX (Musketeer Fury '75- '78, Tender Panther '78- '79, Margarita '79- '83, Vortice '83- '99, Norfolk '99-'06)							
L-3	**LAKE COUNTY HISTORICAL SOCIETY, TWO HARBORS, MN** *(northshorehistory.com)*							
	Edna G.	MU	1896	R	154*	102' 00"	23' 00"	14' 06"
	Built: Cleveland Shipbuilding Co., Cleveland, OH; former Duluth, Missabe & Iron Range Railroad tug last operated in 1981; open to the public at Two Harbors, MN							
L-4	**LAKE EXPRESS LLC, MILWAUKEE, WI** *(lake-express.com)*							
	Lake Express	PA/CF	2004	D	96*	179' 02"	57' 07"	16' 00"
	Built: Austal USA, Mobile, AL; high-speed ferry in service from Milwaukee, WI, to Muskegon, MI							
L-5	**LAKE MICHIGAN CARFERRY SERVICE INC., LUDINGTON, MI** *(ssbadger.com)*							
	Badger	PA/CF	1953	S	4,244*	410' 06"	59' 06"	24' 00"
	Built: Christy Corp., Sturgeon Bay, WI; traditional ferry in service from Ludington, MI, to Manitowoc, WI							
	Spartan	PA/CF	1952	S	4,244*	410' 06"	59' 06"	24' 00"
	Built: Christy Corp., Sturgeon Bay, WI; last operated Jan. 20, 1979; in long-term lay-up at Ludington, MI							
L-6	**LAKE TOWING INC., CLEVELAND, OH**							
	Menominee	TB	1967	D	235*	108' 00"	29' 00"	14' 00"
	Upper Canada	PA/CF	1949	D	165*	143' 00"	36' 00"	11' 00"
	Vessel laid up in Lorain, OH (Romeo and Annette '49-'66)							
L-7	**LAKEN SHIPPING CORP., CLEVELAND, OH** *(www.seawaymarinetransport.com)*							
	VESSELS CHARTERED AND COMMERCIALLY MANAGED BY SMT (USA) INC.							
	Cleveland	TB	1999	D	392*	105' 02"	34' 01"	15' 00"
	Built: C & G Boat Works, Bayou La Batre, AL (James Palladino '99-'04)							
	Cleveland Rocks	SU	1957	B	6,280*	390' 00"	71' 00"	27' 00"
	Built: Todd Shipyards Corp., Houston, TX (M-211 '57-'81, Virginia '81-'88, C-11 '88-'93, Kellstone 1 '93-'04)							
L-8	**LAKES PILOTS ASSOCIATION, PORT HURON, MI** *(lakespilots.com)*							
	Huron Belle	PB	1979	D	21*	50' 00"	16' 00"	7' 09"
	Built: Gladding-Hearn Shipbuilding, Somerset, MA; vessel offers pilot service at Port Huron, MI							
	Huron Maid	PB	1976	D	26*	46' 00"	16' 00"	3' 05"
	Built: Hans Hansen Welding Co., Toledo, OH; vessel offers pilot service at Detroit, MI							
L-9	**LE BATEAU-MOUCHE AU VIEUX-PORT INC., MONTREAL, QC** *(bateaumouche.ca)*							
	Le Bateau-Mouche	ES	1992	D	190*	108' 00"	22' 00"	3' 00"
L-10	**LE GROUPE OCÉAN INC., QUÉBEC, QC** *(groupocean.com)*							
	Basse-Cote	DB	1932	B	400	201' 00"	40' 00"	12' 00"
	Betsiamites	SU	1969	B	11,600	402' 00"	75' 00"	24' 00"
	Coo-Coo	TB	1956	D	11*	35' 00"	10' 00"	4' 04"
	Coucoucache	TB	1934	D	95*	34' 01"	9' 05"	4' 02"
	David T. D.	TB	1947	D	22*	42' 01"	12' 03"	5' 08"
	H. E. Graham	TB	1964	D	7*	32' 09"	9' 05"	3' 05"
	J. V. Perrin	TB	1958	D	8*	34' 01"	10' 00"	3' 09"
	Jerry G.	TB	1960	D	202*	91' 06"	27' 03"	12' 06"
	Built: Davie Shipbuilding Co., Lauzon, QC							
	Kim R. D.	TB	1954	D	30*	48' 07"	14' 01"	5' 08"
	La Croche	TB	1940	D	7*	32' 07"	9' 05"	3' 05"
	La Prairie	TB	1975	D	110*	73' 09"	25' 09"	11' 08"
	Built: Georgetown Shipyard, Georgetown, PEI							
	Lac St-Francois	BC	1979	B	1,200	195' 00"	35' 00"	12' 00"
	Built: Nashville Bridge Co., Nashhville, TN							
	Le Phil D.	TB	1961	D	38*	56' 01"	16' 00"	5' 08"
	Mado-Ray	TB	1954	D	12*	38' 00"	12' 01"	3' 03"

Fleet #	Fleet Name / Vessel Name	Type of Vessel	Year Built	Type of Engine	Cargo Cap. or Gross*	Overall Length	Breadth	Depth or Draft*
	Navcomar No. 1	DB	1955	B	500	135' 00"	35' 00"	9' 00"
	Ocean Abys	DB	1948	B	1,000	140' 00"	40' 00"	9' 00"
	Ocean Bertrand Jeansonne	TB	2008	D	402*	94' 05"	36' 05"	17' 02"
	Built: East Isle Shipyard, Georgetown, PEI							
	Ocean Bravo	TB	1970	D	320*	110' 00"	28' 06"	17' 00"
	Built: Davie Shipbuilding Co., Lauzon, QC (Takis V. '70-'80, Donald P '80-'80, Nimue '80-'83, Donald P. '83-'98)							
	Ocean Delta	TB	1973	D	722*	136' 08"	35' 08"	22' 00"
	Built: Ulstein Mek. Verksted A.S., Ulsteinvik, Norway (Sistella '73-'78, Sandy Cape '78-'80, Captain Ioannis S. '80-'99)							
	Ocean Golf	TB	1959	D	159*	103' 00"	25' 10"	11' 09"
	Built: P.K. Harris & Sons, Appledore, England (Launched as Stranton. Helen M. McAllister '59-'97)							
	Ocean Henry Bain	TB	2006	D	402*	94' 08"	30' 01"	14' 09"
	Built: East Isle Shipyard, Georgetown, PEI							
	Ocean Hercule	TB	1976	D	448*	120' 00"	32' 00"	19' 00"
	(Stril Pilot '76-'81, Spirit Sky '81-'86, Ierland '86-'89, Ierlandia '89-'95, Charles Antoine '95-'97)							
	Ocean Intrepide	TT	1998	D	302*	80' 00"	30' 01"	14' 09"
	Built: Industries Ocean Inc., Ile-Aux-Coudres, QC							
	Ocean Jupiter {2}	TT	1999	D	302*	80' 00"	30' 00"	13' 04"
	Built: Industries Ocean Inc., Ile-Aux-Coudres, QC							
	Ocean K. Rusby	TB	2005	D	402*	94' 08"	30' 01"	14' 09"
	Built: East Isle Shipyard, Georgetown, PEI							
	Ocean Raymond Lemay	TB	2006	D	402*	94' 08"	30' 01"	14' 09"
	Built: East Isle Shipyard, Georgetown, PEI							
	Omni-Atlas	CS	1913	B	479*	133' 00"	42' 00"	10' 00"
	Omni-Richelieu	TB	1969	D	144*	83' 00"	24' 06"	13' 06"
	Built: Pictou Industries Ltd., Pictou, NS (Port Alfred II '69-'82)							
	Omni St. Laurent	TB	1957	D	161*	99' 02"	24' 09"	12' 06"
	Built: P.K. Harris & Sons, Appledore, England (Diligent '57-'89)							
	Rapide Blanc	TB	1951	D	10*	34' 00"	10' 00"	4' 03"
	Roxane D.	TB	1945	D	50*	60' 06"	16' 06"	6' 07"

***Manistee* gets underway.**
(Herm Phillips)

MANISTEE

OCÉAN REMORQUAGE TROIS-RIVIÈRES INC. – SUBSIDIARY OF LE GROUPE OCÉAN INC.

Vessel Name	Type	Year	Eng	Cargo	Length	Breadth	Depth
Andre H.	TB	1963	D	317*	126' 00"	28' 06"	15' 06"

Built: Davie Shipbuilding Co., Lauzon, QC (Foundation Valiant '63-'73, Point Valiant {1} '73-'95)

Avantage	TB	1969	D	367*	116' 10"	32' 09"	16' 03"

Built: J. Boel En Zonen, Temse, Belgium (Sea Lion '69-'97)

Duga	TB	1977	D	403*	111' 00"	33' 00"	16' 01"

Built: Langsten Slip & Båtbyggeri A/S, Lanste, Norway

Escorte	TT	1964	D	120*	85' 00"	23' 08"	11' 00"

Built: Jakobson Shipyard, Oyster Bay, NY (USS Menasha [YTB / YTM-773, YTM-761] '64-'92, Menasha {1} '92-'95)

Josee H.	PB	1961	D	66*	63' 50"	16' 02"	9' 50"
Ocean Charlie	TB	1973	D	448*	123' 02"	31' 06"	18' 09"

Built: Davie Shipbuilding Co., Lauzon, QC (Leonard W. '73-'98)

Ocean Echo II	AT	1969	D	438*	104' 08"	35' 05"	18' 00"

Built: Port Weller Dry Docks, Port Weller, ON (Atlantic '69-'75, Laval '75-'96)

Ocean Foxtrot	TB	1971	D	700*	184' 05"	38' 05"	16' 07"

Built: Cochrane & Sons Ltd., Selby, England (Polar Shore '71-'77, Canmar Supplier VII '77-'95)

R. F. Grant	TB	1969	D	78*	71' 00"	17' 00"	8' 00"

Built: Canadian Vickers Ltd., Montreal, QC

Service Boat No. 1	PB	1965	D	55*	57' 08"	16' 01"	7' 06"
Service Boat No. 4	PB	1959	D	26*	39' 01"	14 02"	6' 03"

L-11   LE SAULT DE SAINTE MARIE HISTORIC SITES INC., SAULT STE. MARIE, MI *(saulthistoricsites.com)*

Valley Camp {2}	MU	1917	R	12,000	550' 00"	58' 00"	31' 00"

Built: American Shipbuilding Co., Lorain, OH; former Hanna Mining Co./Wilson Marine Transit Co./Republic Steel Corp. bulk carrier last operated in 1966; open to the public at Sault Ste. Marie, MI (Louis W. Hill '17-'55)

L-12   LEE MARINE LTD., SOMBRA, ON *(hammondbaycruises.com)*

Hammond Bay	ES	1992	D	43*	54' 00"	16' 00"	3' 00"

Built: Donald Mummery, Port Dover, ON (Scrimp & Scrounge '92-'95)

Nancy A. Lee	TB	1939	D	9*	40' 00"	12' 00"	3' 00"

L-13   LOCK TOURS CANADA BOAT CRUISES, SAULT STE. MARIE, ON *(locktours.com)*

Chief Shingwauk	ES	1965	D	109*	70' 00"	24' 00"	4' 06"

Built: Hike Metal Products Ltd., Wheatley, ON

L-14   LOWER LAKES TOWING LTD., PORT DOVER, ON *(lowerlakes.com)*

Cuyahoga	SU	1943	D	15,675	620' 00"	60' 00"	35' 00"

Built: American Shipbuilding Co., Lorain, OH; converted to a self-unloader by Manitowoc Shipbuilding Co., Manitowoc, WI, in 74; repowered in '01 (J. Burton Ayers '43-'95)

Kaministiqua	BC	1983	D	33,824	730' 00"	75' 09"	48' 00"

Built: Govan Shipyards, Glasgow, Scotland (Saskatchewan Pioneer '83-'95, Lady Hamilton '95-'06, Voyageur Pioneer '06-'08)

Michipicoten {2}	SU	1952	T	22,300	698' 00"	70' 00"	37' 00"

Built: Bethlehem Shipbuilding & Drydock Co., Sparrows Point, MD; lengthened 72' by American Shipbuilding, S. Chicago, IL, in '57; converted to a self-unloader by American Shipbuilding, Toledo, OH, in '80 (Elton Hoyt 2nd '52-'03)

Mississagi	SU	1943	D	15,800	620' 06"	60' 00"	35' 00"

Built: Great Lakes Engineering Works, River Rouge, MI; converted to a self-unloader by Fraser Shipyards, Superior, WI, in '67; repowered in '85 (Hill Annex '43-'43, George A. Sloan '43-'01)

Ojibway	BC	1952	D	20,668	642' 03"	67' 00"	35' 00"

Built: Defoe Shipbuilding Co., Bay City, MI; repowered in '05 (Charles L. Hutchinson {3} '52-'62, Ernest R. Breech '62-'88, Kinsman Independent '88-'05, Voyageur Independent '05-'08)

Robert S. Pierson	SU	1974	D	19,650	630' 00"	68' 00"	36' 11"

Built: American Shipbuilding Co., Lorain, OH (Wolverine {2} '74-'08)

Saginaw {3}	SU	1953	D	20,200	639' 03"	72' 00"	36' 00"

Built: Manitowoc Shipbuilding Co., Manitowoc, WI, repowered in '08 (John J. Boland {3} '53-'99)

L-15   LOWER LAKES TRANSPORTATION CO., WILLIAMSVILLE, NY
A DIVISION OF LOWER LAKES TOWING LTD. *(lowerlakes.com)*

GRAND RIVER NAVIGATION CO., CLEVELAND, OH – OWNER – AFFILIATE OF LOWER LAKES TOWING LTD.

Calumet {3}	SU	1973	D	19,650	630' 00"	68' 00"	36' 11"

Built: American Shipbuilding Co., Lorain, OH (William R. Roesch '73-'95, David Z. Norton {3} '95-'07, David Z. '07-'08)

| | Invincible | ATB | 1979 | D | 180* | 100' 00" | 35' 00" | 22' 06" |

Built: Atlantic Marine Inc., Fort George Island, FL (R. W. Sesler '79-'91)

| | Manistee | SU | 1943 | D | 14,900 | 620' 06" | 60' 03" | 35' 00" |

Built: Great Lakes Engineering Works, River Rouge, MI; converted to a self-unloader by Manitowoc Shipbuilding Co., Manitowoc, WI, in '64; repowered in '76 (Launched as Adirondack. Richard J. Reiss {2} '43-'86, Richard Reiss '86-'05)

| | Manitowoc | SU | 1973 | D | 19,650 | 630' 00" | 68' 00" | 36' 11" |

Built: American Shipbuilding Co., Lorain, OH (Paul Thayer '73-'95, Earl W. Oglebay '95-'07, Earl W. '07-'08)

| | Maumee | SU | 1929 | D | 12,650 | 604' 09" | 60' 00" | 32' 00" |

Built: American Shipbuilding Co., Lorain, OH; converted to a self-unloader by Manitowoc Shipbuilding Co., Manitowoc, WI, in '61; repowered in '64 (William G. Clyde '29-'61, Calcite II '61-'01)

LAKE SERVICE SHIPPING CO., GROSSE POINTE FARMS, MI – OWNER

| | McKee Sons | SU | 1945 | B | 19,900 | 579' 02" | 71' 06" | 38' 06" |

Built: Sun Shipbuilding and Drydock Co., Chester, PA; converted from saltwater vessel to a self-unloading Great Lakes bulk carrier by Maryland Drydock, Baltimore, MD, in '52; completed as a self-unloader by Manitowoc Shipbuilding Co., Manitowoc, WI, in '53; engine removed and converted to a self-unloading barge by Upper Lakes Towing, Escanaba, MI, in '91 (USNS Marine Angel '45-'52)

[ATB McKee Sons / Invincible OA dimensions together] | | 615' 00" | 71' 06" | 38' 06" |

| L-16 | **LUEDTKE ENGINEERING CO., FRANKFORT, MI** *(luedtke-eng.com)* | | | | | | | |

| | Alan K. Luedtke | TB | 1944 | D | 149* | 86' 04" | 23' 00" | 10' 03" |

Built: Allen Boat Co., Harvey, LA (U. S. Army ST-527 '44-'55, USCOE Two Rivers '55-'90)

| | Ann Marie | TB | 1954 | D | 119* | 71' 00" | 19' 06" | 9' 06" |

Built: Smith Basin & Drydock, Pensacola, FL (ST-9684 '54- '80, Lewis Castle '80-'97, Apache '97-'01)

	Chris E. Luedtke	TB	1936	D	18*	42' 05"	11' 09"	5' 00"
	Erich R. Luedtke	TB	1939	D	18*	42' 05"	11' 09"	5' 00"
	Gretchen B.	TB	1943	D	18*	41' 09"	12' 05"	6' 00"
	Karl E. Luedtke	TB	1928	D	32*	55' 02"	14' 09"	6' 00"

Built: Leathem D. Smith Dock Co., Sturgeon Bay, WI

| | Kurt R. Luedtke | TB | 1956 | D | 96* | 72' 00" | 22' 06" | 7' 06" |

Built: Lockport Shipyard, Lockport, LA (Jere C. '56-'90)

| M-1 | **M. C. M. MARINE INC., SAULT STE. MARIE, MI** *(mcmmarine.com)* | | | | | | | |

| | Beaver State | TB | 1935 | D | 18* | 43' 07" | 12' 00" | 5' 02" |
| | Drummond Islander II | CF | 1961 | D | 97* | 65' 00" | 36' 00" | 9' 00" |

Built: Marinette Marine Corp., Marinette, WI

| | Mackinaw City | TB | 1943 | D | 23* | 38' 00" | 11' 05" | 4' 07" |
| | Mohawk | TB | 1945 | D | 46* | 65' 00" | 19' 00" | 10' 06" |

Built: Robert Jacob Inc., City Island, NY

	No. 55	DR	1927	DE	721*	165' 00"	42' 08"	12' 00"
	No. 56	DS	1927	DE	721*	165' 00"	42' 08"	12' 00"
	Ojibway	SB	1945	D	65*	53' 00"	28' 00"	7' 00"

Built: Great Lakes Engineering Works, Ashtabula, OH

| | Peach State | TB | 1961 | D | 19* | 42' 01" | 12' 04" | 5' 03" |
| | Sioux | DS | 1954 | B | 504* | 120' 00" | 50' 00" | 10' 00" |

Built: St. Louis Shipbuilding & Steel Co., St. Louis, MO

| | William C. Gaynor | TB | 1956 | D | 146* | 94' 00" | 27' 00" | 11' 09" |

Built: Defoe Shipbuilding Co., Bay City, MI (William C. Gaynor '56-'88, Captain Barnaby '88-'02)

| M-2 | **MACASSA BAY LIMITED, CORUNNA, ON** *(macassabay.com)* | | | | | | | |

| | Macassa Bay | ES | 1986 | D | 200* | 93' 07" | 29' 07" | 10' 04" |

Built: Boiler Pump & Marine Works Ltd., Hamilton, ON

| M-3 | **MacDONALD MARINE LTD., GODERICH, ON** *(mactug.com)* | | | | | | | |

| | Debbie Lyn | TB | 1950 | D | 10* | 45' 00" | 14' 00" | 10' 00" |

Built: Mathieson Boat Works, Goderich, ON (Skipper '50-'60)

| | Donald Bert | TB | 1953 | D | 11* | 45' 00" | 14' 00" | 10' 00" |

Built: Mathieson Boat Works, Goderich, ON

| | Dover | TB | 1931 | D | 70* | 84' 00" | 17' 00" | 6' 00" |

Built: Canadian Mead-Morrison Co. Ltd., Welland, ON (Earleejune, Iveyrose)

| | Ian Mac | TB | 1955 | D | 12* | 45' 00" | 14' 00" | 10' 00" |

Built: Mathieson Boat Works, Goderich, ON

OLDEST: ST. MARYS CHALLENGER

True, "Know Your Ships" is 50 years old, but the venerable *St. Marys Challenger* has that record beat. Launched in 1906, the steamer embarks on its 103rd season this year.

Built as a traditional Great Lakes bulk carrier by the Great Lakes Engineering Works, Ecorse, Mich., in 1906, this veteran was launched Feb. 7, 1906, as *William P. Snyder* for Shenango Steamship & Transportation Co. (subsidiary of Shenango Furnace Co.), Cleveland, Ohio. Over the years, the vessel has retained her original dimensions but was repowered in 1950 and converted to an automated self-unloading bulk cement carrier in the mid-1960s.

By today's standards, the *St. Marys Challenger* is one of the smaller boats still in service, and if it weren't for her conversion to a cement carrier, the vessel probably would have been scrapped many years ago. The vessel's smaller size is now looked upon as an asset, allowing for the delivery of powdered cement products to cement silos located in smaller ports along the shores of and up some of the rivers feeding into the Great Lakes.

St. Marys Challenger unloads a storage cargo into *C.T.C. #1.* (Peter Groh)

The *Challenger* on the St. Clair River. (Wade P. Streeter)

Sailing as _Alex D. Chisholm_ in the 1950s. _(Tom Manse)_

At the time of her launch, the _William P. Snyder_ was one of the largest ships on the Great Lakes. Coal and iron ore were among the principle cargoes carried. In 1926, she became part of the Pickands Mather/Interlake Steamship fleet as _Elton Hoyt II_, a name she retained until 1952, when she was renamed _Alex D. Chisholm_.

When Medusa Portland Cement Co. acquired the vessel in 1966, it renamed its newly converted cement carrier _Medusa Challenger_. A 1998 takeover of her owners by Southdown Inc. brought a name change to _Southdown Challenger,_ and a further takeover in 2005 resulted in another renaming to _St. Marys Challenger._ Most of the recent trade routes of the _St. Marys Challenger_ have been concentrated in Lake Michigan and upper Lake Huron, with the occasional trip further south as needed. – _George Wharton_

Lake Michigan sunset from on board the _St. Marys Challenger._ _(Blake Kishler)_

Medusa Challenger in the late 1960s. _(Peter Worden)_

M-4   MADELINE ISLAND FERRY LINE INC., LaPOINTE, WI *(madferry.com)*

Bayfield {2}	PA/CF	1952	D	83*	120' 00"	43' 00"	10' 00"
Built: Chesapeake Marine Railway, Deltaville, VA (Charlotte '52-'99)							
Island Queen {2}	PA/CF	1966	D	90*	75' 00"	34' 09"	10' 00"
Madeline	PA/CF	1984	D	97*	90' 00"	35' 00"	8' 00"
Nichevo II	PA/CF	1962	D	89*	65' 00"	32' 00"	8' 09"

M-5   MAID OF THE MIST STEAMBOAT CO. LTD., NIAGARA FALLS, ON *(maidofthemist.com)*

Maid of the Mist IV	ES	1976	D	74*	72' 00"	16' 00"	7' 00"
Maid of the Mist V	ES	1983	D	74*	72' 00"	16' 00"	7' 00"
Maid of the Mist VI	ES	1990	D	155*	78' 09"	29' 06"	7' 00"
Maid of the Mist VII	ES	1997	D	160*	80' 00"	30' 00"	7' 00"

M-6   MALCOLM MARINE, ST. CLAIR, MI

Manitou {2}	TB	1942	D	491*	110' 00"	26' 05"	11' 06"
Built: U.S. Coast Guard, Curtis Bay, MD (USCGC Manitou [WYT-60] '43-'84)							

M-7   MANITOU ISLAND TRANSIT, LELAND, MI *(leelanau.com/manitou)*

Manitou Isle	PA/PK	1946	D	39*	52' 00"	14' 00"	8' 00"
(Namaycush '46-'59)							
Mishe Mokwa	PA/CF	1966	D	49*	65' 00"	17' 06"	8' 00"
Built: J. W. Nolan & Sons, Erie, PA							

M-8   MARINE ONE TOWING & SALVAGE LTD., DETROIT, MI *(marineonetowing.com)*

Sheila Kaye	TB	1943	D	58*	65' 00"	18' 00"	7' 03"
Built: Sturgeon Bay Shipbuilding & Dry Dock Co., Sturgeon Bay, WI (Acushnet '43-'08)							

M-9   MARINE MUSEUM OF THE GREAT LAKES AT KINGSTON, KINGSTON, ON *(marmuseum.ca)*

Alexander Henry	MU	1959	D	1,674*	210' 00"	44' 00"	17' 09"
Built: Port Arthur Shipbuilding Co., Port Arthur, ON; former Canadian Coast Guard icebreaker was retired in 1985; open to the public at Kingston, ON							

M-10   MARINE TECH LLC, DULUTH, MN *(marinetechduluth.com)*

Alton Andrew	CS	1958	B		70' 00"	50' 00	6' 00"
Callie M.	TB	1910	D	51*	64' 03"	16' 09"	8' 06"
Built: Houma Shipbuilding Co., Houma, LA (Chattanooga '10-'79, Howard T. Hagen '79-'94, Nancy Ann '94-'01)							
Dean R. Smith	DR	1985	B	338*	120' 00"	48' 00"	7' 00"
(No. 2 '85-'94, B. Yetter '94-'01)							
Miss Laura	TB	1943	D	146*	81' 01"	24' 00"	9' 10"
Built: Lawley & Son Corp., Neponset, MA (DPC-3 '43-'46, DS-43 '46-'50, Fresh Kills '50-'69, Richard K. '69-'93, Leopard '93-'03)							

M-11   MARIPOSA CRUISE LINE LTD., TORONTO, ON *(mariposacruises.com)*

Capt. Matthew Flinders	ES	1982	D	696*	144' 00"	40' 00"	8' 06"
Built: North Arm Slipway Pty. Ltd., Port Adelaide, Australia							
Mariposa Belle	ES	1970	D	195*	93' 00"	23' 00"	8' 00"
Built: Hike Metal Products, Wheatley, ON (Niagara Belle '70-'73)							
Rosemary	ES	1960	D	52*	68' 00"	15' 06"	6' 08"
Built: Bender Ship Repairs, Mobile, AL							
Showboat Royal Grace	ES	1988	D	135*	58' 00"	18' 00"	4' 00"
Torontonian	ES	1962	D	68*	68' 00"	18' 06"	6' 08"
Built: Canadian Shipbuilding & Engineering, Kingston, ON (Shiawassie '62-'82)							

M-12   MAXIMUS CORP., BLOOMFIELD HILLS, MI *(boblosteamers.com)*

Ste. Claire	PA	1910	R	870*	197' 00"	65' 00"	14' 00"
Built: Detroit Dry Dock Co., Detroit, MI; former Detroit to Bob-Lo Island passenger steamer last operated Sept. 2, 1991; undergoing restoration at Detroit, MI							

M-13   McASPHALT MARINE TRANSPORTATION LTD., SCARBOROUGH, ON *(mcasphalt.com)*

Everlast	ATB	1976	D	1,361*	143' 04"	44' 04"	21' 04"
Built: Hakodate Dock Co., Hakodate, Japan (Bilibino '77-'96)							
John J. Carrick	TK	2008	B	11,613	407' 06"	71' 07"	30' 00"
Built: Penglai Bohai Shipyard Co. Ltd., Penglai, China							
McAsphalt 401	TK	1966	B	7,399	300' 00"	60' 00"	23' 00"
Built: Todd Shipyards Corp., Houston, TX (Pittson 200 '66-'73, Pointe Levy '73-'87)							

	Type	Year			Length	Breadth	
Norman McLeod	TK	2001	B	6,809*	379' 02"	71' 06"	30' 02"
Built: Jinling Shipyard, Nanjing, China							
[ATB Everlast / Norman McLeod OA dimensions together]					500' 00"	71' 06"	30' 02"
Victorious	ATB	2009	D	1,299	117' 15"	44' 03"	26' 02
Built: Penglai Bohai Shipyard Co. Ltd., Penglai, China							

M-14 McKEIL MARINE LTD., HAMILTON, ON *(mckeilmarine.com)*

	Type	Year			Length	Breadth	
AGS-359	DH	1966	B	1,500	187' 00"	35' 00"	11' 00"
Built: Dravo Corp., Neville Island, PA							
Alouette Spirit	DB	1969	B	11,318*	415' 06"	74' 01"	29' 05"
Built: Gulfport Shipbuilding Co., Port Arthur, TX (KTC 135 '69-'04, Lambert's Spirit '04-'05)							
Black Carrier	DB	1908	B	1,300	200' 02"	43' 00"	10' 05"
Built: Vickers Sons Maxim Ltd., Barrows, UK (J.P.P. No. 540)							
Bonnie B. III	TB	1969	D	308*	100' 03"	32' 00"	17' 00"
(Esso Oranjestad '69-'85, Oranjestad '85-'86, San Nicolas '86-'87, San Nicolas I '87-'88)							
Carrol C. 1	TB	1969	D	291*	100' 03"	32' 00"	17' 00"
Built: Gulfport Shipbuilding Corp., Port Arthur, TX (Esso San Nicolas '69-'86, San Nicolas '86-'87, Carrol C '87-'88)							
Condarrell	DH	1953	D	3,017	259' 00"	43' 06"	21' 00"
Built: Canadian Shipbuilding & Engineering, Kingston, ON; laid up at Port Colborne, ON (D. C. Everest '53-'81)							
D.T. Derrick No. 2	CS	1935	B	205*	80' 00"	27' 00"	6' 07"
Built: Canadian Vickers Ltd., Montreal, QC (H.C.M. Derrick No 5)							
Erie-West	DB	1951	B	1,800	290' 00"	50' 00"	12' 00"
Built: Dravo Corp., Pittsburgh, PA Dover Light)							
Evans McKeil	TB	1936	D	284*	110' 07"	25' 06"	11' 06"
Built: Panama Canal Co., Balboa, Panama (Alhajuela '36-'70, Barbara Ann {2} '70-'89)							
Flo-Mac	TB	1960	D	15*	40' 00"	13' 00"	6' 00"
Florence M.	TB	1961	D	236*	96' 03"	28' 00"	14' 06"
Built: P.K. Harris & Sons, Appledore, England (Foundation Vibert '61-'73, Point Vibert '73-'06)							
General Chemical No. 37	TK	1956	D	883*	208' 08"	42' 08"	13' 07"
Built: Todd Shipyard, Houston, TX							
Jarrett M	TB	1945	D	96*	82' 00"	20' 00"	10' 00"
Built: Russel Brothers Ltd., Owen Sound, ON (Atomic '45-'06)							
Jarrett McKeil	TB	1956	D	197*	91' 08"	27' 04"	13' 06"
Built: Davie Shipbuilding Co., Lauzon, QC (Robert B. No. 1 '56-'97)							
Jean-Raymond	DB	1941	B	6,800	409' 00"	57' 00"	18' 00"
John Spence	TB	1972	D	719*	171' 00"	38' 00"	15' 01"
Built: Star Shipyard, New Westminister, BC (Mary B. VI '72-'81, Mary B. '81-'82, Mary B. VI '82-'83, Artic Tuktu '83-'94)							
Lac Manitoba	TB	1944	D	65*	65' 00"	16' 10"	7' 07"
Built: Central Bridge Co., Trenton, ON (Tanac 75 '44-'52, Manitoba '52-'57)							
Lac St. Jean	DB	1971	B	1,000	150' 00"	55' 00"	11' 00"
Built: Canadian Vickers Ltd., Montreal, QC (OH-VIC-1A)							
Lambert Spirit	DB	1968	B	9,645	393' 07"	69' 08"	27' 05"
Built: Avondale Shipyards Inc., Avondale, LA (KTC 115 '68-'06)							
Molly M. 1	DB	1962	D	207*	98' 05"	26' 10"	13' 05"
Built: Davie Shipbuilding Co., Lauzon, QC (Foundation Vigour '62-'74, Point Vigour '74-'07)							
Niagara Spirit	TK	1984	D	418*	340' 00"	78' 00"	19' 00"
Built: FMC Corp., Portland, OR (Alaska Trader '84-'99, Timberjack '99-'08)							
OC 181	DB	1972	B	2,000	180' 00"	54' 00"	12' 00"
Built: National Bridge Co., Nashville, TN							
Pacific Standard	TB	1967	D	451*	127' 08"	31' 00"	15' 06"
Built: Cochrane & Sons Ltd., Selby, Yorkshire, England (Irishman '67-'76, Kwakwani '76-'78, Lorna B. '78-'81)							
Salvor	TB	1963	D	426*	120' 00"	32' 09"	18' 09"
Built: Jakobson Shipyard, Oyster Bay, NY (Esther Moran '63-'00)							
Sault au Cochon	DH	1969	B	9,600	337' 10"	74' 10"	25' 07"
Built: Port Weller Dry Dock, Port Weller, ON							
Stormont	TB	1953	D	108*	80' 00"	20' 00"	15' 00"
Built: Canadian Dredge & Dock Co., Kingston, ON							
S/VM 86	DB	1958	B	487*	161' 01"	40' 00"	10' 00"
Built: Canadian Shipbuilding & Engineering Ltd., Collingwood, ON (S.L.S. 86)							
Tony MacKay	TB	1973	D	366*	127' 00"	30' 05"	14' 05"
Built: Richard Dunston Ltd., Hessle, England (Point Carroll '73-'01)							

Viateur's Spirit	DB	2004	D	253*	141' 01"	52' 03"	5' 01"

Built: Port Weller Dry Dock, Port Weller, ON (Traverse René Lavasseur '04-'06)

Wilf Seymour	TB	1961	D	429*	120' 00"	32' 09"	18' 09"

Built: Gulfport Shipbuilding, Port Arthur, TX (M. Moran '61-'70, Port Arthur '70-'72, M. Moran '72-'00, Salvager '00-'04)

Wyatt M.	TB	1948	D	123*	86' 00"	21' 00"	10' 00"

Built: Russel Brothers Ltd., Owen Sound, ON (P. J. Murer '48-'81, Michael D. Misner '81-'93, Thomas A. Payette '93-'96, Progress '96-'06)

McKEIL SHIPS LTD. – A SUBSIDIARY OF McKEIL MARINE LTD., HAMILTON, ON

Kathryn Spirit	GC	1967	D	12,497	503' 03"	66' 07"	36' 09"

Built: Lindholmen Shipyard, Gothenburg, Sweden (Holmsund '67-'97, Menominee '97-'06)

MONTREAL BOATMEN LTD. – A SUBSIDIARY OF McKEIL MARINE LTD., PORT COLBORNE, ON

Aldo H.	PB	1979	D	37*	56' 04"	15' 04"	6' 02"
Boatman No. 3	PB	1965	D	13*	33' 08"	11' 00"	6' 00"
Boatman No. 6	PB	1979	D	39*	56' 07"	18' 07"	6' 03"
Dredge Primrose	DR	1915	B	916*	136' 06"	42' 00"	10' 02"

M-15   **McMULLEN & PITZ CONSTRUCTION CO., MANITOWOC, WI** (mcmullenandpitz.net)

Dauntless	TB	1937	D	25*	52' 06"	15' 06"	5' 03"
Erich	TB	1943	D	19*	45' 00"	12' 07"	5' 09"

M-16   **McNALLY CONSTRUCTION INC., HAMILTON, ON** (mcnallycorp.com)

Bagotville	TB	1964	D	65*	65' 00"	18' 06"	10' 00"

Built: Verreault Navigation, Les Méchins, QC

Canadian	DR	1954	B	1,087*	173' 08"	49' 08"	13' 04"
Canadian Argosy	DR	1978	B	951*	149' 09"	54' 01"	10' 08"

Edgar B. Speer leaves port at Duluth/Superior.
(Mike Sipper)

Fleet #	Fleet Name / Vessel Name	Type of Vessel	Year Built	Type of Engine	Cargo Cap. or Gross*	Overall Length	Breadth	Depth or Draft*
	Cargo Master	CS	1964	B	561*	136' 00"	50' 00"	9' 00"
	Carl M.	TB	1957	D	21*	47' 00"	14' 06"	6' 00"
	F. R. McQueen	DB	1959	B	180*	79' 09"	39' 09"	5' 07"
	Greta V	TB	1951	D	14*	44' 00"	12' 00"	5' 00"
	Handy Andy	DB	1925	B	313*	95' 09"	43' 01"	10' 00"
	Idus Atwell	DR	1962	B	366*	100' 00"	40' 00"	8' 05"
	Jerry Newberry	TB	1956	D	244*	98' 00"	28' 02"	14' 04"
	Built: Davie Shipbuilding Co., Lauzon, QC (Foundation Victor '56-'73, Point Victor '73-'77, Kay Cole '77-'95)							
	John Holden	DR	1954	B	148*	89' 08"	30' 01"	6' 02"
	Lac Como	TB	1944	D	63*	65' 00"	16' 10"	7' 10"
	Built: Canadian Bridge Co., Walkerville, ON (Tanac 74 '44-'64)							
	Lac Vancouver	TB	1943	D	65*	65' 00"	16' 10"	7' 07"
	Built: Central Bridge Co., Trenton, ON (Vancouver '43-'74)							
	Paula M.	TB	1959	D	12*	46' 06"	16' 01"	4' 10"
	R. C. L. Tug II	TB	1958	D	20*	42' 09"	14' 03"	5' 09"
	Sandra Mary	TB	1962	D	97*	80' 00"	21' 00"	10' 09"
	Built: Russel Brothers Ltd., Owen Sound, ON (Flo Cooper '62-'00)							
	Willmac	TB	1959	D	16*	40' 00"	13' 00"	3' 07"
	Whitby	TB	1978	D	24*	45' 00"	14' 00"	5' 00"

BEAVER MARINE LTD. – A SUBSIDIARY OF McNALLY CONSTRUCTION INC., HALIFAX, NS

		Type of Vessel	Year Built	Type of Engine	Cargo Cap. or Gross*	Overall Length	Breadth	Depth or Draft*
	Beaver Delta II	TB	1959	D	14*	35' 08"	12' 00"	4' 04"
	(Halcyon Bay)							
	Beaver Gamma	TB	1960	D	17*	37' 01"	12' 09"	6' 00"
	(Burlington Bertie)							
	Beaver Kay	GC	1953	B	614*	115' 01"	60' 00"	9' 05"
	Dapper Dan	TB	1948	D	21*	41' 03"	12' 07"	5' 09"
	Jamie L.	TB	1988	D	25*	36' 04"	14' 07"	5' 09"
	(Baie Ste-Anne II '88-'05)							
	Mister Joe	TB	1964	D	70*	61' 00"	19' 00"	7' 02"
	Built: Russel Brothers Ltd., Owen Sound, ON							
	Oshawa	TB	1969	D	24*	42' 09"	13' 08"	5' 04"
	William B. Dilly	DR	1957	B	473*	116' 00"	39' 10"	9' 01"

M-17 MENASHA TUGBOAT CO., SARNIA, ON

	Menasha {2}	TB	1949	D	147*	78' 00"	24' 00"	9' 08"
	Built: Bludworth, Houston, TX (W. C. Harms '49-'54, Hamilton '54-'86, Ruby Casho '86-'88, W. C. Harms '88-'97)							

M-18 MERCURY CHICAGO'S SKYLINE CRUISELINE, CHICAGO, IL (mercuryskylinecruiseline.com)

	Chicago's First Lady	ES	1991	D	62*	96' 00"	22' 00"	9' 00"
	Chicago's Little Lady	ES	1999	D	70*	69' 02"	22' 08"	7' 00"
	Skyline Princess	ES	1956	D	56*	59' 04"	16' 00"	4' 08"
	Skyline Queen	ES	1959	D	45*	61' 05"	16' 10"	6' 00"

M-19 MICHIGAN DEPARTMENT OF NATURAL RESOURCES, LANSING, MI (michigan.gov/dnr)

	Channel Cat	RV	1968	D	24*	46' 00"	13' 06"	4' 00"
	Lake Char	RV	2006	D	26*	56' 00"	16' 00"	4' 05"
	Steelhead	RV	1967	D	70*	63' 00"	16' 04"	6' 06"

M-20 MIDLAND TOURS INC., MIDLAND, ON (midlandtours.com)

	Miss Midland	ES	1974	D	119*	68' 07"	19' 04"	6' 04"
	Serendipity Princess	ES	1982	D	93*	69' 00"	23' 00"	4' 03"
	(Trent Voyageur '82-'87, Serendipity Lady '87-'95)							

M-21 MIDWEST MARITIME CORP., MILWAUKEE, WI

	Leona B.	TB	1972	D	99*	59' 08"	24' 01"	10' 03"
	(Kings Squire '72-'89, Juanita D. '78-'89, Peggy Ann '89-'93, Mary Page Hannah {2} '93-'04)							

M-22 MILLER BOAT LINE, PUT-IN-BAY, OH (millerferry.com)

	Islander {3}	PA/CF	1983	D	92*	90' 03"	38' 00"	8' 03"
	Put-In-Bay {3}	PA/CF	1997	D	95*	96' 00"	38' 06"	9' 06"
	Built: Sturgeon Bay Shipbuilding Co., Sturgeon Bay, WI							
	South Bass	PA/CF	1989	D	95*	96' 00"	38' 06"	9' 06"

Great Lakes Towing Co. tug *Florida*, U.S. Coast Guard cutter *Katmai Bay* and the ULS steamer *Montrealais* at Sault Ste. Marie, Mich., in December 2008. *(Roger LeLievre)*

Vessel Name	Type	Year			Overall Length	Breadth	
Wm. Market	PA/CF	1993	D	95*	96' 00"	38' 06"	8' 09"

Built: Peterson Builders Inc., Sturgeon Bay, WI

M- 23 MILWAUKEE BOAT LINE, MILWAUKEE, WI (mkeboat.com)

Iroquois	PA	1922	D	91*	61' 09"	21' 00"	6' 04"
Voyageur	PA	1988	D	94*	67' 02"	21' 00"	7' 04"

M-24 MONTREAL PORT AUTHORITY, MONTREAL, QC (port-montreal.com)

Denis M	TB	1942	D	21*	46' 07"	12' 08"	4' 01"

Built: Russel Brothers Ltd., Owen Sound, ON

Maisonneuve	TB	1972	D	103*	63' 10"	20' 07"	9' 03"

Built: Fercraft Marine Inc., Ste. Catherine D'Alexandre, QC

M-25 MUSÉE MARITIME DU QUÉBEC, L' ISLET, QC (mmq.qc.ca)

Ernest Lapointe	MU	1941	R	1,179*	185' 00"	36' 00"	22' 06"

Built: Davie Shipbuilding Co., Lauzon, QC; former Canadian Coast Guard icebreaker; open to the public at L'Islet, QC

M-26 MUSEUM SHIP WILLIAM G. MATHER, CLEVELAND, OH (wgmather.nhlink.net)

William G. Mather {2}	MU	1925	T	13,950	618' 00"	62' 00"	32' 00"

Built: Great Lakes Engineering Works, Ecorse, MI; former Cleveland-Cliffs Steamship Co. bulk carrier last operated Dec. 21, 1980; open to the public at Cleveland, OH

M-27 MUSEUM SHIP WILLIS B. BOYER, TOLEDO, OH (willisbboyer.org)

Willis B. Boyer	MU	1911	T	15,000	617' 00"	64' 00"	33' 01"

Built: Great Lakes Engineering Works, Ecorse, MI; former Shenago Furance Co./Republic Steel Co./Cleveland-Cliffs Steamship Co. bulk carrier last operated in 1980; open to the public at Toledo, OH
(Col. James M. Schoonmaker '11-'69)

M-28 MUSKOKA STEAMSHIP AND HISTORICAL SOCIETY, GRAVENHURST, ON (realmuskoka.com)

Segwun	PA	1887	R	168*	128' 00"	24' 00"	7' 06"

Built: Melancthon Simpson, Toronto, ON (Nipissing {2} 1887-'25)

Wanda III	PA	1915	R	60*	94' 00"	12' 00"	5' 00"

Built: Poulson Iron Works Ltd., Toronto, ON

Wenonah II	PA	2001	D	470*	127' 00"	28' 00"	6' 00"

Built: McNally Construction Inc., Belleville, ON

N-1 NADRO MARINE SERVICES LTD., PORT DOVER, ON (nadromarine.ca)

Ecosse	TB	1979	D	146*	91' 00"	26' 01"	8' 06"

Built: Hike Metal Products Ltd., Wheatley, ON (R & L No. 1 '79-'96)

Intrepid III	TB	1976	D	39*	66' 00"	17' 00"	7' 06"

Built: Halter Marine Ltd., Chalmette, LA

Seahound	TB	1941	D	60*	65' 06"	17' 00"	7' 00"

Built: Equitable Equipment Co., New Orleans, LA ([Unnamed] '41-'56, Sea Hound '56-'80, Carolyn Jo '80-'00)

Vac	TB	1942	D	37*	65' 00"	21' 00"	6' 06"

Built: George Gamble, Port Dover, ON

Vigilant 1	TB	1944	D	111*	76' 08"	20' 09"	10' 02"

Built: Russell Brothers Ltd., Owen Sound, ON (HMCS Glenlivet [W-43] '44-'75, Glenlivet II '75-'77, Canadian Franko '77-'82, Glenlivet II '82-'00)

N-2 NAUTICA QUEEN CRUISE DINING, CLEVELAND, OH (nauticaqueen.com)

Nautica Queen	ES	1981	D	95*	124' 00"	31' 02"	8' 10"

Built: Blount Marine Corp., Warren, RI (Bay Queen '81-'85, Arawanna Queen '85-'88, Star of Nautica '88-'92)

N-3 NAUTICAL ADVENTURES, TORONTO, ON (nauticaladventure.com)

Empire Sandy	ES/3S	1943	D/W	434*	140' 00"	32' 08"	14' 00"

Built: Clellands Ltd., Wellington-Quay-on-Tyne, UK (Empire Sandy '43-'48, Ashford '48-'52, Chris M. '52-'79)

Wayward Princess	ES	1976	D	325*	92' 00"	26' 00"	10' 00"

Built: Marlin Yacht Co., Summerstown, ON (Cayuga II '76-'82)

N-4 NAVETTES MARITIMES DU SAINT-LAURENT INC., QUÉBEC, QC (navettesmaritimes.com)

Miss Olympia	ES	1972	D	29*	62' 08"	14' 00"	4' 08"
Tandem I	PA	1991	D	108*	87' 01"	22' 00"	4' 05"
Transit	PA	1992	D	120*	68' 00"	22' 09"	4' 05"

N-5   NAVY MARINE CORPS RESERVE CENTER, BUFFALO, NY

Vessel Name	Type	Year	Engine	Tonnage	Length	Breadth	Depth
LCU 1680	TV	1943	D	170*	135' 00"	29' 00"	

N-6   NEW YORK STATE MARINE HIGHWAY TRANSPORTATION CO., TROY, NY (nysmarinehighway.com)

Vessel Name	Type	Year	Engine	Tonnage	Length	Breadth	Depth
Margot	TB	1958	D	141*	90' 00"	25' 00"	10' 00"

Built: Jakobson Shipyard, Oyster Bay, NY (Jolene Rose, Margot Moran)

N-7   NORLAKE TRANSPORTATION CO., PORT COLBORNE, ON (norlaketransportation.com)

Vessel Name	Type	Year	Engine	Tonnage	Length	Breadth	Depth
Radium Yellowknife	TB	1948	D	235*	120' 00"	28' 00"	6' 06"

Built: Yarrow's Ltd., Esquimalt, BC

N-8   NORTHEASTERN MARITIME HISTORICAL FOUNDATION INC., SUPERIOR, WI
(northeasternmaritime.org)

Vessel Name	Type	Year	Engine	Tonnage	Length	Breadth	Depth
Islay	TB	1892	D	19*	60' 00"	13' 00"	5' 00"

Built: American Steel Barge Co., Superior, WI; laid up at Manitowoc, WI (Islay 1892-'1947, Bayfield {1} '47-'83)

Vessel Name	Type	Year	Engine	Tonnage	Length	Breadth	Depth
Mount McKay	TB	1908	D	99*	80' 00"	21' 06"	9' 00"

Built: Benjamin Cowles, Buffalo, NY (Walter F. Mattick '08-' 19, Merchant '19-'24, Marinette '24-'47, Esther S. '47-'66)

Vessel Name	Type	Year	Engine	Tonnage	Length	Breadth	Depth
Reiss	TB	1913	R	99*	71' 00"	20' 00"	12' 06"

Built: Great Lakes Towing Co., Cleveland, OH; former Reiss Steamship Co. tug last operated in 1969; at anchor in the Kalamazoo River, Saugatuck, MI (Q. A. Gillmore '13-'32)

N-9   NORTHERN MARINE TRANSPORTATION INC., SAULT STE. MARIE, MI

Vessel Name	Type	Year	Engine	Tonnage	Length	Breadth	Depth
Empire State	PB	1951	D	21*	41' 09"	12' 04"	6' 06"
David Allen	PB	1964	D	32*	56' 04"	13' 03"	6' 00"
Linda Jean	PB	1950	D	17*	38' 00"	10' 00"	5' 00"

O-1   OLSON DREDGE & DOCK CO., ALGONAC, MI

Vessel Name	Type	Year	Engine	Tonnage	Length	Breadth	Depth
John Michael	TB	1913	D	41*	55' 04"	15' 01"	7' 06"

Built: Cowles Shipyard Co., Buffalo, NY (Colonel Ward, Ross Coddington, Joseph J. Olivieri)

O-2   OLYMPIA CRUISE LINE INC., THORNHILL, ON

Vessel Name	Type	Year	Engine	Tonnage	Length	Breadth	Depth
Enterprise 2000	ES	1998	D	370*	121' 06"	35' 00"	6' 00"

Built: Galactica 001 Enterprises Ltd., Toronto, ON

O-3   ONTARIO MINISTRY OF NATURAL RESOURCES, UPPER GREAT LAKES MANAGEMENT UNIT, PETERBOROUGH, ON (mnr.gov.on.ca)

Vessel Name	Type	Year	Engine	Tonnage	Length	Breadth	Depth
Atigamayg	RV	1954	D	82*	43' 09"	20' 02"	5' 07"
Erie Explorer	RV	1981	D	72*	53' 05"	20' 01"	4' 08"
K. H. Loftus	RV	1990	D	27*	37' 00"	14' 00"	4' 04"
Keenosay	RV	1957	D	68*	51' 04"	20' 07"	2' 07"
Namaycush	RV	1954	D	28*	65' 03"	12' 00"	4' 01"
Nipigon Osprey	RV	1990	D	33*	42' 04"	14' 09"	6' 08"

O-4   ONTARIO MINISTRY OF TRANSPORTATION, DOWNSVIEW, ON

Vessel Name	Type	Year	Engine	Tonnage	Length	Breadth	Depth
Frontenac II	PA/CF	1962	D	666*	181' 00"	45' 00"	10' 00"

Built: Chantier Maritime de Saint Laurent, St. Laurent, QC (Charlevoix {2} '62-'92)

Vessel Name	Type	Year	Engine	Tonnage	Length	Breadth	Depth
Frontenac Howe Islander	PF/CF	2004	D	130*	100' 00"	32' 03"	5' 05"

Built: Heddle Marine Service Inc., Hamilton, ON

Vessel Name	Type	Year	Engine	Tonnage	Length	Breadth	Depth
Glenora	PA/CF	1952	D	209*	127' 00"	33' 00"	9' 00"

Built: Erieau Shipbuilding & Drydock Co. Ltd., Erieau, ON (The St. Joseph Islander '52-'74)

Vessel Name	Type	Year	Engine	Tonnage	Length	Breadth	Depth
Jiimaan	PA/CF	1992	D	2,830*	176' 09"	42' 03"	13' 06"

Built: Port Weller Drydock, Port Weller, ON

Vessel Name	Type	Year	Engine	Tonnage	Length	Breadth	Depth
Pelee Islander	PA/CF	1960	D	334*	145' 00"	32' 00"	10' 00"

Built: Erieau Shipbuilding & Drydock Co. Ltd., Erieau, ON

Vessel Name	Type	Year	Engine	Tonnage	Length	Breadth	Depth
Quinte Loyalist	PA/CF	1954	D	209*	127' 00"	32' 00"	8' 00"

Built: Erieau Shipbuilding & Drydock Co. Ltd., Erieau, ON

Vessel Name	Type	Year	Engine	Tonnage	Length	Breadth	Depth
Wolfe Islander III	PA/CF	1975	D	985*	205' 00"	68' 00"	6' 00"

Built: Port Arthur Shipbuilding Co., Port Arthur, ON

O-5   ONTARIO POWER GENERATION INC., TORONTO, ON

Vessel Name	Type	Year	Engine	Tonnage	Length	Breadth	Depth
Niagara Queen II	IB	1992	D	57*	56' 01"	18' 00"	6' 08"

O-6   OSBORNE COMPANIES INC., GRAND RIVER, OH

Emmet J. Carey		SC	1948	D	900	114' 00"	23' 00"	11' 00"

Built: Hugh E. Lee Iron Works, Saginaw, MI; laid up at Fairport, OH (Beatrice Ottinger '48-'63, James B. Lyons '63-'88)

Emmet J. Carey								
F. M. Osborne {2}		SC	1910	D	500	150' 00"	29' 00"	11' 03"

Built: J. Butman & T. Horn, Buffalo, NY (Grand Island {1} '10-'58, Lesco '58-'75)

O-7   OWEN SOUND TRANSPORTATION CO. LTD., OWEN SOUND, ON *(ontarioferries.com)*

Chi-Cheemaun	PA/CF	1974	D	6,991*	365' 05"	61' 00"	21' 00"

Built: Canadian Shipbuilding and Engineering Ltd., Collingwood, ON

P-1   PERE MARQUETTE SHIPPING CO., LUDINGTON, MI *(pmship.com)*

Pere Marquette 41	SU	1941	B	4,545	403' 00"	58' 00"	23' 06"

Built: Manitowoc Shipbuilding Co., Manitowoc, WI; converted from powered train/car ferry to a self-unloading barge in '97 (City of Midland 41 '41-'97)

Undaunted	AT	1944	DE	860*	143' 00"	33' 01"	18' 00"

Built: Gulfport Boiler/Welding, Port Arthur, TX (USS Undaunted [ATR-126, ATA-199] '44-'63, USMA Kings Pointer '63-'93, Krystal K. '93-'97)

    [ATB Undaunted / PM 41 OA dimensions together]   493' 06"   58' 00"   23' 06"

P-2   PETERSEN STEAMSHIP CO., DOUGLAS, MI *(keewatinmaritimemuseum.com)*

Keewatin {2}	MU	1907	Q	3,856*	346' 00"	43' 08"	26' 06"

Built: Fairfield Shipbuilding, Govan, Scotland; former Canadian Pacific Railway Co. passenger vessel last operated Nov. 29, 1965; open to the public at Douglas, MI

P-3   PICTURED ROCKS CRUISES INC., MUNISING, MI *(picturedrocks.com)*

Grand Island {2}	ES	1989	D	52*	68' 00"	16' 01"	7' 01"
Grand Portal	ES	2004	D	76*	64' 08"	20' 00"	8' 08"
Miners Castle	ES	1974	D	82*	68' 00"	16' 06"	6' 04"
Miss Superior	ES	1984	D	83*	68' 00"	16' 09"	10' 04"
Pictured Rocks	ES	1972	D	53*	55' 07"	13' 07"	4' 04"

P-4   PIER WISCONSIN, MILWAUKEE, WI *(voyage.pierwisconsin.org)*

Denis Sullivan	TV/ES	1994	W/D	99*	138' 00"	24' 00"	8' 09"

Built: Wisconsin Lake Schooner, Milwaukee, WI

P-5   PLAUNT TRANSPORTATION CO. INC., CHEBOYGAN, MI *(bbiferry.com)*

Kristen D	CF	1988	D	83*	64' 11"	36' 00"	6' 05"

P-6   PORT CITY CRUISE LINE INC., MUSKEGON, MI *(portcityprincesscruises.com)*

Port City Princess	ES	1966	D	79*	64' 09"	30' 00"	5' 06"

Built: Blount Marine Corp., Warren, RI (Island Queen {1} '66-'87)

P-7   PORT CITY TUG INC., MUSKEGON, MI

Prentiss Brown	TB	1967	D	197*	123' 05"	31' 06"	19' 00"

Built: Gulfport Shipbuilding, Port Arthur, TX (Betty Culbreath, Micheala McAllister)

P-8   PORT HURON MUSEUM, PORT HURON, MI *(phmuseum.org)*

Bramble	MU	1944	DE	1,025*	180' 00"	37' 00"	17' 04"

Built: Zenith Dredge Co., Duluth, MN; former U.S. Coast Guard buoy tender/icebreaker was retired in 2003; open to the public at Port Huron, MI (USCGC Bramble [WLB-392] '44-'03)

Huron	MU	1920	D	392*	96' 05"	24' 00"	10' 00"

Built: Charles L. Seabury Co., Morris Heights, NY; former U.S. Coast Guard lightship WLV-526 was retired Aug. 20, 1970; open to the public at Port Huron, MI (Lightship 103 – Relief [WAL-526] '20-'36)

P-9   PORTOFINO ON THE RIVER, WYANDOTTE, MI *(portofinoontheriver.com)*

Friendship	ES	1968	D	110*	85' 00"	30' 06"	7' 03"

Built: Hike Metal Products Ltd., Wheatley, ON (Peche Island V '68-'71, Papoose V '71-'82)

P-10   PROTEUS CO., PORTSMOUTH, VA

Atchafalaya	DR	1972	D	760*	197' 00"	40' 08"	16' 05"
Columbia	DR	1944	D	2,923*	315' 00"	50' 00"	20' 04"

(LST 987, Millard County, Espernace III)

American Century passes under the
Aerial Lift Bridge at Duluth. *(Mike Sipper)*

Fleet #	Fleet Name / Vessel Name	Type of Vessel	Year Built	Type of Engine	Cargo Cap. or Gross*	Overall Length	Breadth	Depth or Draft*
P-11	**PURVIS MARINE LTD., SAULT STE. MARIE, ON** *(purvismarine.com)*							
	Adanac	TB	1913	D	108*	80' 03"	19' 02"	10' 06"
	Built: Western Drydock & Shipbuilding Co., Port Arthur, ON (Edward C. Whalen '13-'66, John McLean '66-'95)							
	Anglian Lady	TB	1953	D	398*	136' 06"	30' 00"	14' 01"
	Built: John I. Thornecroft & Co., Southampton, England (Hamtun '53-'72, Nathalie Letzer '72-'88)							
	Avenger IV	TB	1962	D	293*	120' 00"	30' 05"	17' 05"
	Built: Cochrane & Sons Ltd., Selby, Yorkshire, England (Avenger '62-'85)							
	Chief Wawatam	DB	1911	B	4,500	347' 00"	62' 03"	15' 00"
	Built: Toledo Shipbuilding Co., Toledo, OH; converted from a powered train ferry to a barge in '88							
	E. M. Ford	CC	1898	Q	7,100	428' 00"	50' 00"	28' 00"
	Built: Cleveland Shipbuilding Co., Cleveland, OH; converted to a self-unloading cement carrier at Christy Corp., Sturgeon Bay, WI, in '56; last operated Sept. 16, 1996; awaiting scrapping at Sault Ste. Marie, ON (Presque Isle {1} 1898-'56)							
	G.L.B. No. 1	DB	1953	B	3,215	305' 00"	50' 00"	12' 00"
	Built: Nashville Bridge Co., Nashville, TN (Joe Baugh Jr. '53-'66, ORG 5503 '66-'75)							
	G.L.B. No. 2	DB	1953	B	3,215	305' 02"	50' 00"	12' 00"
	Built: Ingalls Shipbuilding Corp., Birmingham, AL (Jane Newfield '53-'66, ORG 6502 '66-'75)							
	Joyce B. Gardiner	TB	1962	D	71*	72' 00"	19' 00"	12' 00"
	Built: McNamara Marine Ltd., Toronto, ON (Angus M. '62-'92, Omni Sorel '92-'02)							
	Malden	DB	1946	B	1,075	150' 00"	41' 09"	10' 03"
	Martin E. Johnson	TB	1959	D	26*	46' 00"	16' 00"	5' 09"
	Nindawayma	PA/CF	1976	D	6,197*	333' 06"	55' 00"	36' 06"
	Last operated in 1992; laid up at Sault Ste. Marie, ON (Monte Cruceta '76-'76, Monte Castillo '76-'78, Manx Viking '78-'87, Manx '87-'88, Skudenes '88-'89, Ontario No.1 {2} '89-'89)							
	Osprey	TB	1944	D	36*	45' 00"	13' 06"	7' 00"
	P.M.L. Alton	DB	1951	B	150	93' 00"	30' 00"	8' 00"
	P.M.L. 357	DB	1944	B	600	138' 00"	38' 00"	11' 00"
	P.M.L. 2501	TK	1980	B	1,954*	302' 00"	52' 00"	17' 00"
	Built: Cenac Shipyard, Houma, LA (CTCO 2505 '80-'96)							
	P.M.L. 9000	TK	1968	B	4,285*	400' 00"	76' 00"	20' 00"
	Built: Bethlehem Steel – Shipbuilding Division, San Francisco, CA (Palmer '68-'00)							
	P.M.L. Tucci	CS	1958	B	1,000	150' 00"	52' 00"	10' 00"
	Built: Calumet Shipyard & Drydock Co., Chicago, IL (MCD '58-'73, Minnesota '73-'88, Candace Andrie '88-'08)							
	P.M.L. Tucker	DS	1971	B	521*	140' 00"	50' 00"	9' 00"
	Built: Twin City Shipyard, St. Paul, MN (Illinois '71-'02, Meredith Andrie '02-'08)							
	Reliance	TB	1974	D	708*	148' 04"	35' 07"	21' 06"
	Built: Ulstein Hatlo A/S, Ulsteinvik, Norway (Sinni '74-'81, Irving Cedar '81-'96, Atlantic Cedar '96-'02)							
	Rocket	TB	1901	D	39*	70' 00"	15' 00"	8' 00"
	Built: Buffalo Shipbuilding Co., Buffalo, NY							
	Sheila P.	TB	1940	D	15*	40 00"	14' 00"	x' 00"
	Tecumseh II	DB	1976	B	2,500	180' 00"	54' 00"	12' 00"
	(U-727 '76-'94)							
	Wilfred M. Cohen	TB	1948	D	284*	104' 00"	28' 00"	14' 06"
	Built: Newport News Shipbuilding and Drydock Co., Newport News, VA (A. T. Lowmaster '48-'75)							
	W. I. Scott Purvis	TB	1938	D	206*	96' 06"	26' 04"	10' 04"
	Built: Marine Industries, Sorel, QC (Orient Bay '38-'75, Guy M. No. 1 '75-'90)							
	W. J. Ivan Purvis	TB	1938	D	191*	100' 06"	25' 06"	9' 00"
	Built: Marine Industries, Sorel, QC (Magpie '38-'66, Dana T. Bowen '66-'75)							
	Yankcanuck {2}	CS	1963	B	4,760	324' 03"	49' 00"	26' 00"
	Built: Collingwood Shipyards, Collingwood, ON							
P-12	**PUT-IN-BAY BOAT LINE CO., PORT CLINTON, OH** *(jet-express.com)*							
	All vessels built at Gladding-Hearn Shipbuilding, Somerset, MA							
	Jet Express	PF/CA	1989	D	93*	92' 08"	28' 06"	8' 04"
	Jet Express II	PF/CA	1992	D	85*	92' 06"	28' 06"	8' 04"
	Jet Express III	PF/CA	2001	D	70*	78' 02"	27' 06"	8' 02"
Q-1	**QUEBEC PORT AUTHORITY, QUÉBEC, QC** *(portquebec.ca)*							
	Beaupre	TB	1952	D	13*	37' 05"	10' 49"	4' 08"
	Built: Russel-Hipwell Engines Ltd., Owen Sound, ON							

Fleet #	Fleet Name / Vessel Name	Type of Vessel	Year Built	Type of Engine	Cargo Cap. or Gross*	Overall Length	Breadth	Depth or Draft*
R-1	**RANKIN CONSTRUCTION INC., ST. CATHARINES, ON**							
	Judique Flyer	DB	1967	D	67.7*	60' 00"	29' 08"	3' 09"
	Built: Erieau Shipbuilding & Drydock Co. Ltd., Erieau, ON (Sweep Scow No. 4 '67-'03)							
R-2	**REBELLION TUG & BARGE INC., LOCKPORT, N.Y.** *(rebelliontug.com)*							
	Shenandoah	TB	1941	D	29*	49' 03"	14' 00"	6' 01"
	Built: Sturgeon Bay Shipbuilding Co., Sturgeon Bay, WI (Lauren E., R. H. Vaughn)							
R-3	**RJ MARINE ASSOCIATES, CLAYTON, NY** *(americanmetalcraftmarine.com)*							
	Abaco	TB	1953	D	27*	45' 00"	12' 05"	7' 02"
	Built: National Steel & Shipbuilding Co., San Diego, CA (ST 2141, Buffalo)							
	Carina	TB	1954	D	64*	61' 05"	17' 09"	8' 03"
	Maple Grove	PK	1954	D	55*	73' 07"	20' 00"	9' 00"
R-4	**ROCKPORT BOAT LINE LTD., ROCKPORT, ON** *(rockportcruises.com)*							
	Ida M.	ES	1970	D	29*	55' 00"	14' 00"	3' 00"
	Ida M. II	ES	1973	D	116*	63' 02"	22' 02"	5' 00"
	Sea Prince II	ES	1978	D	172*	83' 00"	24' 02"	6' 08"
R-5	**ROEN SALVAGE CO., STURGEON BAY, WI** *(roensalvage.com)*							
	Chas. Asher	TB	1967	D	10*	50' 00"	18' 00"	8' 00"
	Built: Sturgeon Bay Shipbuilding Co., Sturgeon Bay, WI							
	John R. Asher	TB	1943	D	93*	70' 00"	20' 00"	8' 06"
	Built: Platzer Boat Works, Houston, TX (U. S. Army ST-71 '43-'46, Russell 8 '46-'64, Reid McAllister '64-'67, Donegal '67-'85)							
	Louie S.	TB	1956	D	43*	37' 00"	12' 00"	5' 00"
	Spuds	TB	1944	D	19*	42' 00"	12' 06"	6' 00"
	Stephan M. Asher	TB	1954	D	60*	65' 00"	19' 01"	5' 04"
	Built: Burton Shipyard Inc., Port Arthur, TX (Captain Bennie '54-'82, Dumar Scout '82-'87)							
	Timmy A.	TB	1953	D	12*	33' 06"	10' 08"	5' 02"
R-6	**ROGER CHAPMAN, MILWAUKEE, WI**							
	Mermaid	TB	1936	D	11*	41'00"	10'00"	4' 9"
	(Jake M. Kadinger)							

Pilot boat alongside *Gordon C. Leitch* at Sorel, Quebec. *(Sam Lapinski)*

R-7	**ROYAL CANADIAN YACHT CLUB, TORONTO, ON** (rcyc.ca)							
	Elsie D.	PA	1958	D	9*	34' 07"	10' 08"	3' 06"
	Esperanza IV	PA	1953	D	14*	38' 06"	11' 02"	4' 06"
	Hiawatha	PA	1895	D	46*	56' 01"	14' 04"	6' 02"
	Kwasind	PA	1912	D	47*	70' 08"	15' 09"	5' 05"

R-8	**ROYAL WINDSOR CRUISES, WINDSOR, ON** (senatorofwindsor.com)							
	The Senator	ES	1986	D	105*	65' 00"	20' 00"	6' 7"

Built: Duratug Shipyard & Fabricating Ltd., Port Dover, ON

R-9	**RUSSELL ISLAND TRANSIT CO., ALGONAC, MI**							
	Islander {2}	PA/CF	1967	D	38*	41' 00"	15' 00"	3' 06"

R-10	**RYBA MARINE CONSTRUCTION CO., CHEBOYGAN, MI** (rybamarine.com)							
	Alcona	TB	1957	D	18*	40' 00"	12' 06"	5' 06"
	Amber Mae	TB	1922	D	67*	65' 00"	14' 01"	10' 00"

Built: Glove Shipyard Inc. Buffalo, NY (E. W. Sutton '22-'52, Venture '52- '00)

	Jarco 1402	CS	1981	B	473*	140' 00"	39' 00"	9' 00"
	Kathy Lynn	TB	1944	D	140*	85' 00"	24' 00"	9' 06"

Built: Decatur Iron & Steel Co., Decatur, AL (U. S. Army ST-693 '44-'79, Sea Islander '79-'91)

	Rochelle Kaye	TB	1963	D	52*	51' 06"	19' 04"	7' 00"

Built: St. Charles Steel Works Inc., Thibodeaux, LA (Jaye Anne '63-?, Katanni ?-'97)

	Tenacious	TB	1960	D	149*	90' 00"	26' 04"	12' 00"

Built: Ingalls Shipbuilding Corp., Pascagoula, MS (Mobil 8 '60-'91, Tatarrax '91-'93, Nan McKay '93-'95)

S-1	**SABLE POINT MARINE LLC, LUDINGTON, MI**							
	Snohomish	TB	1943	DE	195*	110' 00"	26' 06"	12' 06"

Built: Ira S. Bushey & Sons Inc., Brooklyn, NY (WYTM-98 Snohomish)

S-2	**SCOTLUND STIVERS, MARINETTE, WI**							
	Arthur K. Atkinson	PA	1917	D	3,241*	384' 00"	56' 00"	20' 06"

Built: Great Lakes Engineering Works, Ecorse, MI; last operated in April 1982; laid up at DeTour, MI
(Ann Arbor No. 6 '17-'59)

SEAWAY MARINE TRANSPORT, ST. CATHARINES, ON
PARTNERSHIP BETWEEN ALGOMA CENTRAL CORP. (A-5) AND UPPER LAKES GROUP (U-12)
SEE RESPECTIVE FLEETS FOR VESSELS INVOLVED.

S-3	**SELVICK MARINE TOWING CORP., STURGEON BAY, WI**							
	Carla Anne Selvick	TB	1908	D	191*	96' 00"	23' 00"	11' 02"

Built: Skinner Shipbuilding & Dry Dock Co., Baltimore, MD (S.O. Co. No. 19 '08-'16, S.T. Co. No. 19 '16-'18,
Socony 19 '18-'47, Esso Tug No. 4 '47-'53, McAllister 44 '53-'55, Roderick McAllister '55-'84)

	Cameron O.	TB	1955	D	26*	50' 00"	15' 00"	7' 03"

Built: Peterson Builders Inc., Sturgeon Bay, WI (Escort II '55-'06)

	Jacquelyn Nicole	TB	1913	D	96*	81' 00"	20' 00"	12' 06"

Built: Great Lakes Towing Co., Cleveland, OH (Michigan {4} '13-'78, Ste. Marie II '78-'81, Dakota '81-'92, Ethel E. '92-'02)

	Jimmy L.	TB	1939	D	148*	110' 00"	25' 00"	13' 00"

Built: Defoe Shipbuilding Co., Bay City, MI USCGC Naugatuck [WYT / WYTM-92] '39-'80, Timmy B. '80-'84)

	Mary Page Hannah {1}	TB	1950	DE	461*	143' 00"	33' 01"	14' 06"

Built: Levingston Shipbuilding, Orange, TX (U. S. Army ATA-230 '49-'72, G. W. Codrington '72-'73,
William P. Feeley {2} '73-'73, William W. Stender '73-'78)

	Sharon M. Selvick	TB	1945	D	28*	45' 00"	13' 00"	7' 00"

Built: Kewaunee Shipbuilding & Engineering, Kewaunee, WI (USACE Judson)

	Susan L.	TB	1944	D	163*	86' 00"	23' 00"	10' 04"

Built: Equitable Equipment Co., New Orleans, LA (U. S. Army ST-709 '44-'47, USCOE Stanley '47-'99)

	William C. Selvick	TB	1944	D	142*	85' 00"	22' 11"	10' 04"

Built: Platzer Boat Works, Houston, TX (U. S. Army ST-500 '44-'49, Sherman H. Serre '49-'77)

S-4	**SHAMROCK CHARTERING CO., GROSSE POINTE, MI**							
	Helene	ES	1927	D	99*	96' 09"	17' 00"	8' 00"

Built: Defoe Shipbuilding Co., Bay City, MI; laid up at Ecorse, MI

S-5	**SHELL CANADA PRODUCTS LTD., MONTREAL, QC**							
	Arca	RT	1963	D	1,296	175' 00"	36' 00"	14' 00"

Built: Port Weller Dry Docks, Port Weller, ON (Imperial Lachine '63-'03, Josee M. '03-'03)

S-6   SHEPARD MARINE CONSTRUCTION, ST. CLAIR SHORES, MI

Vessel Name	Type	Year			Overall Length	Breadth	
Geraldine	TW	1988	D	26*	42' 00"	19' 00"	5' 00"
Robin Lynn	TB	1952	D	146*	85' 00"	25' 00"	11' 00"

    Built: Alexander Shipyard Inc., New Orleans, LA (Bonita '52-'85, Susan Hoey {2} '85'-'95, Blackie B '95-'97, Susan Hoey {3} '97-'98)

S-7   SHEPLER'S MACKINAC ISLAND FERRY SERVICE, MACKINAW CITY, MI *(sheplersferry.com)*

Vessel Name	Type	Year			Overall Length	Breadth	
Capt. Shepler	PF	1986	D	71*	84' 00"	21' 00"	7' 10"
Felicity	PF	1972	D	84*	65' 00"	18' 01"	8' 03"
Sacre Bleu	PK	1959	D	92*	94' 10"	31' 00"	9' 09"

    Built: Sturgeon Bay Shipbuilding Co., Sturgeon Bay, WI (Put-In-Bay {2} '59-'94)

Vessel Name	Type	Year			Overall Length	Breadth	
The Hope	PF	1975	D	87*	77' 00"	20' 00"	8' 03"

    Built: Bergeron Boats Inc., Lafitte, LA

Vessel Name	Type	Year			Overall Length	Breadth	
The Welcome	PF	1969	D	66*	60' 06"	16' 08"	8' 02"

    Built: Camcraft Inc., Crown Point, LA

Vessel Name	Type	Year			Overall Length	Breadth	
Wyandot	PF	1979	D	99*	77' 00"	20' 00"	8' 00"

    Built: Bergeron Boats Inc., Lafitte, LA

S-8   SHIPWRECK TOURS INC., MUNISING, MI *(shipwrecktours.com)*

Vessel Name	Type	Year			Overall Length	Breadth	
Miss Munising	ES	1967	D	50*	60' 00"	14' 00"	4' 04"

S-9   SHORELINE CHARTERS, GILLS ROCK, WI *(shorelinecharters.net)*

Vessel Name	Type	Year			Overall Length	Breadth	
The Shoreline	ES	1973	D	12*	33' 00"	11' 4"	3' 00"

S-10   SHORELINE CONTRACTORS INC., WESTLAKE, OH *(shorelinecontractors.com)*

Vessel Name	Type	Year			Overall Length	Breadth	
Eagle	TB	1943	D	31*	57' 09"	14' 05"	6' 10"

    Built: Defoe Shipbuilding Co., Bay City, MI

S-11   SHORELINE SIGHTSEEING CO., CHICAGO, IL *(shorelinesightseeing.com)*

Vessel Name	Type	Year			Overall Length	Breadth	
Cap Streeter	ES	1987	D	28*	63' 06"	24' 04"	7' 07"
Evening Star	ES	2001	D	93*	83' 00"	23' 00"	7' 00"
Marlyn	ES	1961	D	70*	65' 00"	25' 00"	7' 00"
Shoreline II	ES	1987	D	89*	75' 00"	26' 00"	7' 01"
Star of Chicago {2}	ES	1999	D	73*	64' 10"	22' 08"	7' 05"
Voyager	CF	1960	D	98*	65' 00"	35' 00"	8' 00"

Roger Blough in spring ice at the Soo Locks. *(Eric Treece)*

S-12   **SOCIÉTÉ DES TRAVERSIERS DU QUÉBEC, QUÉBEC, QC** *(www.traversiers.gouv.qc.ca)*

Alphonse Desjardins		CF	1971	D	1,741*	214' 00"	71' 06"	20' 00"
Built: Davie Shipbuilding Co., Lauzon, QC								
Armand Imbeau		CF	1980	D	1,285*	203' 07"	72' 00"	18' 04"
Built: Marine Industries Ltd., Sorel, QC								
Camille Marcoux		CF	1974	D	6,122*	310' 09"	62' 09"	39' 00"
Built: Marine Industries Ltd., Sorel, QC								
Catherine-Legardeur		CF	1985	D	1,348*	205' 09"	71' 10"	18' 10"
Built: Davie Shipbuilding Co., Lauzon, QC								
Felix Antoine Savard		CF	1997	D	2,489*	272' 00"	70' 00"	21' 09"
Built: Davie Shipbuilding Co., Lauzon, QC								
Grue-des-Iles		CF	1981	D	447*	155' 10"	41' 01"	12' 06"
Built: Bateaux Tur-Bec Ltd., Ste-Catherine, QC								
Jos. Deschenes		CF	1980	D	1,287*	203' 07"	72' 00"	18' 04"
Built: Marine Industries Ltd., Sorel, QC								
Joseph-Savard		CF	1985	D	1,445*	206' 00"	71' 10"	18' 10"
Built: Davie Shipbuilding Co., Lauzon, QC								
Lomer Gouin		CF	1971	D	1,741*	214' 00"	71' 06"	20' 00"
Built: Davie Shipbuilding Co., Lauzon, QC								
Lucien L.		CF	1967	D	867*	220' 10"	61' 06"	15' 05"
Built: Marine Industries Ltd., Sorel, QC								
Radisson {1}		CF	1954	D	1,043*	164' 03"	72' 00"	10' 06"
Built: Davie Shipbuilding Co., Lauzon, QC								

S-13   **SOO LOCKS BOAT TOURS, SAULT STE. MARIE, MI** *(soolocks.com)*

Bide-A-Wee {3}		ES	1955	D	99*	64' 07"	23' 00"	7' 11"
Built: Blount Marine Corp., Warren, RI								
Hiawatha {2}		ES	1959	D	99*	64' 07"	23' 00"	7' 11"
Built: Blount Marine Corp., Warren, RI								
Holiday		ES	1957	D	99*	64' 07"	23' 00"	7' 11"
Built: Blount Marine Corp., Warren, RI								
Le Voyageur		ES	1959	D	70*	65' 00"	25' 00"	7' 00"
Built: Sturgeon Bay Shipbuilding and Drydock Co., Sturgeon Bay, WI								
Nokomis		ES	1959	D	70*	65' 00"	25' 00"	7' 00"
Built: Sturgeon Bay Shipbuilding and Drydock Co., Sturgeon Bay, WI								

S-14   **SOO RIVER MARINE LLC, WILLIAMSTON, MI**

Soo River Belle		PB	1961	D	25*	40' 00"	14' 00"	6' 00"

S-15   **SPIRIT CRUISE LINE LTD., TORONTO, ON**

Northern Spirit I		ES	1983	D	489*	136' 00"	31' 00"	9' 00"
Built: Blount Marine Corp., Warren, RI (New Spirit '83-'89, Pride of Toronto '89-'92)								
Oriole		ES	1987	D	200*	75' 00"	23' 00"	9' 00"

S-16   **SPIRIT CRUISES LLC, CHICAGO, IL** *(spiritcruises.com)*

Spirit of Chicago		ES	1988	D	92*	156' 00"	35' 00"	7' 01"
Built: Blount Marine Corp., Warren, RI								

S-17   **SPIRIT OF LASALLE CRUISE LINE, MENOMINEE, MI**

Spirit of LaSalle		ES	1978	D	99*	95' 09"	21' 05"	7' 00"
Built: Camcraft Inc., Crown Point, LA (Melissa Briley '78-'98, Grampa Woo '98-'07)								
Isle Royale Queen III		PA	1959	D	88*	74' 03"	18' 04"	6' 05"
Built: T.D. Vinette Co., Escanaba, MI (Isle Royale Queen II)								

S-18   **SPIRIT OF THE SOUND SCHOONER CO., PARRY SOUND, ON** *(spiritofthesound.ca)*

Chippewa III		PA	1954	D	47*	65' 00"	16' 00"	6' 06"
Built: Russel-Hipwell Engines Ltd., Owen Sound, ON (Maid of the Mist III '54-'56, Maid of the Mist '56-'92)								

S-19   **S.S. CITY OF MILWAUKEE-NATIONAL HISTORIC LANDMARK, MANISTEE, MI** *(carferry.com)*

City of Milwaukee		MU	1931	R	26 cars	360' 00"	56' 03"	21' 06"
Built: Manitowoc Shipbuilding Co., Manitowoc, WI; train ferry sailed for the Grand Trunk Railroad '31-'78 and the Ann Arbor Railroad '78-'81; open to the public at Manistee, MI								

Canadian Leader on the **Detroit River.** *(Blake Kishler)*

S-20 **S.S. METEOR WHALEBACK SHIP MUSEUM, SUPERIOR, WI** *(superiorpublicmuseums.org)*

Meteor {2}	MU	1896	R	40,100	380' 00"	45' 00"	26' 00"

Built: American Steel Barge Co., Superior, WI; former ore carrier/auto carrier/tanker is the last vessel of whaleback design surviving on the Great Lakes; Cleveland Tankers vessel last operated in 1969; open to the public at Superior, WI (Frank Rockefeller 1896-'28, South Park '28-'43)

S-21 **ST. JAMES MARINE CO., BEAVER ISLAND, MI**

American Girl	PK	1922	D	67*	62' 00"	14' 00"	6' 00"
Cisco	TB	1951	D	53*	60' 06"	16' 08"	7' 08"
Oil Queen	TK	1949	B	50*	64' 08"	16' 00"	6' 00"

S-22 **ST. LAWRENCE CRUISE LINES INC., KINGSTON, ON** *(stlawrencecruiselines.com)*

Canadian Empress	PA	1981	D	463*	108' 00"	30' 00"	8' 00"

Built: Algan Shipyards Ltd., Gananoque, ON

S-23 **ST. LAWRENCE SEAWAY DEVELOPMENT CORP., MASSENA, NY** *(www.seaway.dot.gov)*

McCauley	CS	1948	B		112' 00"	52' 00"	3' 00"
Robinson Bay	TB	1958	DE	213*	103' 00"	26' 10"	14' 06"

Built: Christy Corp., Sturgeon Bay, WI

Performance	TB	1997	D		50' 00"	16' 06"	7' 05"

Built: Marine Builders Inc., Utica, IN

S-24 **ST. LAWRENCE SEAWAY MANAGEMENT CORP., CORNWALL, ON** *(greatlakes-seaway.com)*

VM/S Hercules	GL	1962	D	2,107*	200' 00"	75' 00"	18' 08"

Built: Marine Industries Ltd., Sorel, QC

VM/S Maisonneuve	TB	1974	D	56*	58' 03"	20' 03"	6' 05"

Built: Fercraft Marine Inc., Ste. Catherine D'Alexandre, QC

VM/S St. Lambert	TB	1974	D	20*	30' 08"	13' 01"	6' 05"
VM/S St. Louis III	TB	1977	D	15*	34' 02"	11' 08"	4' 00"

S-25 **ST. MARYS CEMENT INC. (CANADA), TORONTO, ON** *(stmaryscement.com)*

C.T.C. No. 1	CC	1943	R	16,300	620' 06"	60' 00"	35' 00"

Built: Great Lakes Engineering Works, River Rouge, MI; last operated Nov. 12, 1981; in use as a cement storage/transfer vessel in South Chicago, IL
(Launched as McIntyre. Frank Purnell {1} '43-'64, Steelton {3} '64-'78, Hull No. 3 '78-'79, Pioneer {4} '79-'82)

Sea Eagle II	ATB	1979	D	560*	132' 00"	35' 00"	19' 00"

Built: Modern Marine Power Co., Houma, LA (Sea Eagle '79-'81, Canmar Sea Eagle '81-'91)

St. Marys Cement	CC	1986	B	9,400	360' 00"	60' 00"	23' 03"

Built: Merce Industries East, Cleveland, OH

St. Marys Cement II	CC	1978	B	19,513	496' 06"	76' 00"	35' 00"

Built: Galveston Shipbuilding Co., Galveston, TX (Velasco '78-'81, Canmar Shuttle '81-'90)

THE FOLLOWING VESSEL MANAGED BY PORT CITY STEAMSHIP SERVICES INC., MUSKEGON, MI

St. Marys Challenger	CC	1906	S	10,250	552' 01"	56' 00"	31' 00"

Built: Great Lakes Engineering Works, Ecorse, MI; repowered in '50; converted to a self-unloading cement carrier by Manitowoc Shipbuilding Co., Manitowoc, WI, in '67; celebrated its 100th season in 2006 (William P. Snyder '06-'26, Elton Hoyt II {1} '26-'52, Alex D. Chisholm '52-'66, Medusa Challenger '66-'99, Southdown Challenger '99-'04)

THE FOLLOWING VESSEL MANAGED BY PORT CITY MARINE SERVICES INC., MUSKEGON, MI

St. Marys Conquest	CC	1937	B	8,500	437' 06"	55' 00"	28' 00"

Built: Manitowoc Shipbuilding Co., Manitowoc, WI; converted from a powered tanker to a self-unloading cement barge by Bay Shipbuilding, Sturgeon Bay, WI, in '87 (Red Crown '37-'62, Amoco Indiana '62-'87, Medusa Conquest '87-'99, Southdown Conquest '99-'04)

THE FOLLOWING VESSEL CHARTERED BY ST. MARYS CEMENT CO. FROM GREAT LAKES INTERNATIONAL TOWING & SALVAGE CO., BURLINGTON, ON

Petite Forte	TB	1969	D	368*	127' 00"	32' 00"	14' 06"

Built: Cochrane and Sons Ltd., Selby, Yorkshire, England (E. Bronson Ingram '69-'72, Jarmac 42 '72-'73, Scotsman '73-'81, Al Battal '81-'86)

S-26 **ST. MARYS RIVER MARINE CENTRE, SAULT STE. MARIE, ON** *(norgoma.org)*

Norgoma	MU	1950	D	1,477*	188' 00"	37' 06"	22' 06"

Built: Collingwood Shipyards, Collingwood, ON; former Ontario Northland Transportation Commission passenger vessel last operated in 1974; open to the public at Sault Ste. Marie, ON

S-27 STAR LINE MACKINAC ISLAND FERRY, ST. IGNACE, MI *(mackinacferry.com)*

All vessels built at Gulf Craft Inc., Patterson, LA

Cadillac {5}	PF	1990	D	73*	64' 07"	20' 00"	7' 07"
Joliet {3}	PF	1993	D	83*	64' 08"	22' 00"	8' 03"
La Salle {4}	PF	1983	D	55*	65' 00"	20' 00"	7' 05"
Marquette II {2}	PF	2005	D	65*	74' 00"	23' 06"	8' 00"
Radisson {2}	PF	1988	D	97*	80' 00"	23' 06"	7' 00"

S-28 STATE OF NEW YORK POWER AUTHORITY, LEWISTON, NY

Breaker	TB	1962	D	29*	43' 03"	14' 03"	5' 00"
Daniel Joncaire	TB	1979	D	25*	43' 03"	15' 00"	5' 00"

S-29 STEAMER COLUMBIA FOUNDATION, DETROIT, MI *(boblosteamers.com)*

Columbia {2}	PA	1902	R	968*	216' 00"	60' 00"	13' 06"

Built: Detroit Dry Dock Co, Detroit, MI; former Detroit to Bob-Lo Island passenger steamer last operated Sept. 2, 1991; laid up at Ecorse, MI

T-1 TALISMAN ENERGY INC., CALGARY, AB *(talisman-energy.com)*

Vessels are engaged in oil and gas exploration on Lake Erie

Dr. Bob	DV	1973	B	1,022*	160' 01"	54' 01"	11' 01"

Built: Cenac Shipyard Co. Inc., Houna, LA (Mr. Chris '73-'03)

J.R. Rouble	DV	1958	D	562*	123' 06"	49' 08"	16' 00"

Built: American Marine Machinery Co., Nashville, TN (Mr. Neil)

Miss Libby	DV	1972	B	924*	160' 01"	54' 01"	11' 01"

Built: Service Machine & Shipbuilding Corp., Morgan City, LA

Sarah No. 1	TB	1969	D	43*	72' 01"	17' 03"	6' 08"

Built: Halter Boats Ltd., New Orleans, LA

Timesaver II	DB	1964	B	510*	91' 08"	70' 08"	9' 01"

T-2 TGL MARINE HOLDINGS ULC, TORONTO, ON

Jane Ann IV	ATB	1978	D	954*	137' 06"	42' 08"	21' 04"

Built: Mitsui Engineering & Shipbuilding Co., Tokyo, Japan (Ouro Fino '78-'81, Bomare '81-'93, Tignish Sea '93-'98)

Sarah Spencer	SU	1959	B	23,200	611' 03"	72' 00"	40' 00"

Built: Manitowoc Shipbuilding Co., Manitowoc, WI; engine removed, converted to a self-unloading barge by Halifax Dartmouth Industries, Halifax, NS, in '89 (Adam E. Cornelius {3} '59-'89, Capt. Edward V. Smith '89-'91, Sea Barge One '91-'96)

[Jane Ann IV / Sarah Spencer OA dimensions together]			729' 03"	72' 00"	40' 00"

T-3 THOUSAND ISLANDS AND SEAWAY CRUISES, BROCKVILLE, ON *(1000islandscruises.com)*

General Brock III	ES	1977	D	56*	50' 05"	15' 04"	5' 02"

Built: Gananoque Boat Line Ltd., Gananoque, ON (Miss Peterborough)

Island Heritage	ES	1929	D	21*	63' 09"	9' 08"	4' 09"

(Miss Ivy Lea No. 1)

Sea Fox II	ES	1988	D	55*	39' 08"	20' 00"	2' 00"

T-4 THUNDER BAY TUG SERVICES LTD., THUNDER BAY, ON

Glenada	TB	1943	D	107*	80' 06"	25' 00"	10' 01"

Built: Russel Brothers Ltd., Owen Sound, ON (HMCS Glenada [W-30] '43-'45)

Miseford	TB	1915	D	116*	85' 00"	20' 00"	10' 06"

Built: M. Beatty & Sons Ltd., Welland, ON

Point Valour	TB	1958	D	246*	97' 08"	28' 02"	13' 10"

Built: Davie Shipbuilding Co., Lauzon, QC (Foundation Valour '58-'83)

THUNDER BAY MARINE SERVICES LTD., A DIVISION OF THUNDER BAY TUG SERVICES LTD.

Coastal Cruiser	TB	1939	D	29*	65' 00"	18' 00"	12' 00"

Built: George Gamble, Port Dover, ON

Robert W.	TB	1949	D	48*	60' 00"	16' 00"	8' 06"

Built: Russel Brothers Ltd., Owen Sound, ON

Rosalee D.	TB	1943	D	22*	55' 00"	16' 00"	10' 00"

Built: Northern Shipbuilding & Repair Co. Ltd., Bronte, ON

T-5 TNT DREDGING INC., GRAND RAPIDS, MI

Bonnie G.	TB	1928	D	95*	86' 00"	21' 00"	12' 00"

Built: Manitowoc Shipbuilding Co., Manitowoc, WI (E. James Fucik '28-'77, Bonnie G. Selvick '77-'04)

Joyce Marie	TB	1960	D	36*	46' 02"	15' 02"	6' 03"
(Kendee '60-'71, Morelli, Michelle B, Debra Ann '98-'03)							
Wolverine	TB	1952	D	22*	42' 05"	14' 00"	7' 00"
Built: Hans Hansen Welding Co., Toledo, OH							

T-6   TOBERMORY ADVENTURE TOURS, TOBERMORY, ON

| Dawn Light | TB | 1891 | D | 64* | 75' 00" | 24' 00" | 12' 00" |
| *Built: Craig Shipbuilding Co., Toledo, OH (Le Roy Brooks 1891-1925, Henry Stokes '25-'54, Aburg '54-'81)* | | | | | | | |

T-7   TORONTO BRIGANTINE INC., TORONTO, ON *(tallshipadventures.on.ca)*

| Pathfinder | TV | 1963 | W/D | 35* | 53' 00" | 15' 00" | 6' 09" |
| Playfair | TV | 1973 | W/D | 41* | 53' 07" | 15' 00" | 7' 04" |

T-8   TORONTO DRYDOCK LTD., TORONTO, ON *(torontodrydock.com)*

M. R. Kane	TB	1945	D	51*	60' 06"	16' 05"	6' 07"
Built: Central Bridge Co. Ltd., Trenton, ON (Tanac V-276 '45-'47)							
Menier Consol	FD	1962	B	2,575*	304' 05"	49' 06"	25' 06"
Built: Davie Shipbuilding Co., Lauzon, QC; former pulpwood carrier is now a floating dry dock at Toronto, ON							

T-9   TORONTO FIRE DEPARTMENT, TORONTO, ON

| Wm. Lyon Mackenzie | FB | 1964 | D | 102* | 81' 01" | 20' 00" | 10' 00" |
| *Built: Russel Brothers Ltd., Owen Sound, ON* | | | | | | | |

T-10   TORONTO PADDLEWHEEL CRUISES LTD., NORTH YORK, ON

Pioneer Princess	ES	1984	D	74*	56' 00"	17' 01"	3' 09"
Pioneer Queen	ES	1968	D	110*	85' 00"	30' 06"	7' 03"
Built: Hike Metal Products, Wheatley, ON (Peche Island III '68-'71, Papoose IV '71-'96)							

T-11   TORONTO PARKS & RECREATION DEPARTMENT, TORONTO, ON

Ongiara	PF	1963	D	180*	78' 00"	12' 04"	9' 09"
Built: Russel Brothers Ltd., Owen Sound, ON							
Sam McBride	PF	1939	D	412*	129' 00"	34' 11"	6' 00"
Built: Toronto Dry Dock Co. Ltd., Toronto, ON							
Thomas Rennie	PF	1950	D	419*	129' 00"	32' 11"	6' 00"
Built: Toronto Dry Dock Co. Ltd., Toronto, ON							
Trillium	PF	1910	R	611*	150' 00"	30' 00"	8' 04"
Built: Poulson Iron Works, Toronto, ON							
William Inglis	PF	1935	D	238*	99' 00"	24' 10"	6' 00"
Built: John Inglis Co. Ltd., Toronto, ON (Shamrock {2} '35-'37)							

T-12   TORONTO PORT AUTHORITY, TORONTO, ON *(torontoport.com)*

Brutus I	TB	1992	D	10*	36' 01"	11' 09"	4' 04"
Fred Scandrett	TB	1963	D	52*	62' 00"	17' 00"	8' 00"
Built: Port Weller Dry Docks Ltd., St. Catharines, ON (C. E. "Ted" Smith '63-'70)							
Maple City	PA/CF	1951	D	135*	70' 06"	36' 04"	5' 11"
Built: Muir Brothers Dry Dock Co. Ltd., Port Dalhousie, ON							
TCCA 1	PA/CF	2006	D	219*	95' 10"	37' 07"	7' 05"
Built: Hike Metal Products, Wheatley, ON							
William Rest	TB	1961	D	62*	65' 00"	18' 06"	10' 06"
Built: Erieau Shipbuilding & Drydock Co. Ltd., Erieau, ON							
Windmill Point	PA/CF	1954	D	118*	65' 00"	36' 00"	10' 00"
Built: Kingston Shipyards Ltd., Kingston, ON							

T-13   TORONTO PUBLIC WORKS DEPARTMENT, TORONTO, ON

| Ned Hanlan II | TB | 1966 | D | 26* | 41' 06" | 14' 01" | 5' 05" |
| *Built: Erieau Shipbuilding & Drydock Co. Ltd., Erieau, ON* | | | | | | | |

T-14   TORONTO TOURS LTD., TORONTO, ON *(www.torontotours.com)*

Miss Kim Simpson	ES	1960	D	33*	90' 02"	13' 04"	3' 09"
New Beginnings	ES	1961	D	28*	41' 09"	13' 01"	4' 09"
Shipsands	ES	1972	D	23*	58' 03"	12' 01"	4' 07"

Edward H. at Duluth. *(Pat Ojard)*

Canadian tug Vac. *(Paul Beesley)*

Tugs

Avenger IV, with W.I. Scott Purvis on the hip. *(Roger LeLievre)*

Kurt R. Luedtke and barge. *(Alain Gindroz)*

Jimmy L. assists James R. Barker at Sturgeon Bay. *(Steve Hogler)*

TRANSPORT DESGAGNÉS INC., QUÉBEC, QC *(groupedesgagnes.com)*
A SUBSIDIARY OF GROUPE DESGAGNÉS INC., QUÉBEC CITY, QC

Amelia Desgagnés	GC	1976	D	7,126	355' 00"	49' 00"	30' 06"

Built: Collingwood Shipyards, Collingwood, ON (Soodoc {2} '76-'90)

Anna Desgagnés	RR	1986	D	17,850	565' 00"	75' 00"	45' 00"

Built: Kvaerner Warnow Werft GmbH, Rostock, Germany; re-registered in the Bahamas in 2006
(Truskavets '86-'96, Anna Desgagnés '96-'98, PCC Panama '98-'99)

Camilla Desgagnés	GC	1982	D	7,000	436' 00"	68' 05"	22' 06"

Built: Kroeger Werft GmbH & Co. KG, Rendsburg, Germany (Camilla 1 '82-'04)

Catherine Desgagnés	GC	1962	D	8,350	410' 03"	56' 04"	31' 00"

Built: Hall, Russel and Co., Aberdeen, Scotland (Gosforth '62-'72, Thorold {4} '72-'85)

Melissa Desgagnés	GC	1975	D	7,000	355' 00"	49' 00"	30' 06"

Built: Collingwood Shipyards, Collingwood, ON (Ontadoc {2} '75-'90)

Rosaire A. Desgagnés	GC	2007	D	12,580	452' 11"	70' 01"	36' 01"

Built: Quingshan/Jiangdong/Jiangzhou Shipyards, Jiangzhou, China (Beluga Fortification '07-'07)

Zelada Desgagnés	GC	2009	D	12,491	452' 11"	70' 01"	36' 01"

Built: Quingshan/Jiangdong/Jiangzhou Shipyards, Jiangzhou, China (Beluga Freedom '09-'09)

THE FOLLOWING VESSELS CHARTERED TO PETRO-NAV INC., MONTREAL, QC,
A SUBSIDIARY OF GROUPE DESGAGNÉS INC.

Diamond Star	TK	1992	D	10,511	405' 11"	58' 01"	34' 09"

Built: MTW Shipyard, Wismar, Germany (Elbestern '92-'93)

Emerald Star	TK	1992	D	10,511	405' 11"	58' 01"	34' 09"

Built: MTW Shipyard, Wismar, Germany (Emsstern '92-'92)

Jade Star	TK	1993	D	10,511	405' 11"	58' 01"	34' 09"

Built: MTW Shipyard, Wismar, Germany (Jadestern '93-'94)

Maria Desgagnés	TK	1999	D	14,335	393' 08"	68' 11"	40' 04"

Built: Qiuxin Shipyard, Shanghai, China (Kilchem Asia '99-'99)

Petrolia Desgagnés	TK	1975	D	9,712	441' 05"	56' 06"	32' 10"

Built: Ankerlokken Verft Glommen, Fredrikstad, Norway (Jorvan '75-'79, Lido '79-'84, Ek-Sky '84-'98)

Sarah Desgagnés	TK	2007	D	18,000	483' 11"	73' 06"	41' 04"

Built: Gisan Shipyard, Tuzla, Turkey (Besiktas Greenland '07 - '08)

Thalassa Desgagnés	TK	1976	D	9,748	441' 05"	56' 06"	32' 10"

Built: Ankerlokken Verft Glommen, Fredrikstad, Norway (Joasla '76-'79, Orinoco '79-'82, Rio Orinoco '82-'93)

Vega Desgagnés	TK	1982	D	11,548	461' 11"	69' 08"	35' 01"

Built: Kvaerner Masa-Yards, Helsinki, Finland (Shelltrans '82-'94, Acila '94-'99, Bacalan '99-'01)

THE FOLLOWING VESSEL CHARTERED TO RELAIS NORDIC INC., RIMOUSKI, QC
A SUBSIDIARY OF GROUPE DESGAGNÉS INC.

Nordik Express	CF	1974	D	1,697	219' 11"	44' 00"	16' 01"

Built: Todd Pacific Shipyards Corp., Seattle, WA (Theriot Offshore IV '74-'77, Scotoil 4 '77-'79, Tartan Sea '79-'87)

TRANSPORT INUKSHUK INC., IQALUIT, NUNAVUT TERRITORY, CANADA
THE FOLLOWING VESSEL CHARTERED TO NUNAVUT EASTERN ARCTIC SERVICES INC.

Avataq	GC	2004	D	9,653	370' 07"	62' 00"	37' 00"

Built: Miho Shipbuilding Co. Ltd., Shimizu Shizuoka Prefecture, Japan

TRANSPORT NANUK INC., MONTREAL, QC

Edisongracht	GC	1994	D	12,760	446' 00"	62' 00"	38' 02"

Built: Frisian Shipbuilding Welgelegen B.V., Harlingen, Netherlands (Edisongracht '94-'08, Qamutik '08-'08)

THE FOLLOWING VESSEL CHARTERED TO NUNAVUT EASTERN ARCTIC SERVICES INC.

Umiavut	GC	1988	D	9,653	371' 02"	63' 01"	37' 00"

Built: Miho Shipbuilding Co. Ltd., Shimizu Shizuoka Prefecture, Japan; operated by Spliethoff's, Amsterdam,
Netherlands (Completed as Newca; Kapitan Silin '88-'92, Lindengracht '92-'00)

TRANSPORT IGLOOLIK INC., MONTREAL, QC
THE FOLLOWING VESSEL CHARTERED TO NUNAVUT EASTERN ARCTIC SERVICES INC.

Aivik	HL	1980	D	4,860	359' 08"	63' 08"	38' 09"

Built: ACH - Construction Navale, Le Havre, France (Mont Ventoux '80-'90, Aivik '90-'91, Unilifter '91-'92)

TRAVERSE TALL SHIP CO., TRAVERSE CITY, MI *(tallshipsailing.com)*

Manitou {1}	ES/2S	1983	W	78*	114' 00"	21' 00"	9' 00"

T-20	**30,000 ISLANDS CRUISE LINES INC., PARRY SOUND, ON** *(island-queen.com)*						
Island Queen	ES	1990	D	526*	130' 00"	35' 00"	6' 06"

U-1	**UNCLE SAM BOAT TOURS, ALEXANDRIA, NY** *(usboattours.com)*						
Alexandria Belle	ES	1988	D	92*	82' 00"	32' 00"	8' 00"
Island Duchess	ES	1988	D	73*	90' 03"	27' 08"	9' 00"
Island Wanderer	ES	1971	D	57*	62' 05"	22' 00"	7' 02"
Uncle Sam 7	ES	1976	D	55*	60' 04"	22' 00"	7' 01"

U-2 U.S. ARMY CORPS OF ENGINEERS – GREAT LAKES AND OHIO RIVER DIVISION, CINCINNATI, OH
(usace.army.mil) **U.S. ARMY CORPS OF ENGINEERS – BUFFALO DISTRICT**

Cheraw	TB	1970	D	356*	109' 00"	30' 06"	16' 03"

Built: Southern Shipbuilding Corp., Slidell, LA (USS Cheraw [YTB-802] '70-'96)

Simonsen	CS	1954	B		142' 00"	58' 00"	5' 00"

U.S. ARMY CORPS OF ENGINEERS – DETROIT DISTRICT, LAKE MICHIGAN AREA OFFICE, KEWAUNEE SUB OFFICE

Kenosha	TB	1954	D	82*	70' 00"	20' 00"	9' 08"

Built: Missouri Valley Bridge & Iron Works, Leavenworth, KS (U. S. Army ST-2011 '54-'65)

Manitowoc	CS	1976	B		132' 00"	44' 00"	8' 00"
Racine	TB	1931	D	61*	66' 03"	18' 05"	7' 08"

Built: Marine Iron & Shipbuilding Company, Duluth MN

U.S. ARMY CORPS OF ENGINEERS – DETROIT DISTRICT, DETROIT AREA OFFICE

Demolen	TB	1974	D	356*	109' 00"	30' 06"	16' 03"

Built: Marinette Marine Corp., Marinette, WI (USS Metacom [YTB-829] '74-'01, Metacom '01-'02)

Veler	CS	1991	B	613*	150' 00"	46' 00"	10' 06"

U.S. ARMY CORPS OF ENGINEERS – DETROIT DISTRICT, DULUTH AREA OFFICE

D. L. Billmaier	TB	1968	D	356*	109' 00"	30' 06"	16' 03"

Built: Southern Shipbuilding Corp., Slidell, LA (USS Natchitoches [YTB-799] '68-'95)

H. J. Schwartz	DB	1995	B		150' 00"	48' 00"	11' 00"
Hammond Bay	TB	1953	D	23*	45' 00"	13' 00"	7' 00"

U.S. ARMY CORPS OF ENGINEERS – DETROIT DISTRICT, SOO AREA OFFICE

Harvey	DB	1961	B		120' 00"	40' 00"	8' 00"
Nicolet	DB	1971	B		120' 00"	40' 00"	8' 00"
Owen M. Frederick	TB	1942	D	56*	65' 00"	17' 00"	7' 06"

Built: Sturgeon Bay Shipbuilding Co., Sturgeon Bay, WI

Paul Bunyan	GL	1945	B		150' 00"	65' 00"	12' 06"

Built: Wiley Equipment Co., Port Deposit, MD

Whitefish Bay	TB	1953	D	23*	45' 00"	13' 00"	7' 00"

U-3 U.S. COAST GUARD 9TH COAST GUARD DISTRICT, CLEVELAND, OH *(uscg.mil/d9)*

Alder **[WLB-216]**	BT	2004	D	2,000*	225' 09"	46' 00"	19' 08"

Built: Marinette Marine Corp., Marinette, WI; stationed at Duluth, MN

Biscayne Bay **[WTGB-104]**	IB	1979	D	662*	140' 00"	37' 06"	12' 00"

Built: Tacoma Boatbuilding Co., Tacoma, WA; stationed at St. Ignace, MI

Bristol Bay **[WTGB-102]**	IB	1979	D	662*	140' 00"	37' 06"	12' 00"

Built: Tacoma Boatbuilding Co., Tacoma, WA; stationed at Detroit, MI

Buckthorn **[WLI-642]**	BT	1963	D	200*	100' 00"	24' 00"	4' 08"

Built: Mobile Ship Repair Inc., Mobile, AL; stationed at Sault Ste. Marie, MI

CGB-12000	BT	1991	B	700*	120' 00"	50' 00"	6' 00"
CGB-12001	BT	1991	B	700*	120' 00"	50' 00"	6' 00"
Hollyhock **[WLB-214]**	BT	2003	D	2,000*	225' 09"	46' 00"	19' 08"

Built: Marinette Marine Corp., Marinette, WI; stationed at Port Huron, MI

Katmai Bay **[WTGB-101]**	IB	1978	D	662*	140' 00"	37' 06"	12' 00"

Built: Tacoma Boatbuilding Co., Tacoma, WA; stationed at Sault Ste. Marie, MI

Mackinaw **[WLBB-30]**	IB	2005	D	3,407*	240' 00"	58' 00"	15' 05"

Built: Marinette Marine Corp., Marinette, WI; stationed at Cheboygan, MI

Mobile Bay **[WTGB-103]**	IB	1979	D	662*	140' 00"	37' 06"	12' 00"

Built: Tacoma Boatbuilding Co., Tacoma, WA; stationed at Sturgeon Bay, WI

Neah Bay **[WTGB-105]**	IB	1980	D	662*	140' 00"	37' 06"	12' 00"

Built: Tacoma Boatbuilding Co., Tacoma, WA; stationed at Cleveland, OH

U-4	**U.S. COAST GUARD TUG ASSOCIATION, CLEVELAND, OH** *(76fsa.org/cgta)*							
	Apalachee	TB/MU	1943	DE	224*	104' 03"	26' 04"	15' 01"
	Built: Ira S. Bushey & Sons Inc., Brooklyn, NY; vessel is expected to be moved to Cleveland in 2009 to be restored as a maritime and Coast Guard museum ship (Apalachee WYTM-71)							
U-5	**U.S. ENVIRONMENTAL PROTECTION AGENCY, DULUTH, MN AND CHICAGO, IL**							
	Peter Wise Lake Guardian	RV	1981	D	282*	180' 00"	40' 00"	11' 00"
	Built: Halter Marine Inc., Moss Point MS (Marsea Fourteen '81-'90)							
U-6	**U.S. FISH & WILDLIFE SERVICE, JORDAN RIVER NATIONAL FISH HATCHERY, ELMIRA, MI**							
	Spencer F. Baird	RV	2006	D	256*	95' 00"	30' 00"	9' 05"
U-7	**U.S. NATIONAL PARK SERVICE - ISLE ROYALE NATIONAL PARK, HOUGHTON, MI** *(nps.gov)*							
	Greenstone II	TK	2003	B	114*	70' 01"	24' 01"	8' 00"
	Built: Fraser Shipyards Inc., Superior, WI							
	Ranger III	PK	1958	D	648*	152' 08"	34' 00"	13' 00"
	Built: Christy Corp., Sturgeon Bay, WI							
	Shelter Bay	TB	1953	D		45' 00"	13' 00"	7' 00"
U-8	**U.S. NAVAL SEA CADET CORPS** *(seacadets.org)*							
	Grayfox **[TWR-825]**	TV	1985	D	213*	120' 00"	25' 00"	12' 00"
	Built: Marinette Marine, Marinette, WI; based at Port Huron, MI (USS TWR-825 '85-'97)							
	Manatra **[YP-671]**	TV	1974	D	67*	80' 05"	17' 09"	5' 04"
	Based at Chicago, IL; name stands for MArine NAvigation and TRaining Association (USS YP-671 '74-'89)							
	Pride of Michigan **[YP-673]**	TV	1977	D	70*	80' 06"	17' 08"	5' 03"
	Built: Peterson Builders Inc., Sturgeon Bay, WI; based at Mount Clemens, MI (USS YP-673 '77-'89)							
U-9	**UNIVERSITY OF MINNESOTA-DULUTH, DULUTH, MN** *(www.d.umn.edu)*							
	Blue Heron	RV	1985	D	175*	87' 00"	23' 00"	11' 00"*
	Built: Goudy and Stevens, E. Boothbay, ME (Fairtry '85-'97)							
U-10	**UNIVERSITY OF WISCONSIN, GREAT LAKES WATER INSTITUTE, MILWAUKEE, WI** *(glwi.uwm.edu)*							
	Neeskay	RV	1952	D	75*	71' 00"	17' 06"	7' 06"
U-11	**UNIVERSITY OF WISCONSIN, SUPERIOR, WI** *(uwsuper.edu)*							
	L. L. Smith Jr.	RV	1950	D	38*	57' 06"	16' 06"	6' 06"
U-12	**UPPER LAKES GROUP INC., TORONTO, ON** *(upperlakes.com)*							
	DISTRIBUTION GRANDS LACS/ST-LAURENT LTEE, TROIS RIVIERES, QC – A DIVISION OF UPPER LAKES GROUP INC.							
	BIG 503	BC	2000	B	902*	190' 06"	35' 00"	14' 00"
	BIG 543	BC	2003	B	916*	191' 00"	35' 00"	14' 00"
	BIG 546	BC	2003	B	916*	191' 00"	35' 00"	14' 00"
	BIG 548	BC	2003	B	916*	191' 00"	35' 00"	14' 00"
	BIG 549	BC	2003	B	916*	191' 00"	35' 00"	14' 00"
	BIG 551	BC	2003	B	916*	191' 00"	35' 00"	14' 00"
	BIG 9708 B	BC	1996	B	958*	191' 09"	35' 00"	14' 00"
	BIG 9917 B	BC	1999	B	958*	191' 09"	35' 00"	14' 00"
	Commodore Straits	TB	1966	D	566*	130' 00"	34' 01"	15' 07"
	Built: Dominion Steel & Coal Corp., Halifax, NS (Haida Brave '66-'79)							
	Doc Morin	TB	1954	D	225*	101' 10"	26' 00"	13' 08"
	Built: Davie Shipbuilding Co., Lauzon, QC (Charlie S., Cathy McAllister, Seven Sisters '54-'05)							
	MARINELINK INC., TORONTO, ON – A DIVISION OF UPPER LAKES GROUP INC.							
	MarineLink Explorer	HL	1978	B	3,000*	300' 00"	55' 00"	27' 00"
	Built: Peterson Builders, Sturgeon Bay, WI (John Henry)							
	PROVMAR FUELS INC., HAMILTON, ON – A DIVISION OF UPPER LAKES GROUP INC.							
	Hamilton Energy	TK	1965	D	1,282	201' 05"	34' 01"	14' 09"
	Built: Grangemouth Dockyard Co., Grangemouth, Scotland (Partington '65-'79, Shell Scientist '79-'81, Metro Sun '81-'85)							
	Provmar Terminal	TK	1959	B	7,300	403' 05"	55' 06"	28' 00"
	Built: Sarpsborg Mek, Verksted, Greater Norway; last operated in 1984; in use as a fuel storage barge at Hamilton, ON (Varangnes '59-'70, Tommy Wiborg '70-'74, Ungava Transport '74-'85)							

Fleet #	Fleet Name / Vessel Name	Type of Vessel	Year Built	Type of Engine	Cargo Cap. or Gross*	Overall Length	Breadth	Depth or Draft*
	Provmar Terminal II	TK	1948	B	6,832	408' 08"	53' 00"	26' 00"

Built: Collingwood Shipyards, Collingwood, ON; last operated 1986; in use as a fuel storage barge at Hamilton, ON (Imperial Sarnia {2} '48-'89)

UPPER LAKES SHIPPING LTD., CALGARY, AB – DIVISION OF UPPER LAKES GROUP INC.
* VESSELS OPERATED AND MANAGED BY SEAWAY MARINE TRANSPORT, ST. CATHARINES, ON, A PARTNERSHIP BETWEEN ALGOMA CENTRAL CORP. AND UPPER LAKES GROUP INC.

Fleet #	Fleet Name / Vessel Name	Type of Vessel	Year Built	Type of Engine	Cargo Cap. or Gross*	Overall Length	Breadth	Depth or Draft*
	Canadian Enterprise*	SU	1979	D	35,100	730' 00"	75' 08"	46' 06"

Built: Port Weller Dry Docks, Port Weller, ON

	Canadian Leader*	BC	1967	T	28,300	730' 00"	75' 00"	39' 08"

Built: Collingwood Shipyards, Collingwood, ON; last steam-powered vessel built on lakes (Feux-Follets '67-'72)

	Canadian Miner*	BC	1966	D	28,050	730' 00"	75' 00"	39' 01"

Built: Canadian Vickers, Montreal, QC (Maplecliffe Hall '66-'88, Lemoyne {2} '88-'94); laid up at Toronto, ON

	Canadian Navigator*	SU	1967	D	30,925	728' 11"	75' 10"	40' 06"

Built: J. Readhead & Sons, South Shields, England; converted from a saltwater bulk carrier in '80; converted to a self-unloader in '97; both conversions by Port Weller Dry Docks, St. Catharines, ON (Demeterton '67-'75, St. Lawrence Navigator '75-'80)

	Canadian Olympic*	SU	1976	D	35,100	730' 00"	75' 00"	46' 06"

Built: Port Weller Dry Docks, Port Weller, ON

	Canadian Progress*	SU	1968	D	32,700	730' 00"	75' 00"	46' 06"

Built: Port Weller Dry Docks, Port Weller, ON

	Canadian Prospector*	BC	1964	D	30,500	730' 00"	75' 10"	40' 06"

Built: Short Brothers Ltd., Sunderland, England; converted from a saltwater bulk carrier by St. John Shipbuilding and Drydock, Saint John, NB, in '79 (Carlton '64-'75, St. Lawrence Prospector '75-'79)

	Canadian Provider*	BC	1963	T	27,450	730' 00"	75' 00"	39' 02"

Built: Collingwood Shipyards, Collingwood, ON (Murray Bay {3} '63-'94)

	Canadian Ranger*	SU	1943/67	D	25,900	729' 10"	75' 00"	39' 03"

Canadian Ranger was built by joining the stern section (pilothouse, engine room, machinery) of the former coastal package freighter Chimo with the bow and mid-body of the laker Hilda Marjanne in '84; converted to a self- unloader in '88; all work by Port Weller Dry Docks, St. Catharines, ON (Fore Section) Built: Kaiser Inc., Portland, OR, as Grande Ronde '43-'48, Kate N. L. '48-'61, Hilda Marjanne '61-'84); converted from a saltwater bulk carrier in '61 (Stern Section) Built: Davie Shipbuilding Co., Lauzon, QC, as Chimo '67-'83

	Canadian Transfer*	SU	1943/65	D	22,204	650' 06"	60' 00"	35' 00"

Canadian Transfer was built by joining the stern section of Canadian Explorer (engine room, machinery) with the bow and mid-body of the World War II-era laker Hamilton Transfer in '98; all work by Port Weller Dry Docks, St. Catharines, ON (Fore Section) Built: Great Lakes Engineering Works, Ashtabula, OH, as J. H. Hillman Jr. '43-'74, Crispin Oglebay {2} '74-'95, Hamilton Transfer '95-'98); converted to a self-unloader in '74 (Stern Section) Built: Davie Shipbuilding Co., Lauzon, QC as Cabot {1} '65-'83, Canadian Explorer '83-'98)

	Canadian Transport* {2}	SU	1979	D	35,100	730' 00"	75' 08"	46' 06"

Built: Port Weller Dry Docks, Port Weller, ON

	Gordon C. Leitch* {2}	BC	1968	D	29,700	730' 00"	75' 00"	42' 00"

Built: Canadian Vickers, Montreal, QC; converted from a self-unloader to a bulk carrier by the builders in '77 (Ralph Misener '68-'94)

	James Norris*	SU	1952	S	18,600	663' 06"	67' 00"	35' 00"

Built: Midland Shipyards, Midland, ON; converted to a self-unloader by Port Weller Dry Docks, St. Catharines, ON, in '81

	John D. Leitch*	SU	1967	D	31,600	730' 00"	78' 00"	45' 00"

Built: Port Weller Dry Docks, Port Weller, ON; rebuilt with new mid-body, widened 3' by the builders in '02 (Canadian Century '67-'02)

	Montrealais*	BC	1962	T	27,800	730' 00"	75' 00"	39' 00"

Built: Canadian Vickers, Montreal, QC (Launched as Montrealer)

	Quebecois*	BC	1963	T	27,800	730' 00"	75' 00"	39' 00"

Built: Canadian Vickers, Montreal, QC

U-13 UPPER LAKES TOWING CO., ESCANABA, MI

Fleet #	Fleet Name / Vessel Name	Type of Vessel	Year Built	Type of Engine	Cargo Cap. or Gross*	Overall Length	Breadth	Depth or Draft*
	Joseph H. Thompson	SU	1944	B	21,200	706' 06"	71' 06"	38' 06"

Built: Sun Shipbuilding & Drydock Co., Chester, PA; converted from a saltwater vessel to a Great Lakes bulk carrier by Maryland Dry Dock, Baltimore, MD, and American Shipbuilding Co., South Chicago, IL, in '52; converted to a self-unloading barge by the owners in '91 (USNS Marine Robin '44-'52)

	Joseph H. Thompson Jr.	ATB	1990	D	841*	146' 06"	38' 00"	35' 00"

Built: At Marinette, WI, from steel left over from the conversion of Joseph H. Thompson (see above)

Philip R. Clarke in the St. Marys River. *(Steve Hogler)*

U-14   **USS COD SUBMARINE MEMORIAL, CLEVELAND, OH** *(usscod.org)*
   Cod · MU · 1943 · D/V · 1,525* · 311' 08" · 27' 02" · 33' 09"
   Built: Electric Boat Co., Groton, CT; former U.S. Navy Albacore (Gato) class submarine IXSS-224 open to the public at Cleveland, OH

V-1   **VANENKEVORT TUG & BARGE INC., BARK RIVER, MI**
   Great Lakes Trader · SU · 2000 · B · 39,600 · 740' 00" · 78' 00" · 45' 00"
   Built: Halter Marine, Pearlington, MS
   Joyce L. VanEnkevort · AT · 1998 · D · 1,179* · 135' 04" · 50' 00" · 26' 00"
   Built: Bay Shipbuilding Co., Sturgeon Bay, WI
   [ATB VanEnkevort / GL Trader OA dimensions together] · 844' 10" · 78' 00" · 45' 00"

V-2   **VANGUARD SHIPPING (GREAT LAKES) LTD., INGLESIDE, ON**
   J.W. Shelley · BC · 1968 · D · 28,400 · 730' 00" · 75' 03" · 39' 08"
   Built: Collingwood Shipyards, Collingwood, ON (Algocen '68-'05, Valgocen '05-'08)

V-3   **VIC POWELL, DUNNVILLE, ON**
   Beaver D. · TB · 1955 · D · 15* · 36' 02" · 14' 09" · 4' 04"
   Lac Erie · TB · 1944 · D · 65* · 65' 00" · 16' 10" · 7' 07"
   Built: Central Bridge Co., Trenton, ON (Tanmac '44-'74)
   Toni D · TB · 1959 · D · 15* · 46' 00" · 15' 07" · 4' 01"

V-4   **VICTORIAN PRINCESS CRUISE LINES INC., ERIE, PA** *(victorianprincess.com)*
   Victorian Princess · ES · 1985 · D · 46* · 67' 00" · 24' 00" · 4' 05"
   Built: Mid-City Steel Fabricating Inc., LaCrosse, WI (Rosie 1, Rosie O'Shea)

V-5   **VINCENT KLAMERUS, DRUMMOND ISLAND, MI**
   Lime Island · PA · 1953 · D · 24* · 42' 08" · 12' 00" · 6' 00"

V-6   **VISTA FLEET, DULUTH, MN** *(vistafleet.com)*
   Vista King · ES · 1978 · D · 60* · 78' 00" · 23' 00" · 5' 02"
   Built: Blount Marine Corp., Warren, RI
   Vista Queen · ES · 1987 · D · 97* · 64' 00" · 16' 00" · 6' 02"
   Built: Mid-City Steel Fabricating Inc., LaCrosse, WI
   Vista Star · ES · 1987 · D · 95* · 91' 00" · 24' 09" · 5' 02"
   Built: Freeport Shipbuilding Inc., Freeport, FL (Island Empress '87-'88)

V-7   **VOIGHT'S MARINE SERVICES LTD., ELLISON BAY AND GILLS ROCK, WI** *(islandclipper.com)*
   Island Clipper {2} · ES · 1987 · D · 71* · 65' 00" · 20' 00" · 8' 00"
   Built: Breaux Bros. Enterprises, Loreauville LA
   Yankee Clipper · ES · 1971 · D · 41* · 46' 06" · 17' 00" · 6' 00"

V-8   **VOYAGEUR MARINE TRANSPORT LTD., RIDGEVILLE, ON** *(voyageurtransport.com)*
   Maritime Trader · BC · 1967 · D · 19,093 · 607' 10" · 62' 00" · 36' 00"
   Built: Collingwood Shipyards, Collingwood, ON; commercially operated under contract of affreightment to Lower Lakes Towing Ltd. (Mantadoc '67-'02, Teakglen '02-'05)

W-1   **WARNER PETROLEUM CORP., CLARE, MI** *(warnerpetroleum.com)*
   William L. Warner · RT · 1973 · D · 492* · 120' 00" · 40' 00" · 14' 00"
   Vessel is engaged in bunkering operations in the Indiana Harbor, IN and Chicago, IL., areas
   Built: Halter Marine, New Orleans, LA (Jos. F. Bigane '73-'04)

W-2   **WASHINGTON ISLAND FERRY LINE INC., WASHINGTON ISLAND, WI** *(wisferry.com)*
   Arni J. Richter · PA/CF · 2003 · D · 92* · 104' 00" · 38' 06" · 10' 11"
   Built: Bay Shipbuilding Co., Sturgeon Bay, WI
   C. G. Richter · PA/CF · 1950 · D · 82* · 70' 06" · 25' 00" · 9' 05"
   Built: Sturgeon Bay Shipbuilding, Sturgeon Bay, WI
   Eyrarbakki · PA/CF · 1970 · D · 95* · 87' 00" · 36' 00" · 7' 06"
   Built: Bay Shipbuilding Co., Sturgeon Bay, WI
   Robert Noble · PA/CF · 1979 · D · 97* · 90' 04" · 36' 00" · 8' 03"
   Built: Peterson Builders Inc., Sturgeon Bay, WI
   Washington {2} · PA/CF · 1989 · D · 97* · 100' 00" · 37' 00" · 9' 00"
   Built: Peterson Builders Inc., Sturgeon Bay, WI

W-3	**WENDELLA BOAT TOURS, CHICAGO, IL** (wendellaboats.com)							
	Sunliner	ES	1961	D	35*	62' 00"	14' 04"	6' 04"
	Wendella	ES	1958	D	46*	68' 00"	19' 00"	6' 00"
	Wendella	ES	2007	D	77*	85' 05"	30' 00"	7' 01"
	Wendella LTD	ES	1992	D	66*	68' 00"	20' 00"	4' 09"

W-4	**WESTERN RESERVE STEAMSHIP SUPPLY, LAKEWOOD, OH**							
	Forest City	SB	1934	D	22*	44' 04"	11' 11"	4' 09"

W-5	**WILLY'S CONTRACTING CO., SOUTHAMPTON, ON**							
	Pride	TB	1957	D	47*	52' 06"	29' 08"	5' 01"

W-6	**WINDY OF CHICAGO LTD., CHICAGO, IL** (tallshipwindy.com)							
	Windy	ES/4S	1996	W	75*	148' 00"	25' 00"	8' 00"
	Built: Detyens Shipyards Inc., Charleston, SC							
	Windy II	ES/4S	2000	W	99*	150' 00"	25' 00"	8' 05"
	Built: Detyens Shipyards Inc., Charleston, SC							

W-7	**WISCONSIN DEPARTMENT OF NATURAL RESOURCES, BAYFIELD AND STURGEON BAY, WI**							
	Barney Devine	RV	1937	D	42*	50' 00"	14' 05"	6' 00"
	Hack Noyes	RV	1947	D	50*	56' 00"		4' 00"

W-8	**WISCONSIN MARITIME MUSEUM, MANITOWOC, WI** (wisconsinmaritime.org)							
	Cobia	MU	1944	D/V	1,500*	311' 09"	27' 03"	33' 09"
	Built: Manitowoc Shipbuilding Co., Manitowoc, WI; former U. S. Navy Gato class submarine AGSS-245 is open to the public at Manitowoc, WI							

Z-1	**ZENITH TUGBOAT CO., DULUTH, MN**							
	Anna Marie Altman	TB	1950	D	146*	88' 06"	25' 06"	11' 00"
	Built: Alexander Shipyard Inc., New Orleans, LA (Navajo {1} '50-'52, Seaval '52-'63, Mary T. Tracy '63-'69, Yankee '69-'70, Minn '70-'74, William S. Bell '74-'83, Newcastle '83-'93, Laura Lynn '93-'99, Susan Hoey {3} '99-'06)							
	Sioux	TB	1921	D	96*	81' 00"	20' 00"	12' 06"
	Built: Great Lakes Towing Co., Cleveland, OH (Oregon {1} '21-'78, Ste. Marie I '78-'81, Sioux {2} '81-'91, Susan E. '91-'05)							
	Victor J. Altman	TB	1965	D	195*	108' 00"	27' 10"	12' 00"
	Built: Walter M. Edwards, New Iberia, LA (Trans World '65-'69, Rosemary McAllister '69-'07)							

Know Your SHIPS 50 Years

The information in this book, current as of Feb. 15, 2009, was obtained from the United States Coast Guard, the Lake Carriers' Association, Lloyd's Register of Shipping, Transport Canada, the U.S. Army Corps of Engineers, the St. Lawrence Seaway Authority, "Shipfax," The Tugboat Enthusiasts Society of the Americas, vessel owners and operators, BoatNerd.com and publications of the Toronto Marine Historical Society, the Marine Historical Society of Detroit and the Welland Canal Ship Society.

***Saginaw* on Lake Michigan.**
(Brian Bluekamp)

GREAT LAKES MARITIME ACADEMY

Chart your course as a Merchant Marine Officer aboard the ships of the world. The Academy offers an exciting Bachelor's degree program which includes three semesters at sea and 100% job placement.

www.nmc.edu/maritime | 877.824.SHIP
Great Lakes Maritime Academy, Traverse City, MI

00s-30s 1902: Columbia* 1906: St. Marys Challenger (re: '67) 1910: Ste. Claire* 1927: S.T. Crapo* 1929: Maumee (re: '61) 1936: J.A.W. Iglehart (re: '65)* 1937: St. Marys Conquest (re: '87)

1940s 1941: Pere Marquette 41 (re: '97) 1942: Alpena (re: '91), American Victory (re: '61, '82), Lee A. Tregurtha (re: '61) 1943: Canadian Transfer (re: '98), Cuyahoga (re: '74), Manistee (re: '64), Mississagi (re: '67) 1944: Joseph H. Thompson (re '52 and '91), McKee Sons (re: '53, '91) 1945: Paul H. Townsend (re: '52)* 1949: Wilfred Sykes

1950s 1952: Arthur M. Anderson (re: '75, '82), Kaye E. Barker (re: '76 '81), Cason J. Callaway (re: '74, '82), Philip R. Clarke (re: '74, '82), Lewis J. Kuber (re: '06), Michipicoten (re: '57, '80), Ojibway, John G. Munson, James Norris (re: '81) 1953: American Valor (re: '74, '82), American Fortitude (re: '81), Badger, James J. Kuber (re: '07), Pathfinder (re: '98), Saginaw, Spartan* 1958: John Sherwin* 1959: Cedarglen (re: '77), Charles M. Beeghly (re: '72, '81), Herbert C. Jackson (re: '75), Sarah Spencer (re: '89)

1960s 1960: Algontario (re: '76), Edward L. Ryerson 1961: Canadian Ranger (re: '84), English River (re: 74) 1962: Catherine Desgagnés, Montrealais 1963: Algoisle, Canadian Provider, Halifax, (re: '80), Quebecois, Yankcanuck 1964: Canadian Prospector (re: '79) 1965: Stephen B. Roman (re: '83) 1966: Algosteel (re: '89), Canadian Miner 1967: Algocape, Tim S. Dool (re: '96), Canadian Leader, Canadian Navigator (re: '80, '97), John D. Leitch (re: '02), Maritime Trader 1968: Algomarine (re: '89), Algorail, Canadian Progress, Frontenac (re: '73), Gordon C. Leitch, J.W. Shelley 1969: CSL Tadoussac (re: '01)

1970s 1970: Agawa Canyon, Sauniere (re: '76); 1971: Algonorth 1972: Algoway, Roger Blough, CSL Niagara (re: '99), Stewart J. Cort 1973: Adam E. Cornelius, Calumet, Manitowoc, John J. Boland, Rt. Hon. Paul J. Martin (re: '00), Presque Isle 1974: Algosoo, Chi-Cheemaun, H. Lee White, Robert S. Pierson 1975: Melissa Desgagnés, Petrolia Desgagnés, Sam Laud 1976: James R. Barker, Joseph L. Block, Canadian Olympic, Amelia Desgagnés, Thalassa Desgagnés, St. Clair 1977: Algoeast, Algolake, CSL Assiniboine (re: '05), CSL Laurentien (re: '01), Walter J. McCarthy Jr., Mesabi Miner 1978: Algobay (re: '09), Algosar, American Integrity, American Spirit, Buffalo 1979: Algoport, American Courage, Canadian Enterprise, Canadian Transport, Edwin H. Gott, Indiana Harbor

1980s 1980: American Mariner, Burns Harbor, Nanticoke, Edgar B. Speer, Oakglen, Richelieu 1981: Algowood (re: '00), American Century, American Republic, Capt. Henry Jackman (re: '96), Mapleglen, Saguenay, Paul R. Tregurtha 1982: Algowest, Atlantic Superior, Camilla Desgagnés, Peter R. Cresswell (re: '98), Michigan, Vega Desgagnés 1983: John B. Aird, Birchglen, Spruceglen, Kaministiqua 1984: Atlantic Huron (re: '89, '03) 1985: Atlantic Erie, Pineglen 1986: Anna Desgagnés, Algoma Spirit 1987: Algoma Discovery, Algoma Guardian

1990s 1992: Diamond Star, Emerald Star 1993: Jade Star; 1996: Integrity 1998: Algosea 1999: Maria Desgagnés

2000s 2000: Great Lakes Trader 2004: Algoscotia, Lake Express 2006: Innovation 2007: Rosaire A. Desgagnés 2008: Algocanada, Algonova

*(re = major rebuild; * inactive)*

NORTHERN LIGHTS BOOKS & GIFTS

An independent full-service bookstore specializing in regional titles and Great Lakes Shipping.

Come visit us in historic Canal Park on Duluth's waterfront.

Shop on line at **www.norlights.com**

307 Canal Park Drive
Duluth, MN 55802
800-868-8904

email: norlight@norlights.com

VESSEL ENGINE DATA

bhp: brake horsepower, a measure of diesel engine output measured at the crankshaft before entering gearbox or any other power take-out device

ihp: indicated horsepower, based on an internal measurement of mean cylinder pressure, piston area, piston stroke and engine speed; used for reciprocating engines

shp: shaft horsepower, a measure of engine output at the propeller shaft at the output of the reduction gearbox; used for steam and diesel-electric engines

cpp: controllable pitch propeller

Vessel Name	Engine Manufacturer & Model #	Engine Type	Total Engines	Total Cylinders	Rated HP	Total Props	Speed MPH
Adam E. Cornelius	GM - Electro-Motive Div. - 20-645-E7B	Diesel	2	20	7,200 bhp	1 cpp	16.1
Agawa Canyon	Fairbanks Morse - 10-38D8-1/8	Diesel	4	10	6,662 bhp	1 cpp	13.8
Aivik	Pielstick - 8PA6L280	Diesel	3	8	5,200 bhp	1 cpp	15.0
Alder (USCG)	Caterpillar - 3608TA	Diesel	2	6	3,100 bhp	1 cpp	
Algobay	Pielstick - 10PC2-3V-400	Diesel	2	10	10,700 bhp	1 cpp	13.8
Algocanada	MaK - 9M32C	Diesel	1	9	6,118 bhp	1 cpp	16.1
Algocape	Sulzer - 6RND76	Diesel	1	6	9,600 bhp	1 cpp	17.3
Algoeast	B&W - 6K45GF	Diesel	1	6	5,300 bhp	1 cpp	15.8
Algoisle	M.A.N. - K6Z78/155	Diesel	1	6	9,000 bhp	1 cpp	19.3
Algolake	Pielstick - 10PC2-2V-400	Diesel	2	10	9,000 bhp	1 cpp	17.3
Algoma Discovery	Sulzer - 6RTA62	Diesel	1	6	15,499 bhp	1 cpp	16.4
Algoma Guardian	Sulzer - 6RTA62	Diesel	1	6	15,499 bhp	1 cpp	16.4
Algoma Spirit	Sulzer - 6RTA62	Diesel	1	6	11,284 bhp	1 cpp	16.4
Algomarine	Sulzer - 6RND76	Diesel	1	6	9,600 bhp	1 cpp	17.0
Algonorth	Werkspoor - 9TM410	Diesel	2	9	12,000 bhp	1 cpp	16.1
Algonova	MaK - 9M32C	Diesel	1	9	6,118 bhp	1 cpp	16.1
Algontario	B&W - 7-74VTBF-160	Diesel	1	7	8,750 bhp	1 cpp	14.4
Algoport	Pielstick - 10PC2-3V-400	Diesel	2	10	10,700 bhp	1 cpp	13.8
Algorail	Fairbanks Morse - 10-38D8-1/8	Diesel	4	10	6,662 bhp	1 cpp	13.8
Algosar	Alco - 16V251E	Diesel	2	16	5,150 bhp	2	14.4
Algoscotia	Wartsila - 6L46C	Diesel	1	6	8,445 bhp	1 cpp	16.0
Algosoo	Pielstick - 10PC2-V-400	Diesel	2	10	9,000 bhp	1 cpp	15.0
Algosea	Wartsila - 6L46A	Diesel	1	6	6,434 bhp	1 cpp	15.0
Algosteel	Sulzer - 6RND76	Diesel	1	6	9,599 bhp	1	17.0
Algoway	Fairbanks Morse - 10-38D8-1/8	Diesel	4	10	6,662 bhp	1 cpp	13.8
Algowood	MaK - 6M552AK	Diesel	2	6	10,200 bhp	1 cpp	13.8
Alpena	De Laval Steam Turbine Co.	Turbine	1	**	4,400 shp	1	14.1
Amelia Desgagnés	Allen - 12PVBCS12-F	Diesel	2	12	4,000 bhp	1 cpp	16.1
American Century	GM - Electro-Motive Div. - 20-645-E7B	Diesel	4	20	14,400 bhp	2 cpp	17.3
American Courage	GM - Electro-Motive Div. - 20-645-E7	Diesel	2	20	7,200 bhp	1 cpp	16.1
American Fortitude	General Electric Co.	Turbine	1	**	7,700 shp	1	16.7
American Integrity	GM - Electro-Motive Div. - 20-645-E7	Diesel	4	20	14,400 bhp	2 cpp	18.4
American Mariner	GM - Electro-Motive Div. - 20-645-E7	Diesel	2	20	7,200 bhp	1 cpp	15.0
American Republic	GM - Electro-Motive Div. - 20-645-E7	Diesel	2	20	7,200 bhp	2 cpp	15.0
American Spirit	Pielstick - 16PC2-2V-400	Diesel	2	16	16,000 bhp	2 cpp	17.3
American Valor	Westinghouse Elec. Corp.	Turbine	1	**	7,700 shp	1	16.1
American Victory	Bethlehem Steel Corp.	Turbine	1	**	7,700 shp	1	19.0
Amundson (CCG)	Alco - 16V251F	Diesel	6	16	17,700 bhp	2	18.6
Anglian Lady	*(Tug / Barge, usually paired with PML2501)*						
	Deutz	Diesel	2	12	3,480 bhp	2 cpp	15.5
Anna Desgagnés	M.A.N. - K5SZ70/125B	Diesel	1	5	10,332 bhp	1	17.8
Arctic	M.A.N. 14V52/55A	Diesel	1	14	14,770 bhp	1 cpp	17.8
Arthur M. Anderson	Westinghouse Elec. Corp.	Turbine	1	**	7,700 shp	1	16.1
Atlantic Erie	Sulzer - 6RLB66	Diesel	1	6	11,100 bhp	1 cpp	16.1
Atlantic Huron	Sulzer - 6RLB66	Diesel	1	6	11,094 bhp	1 cpp	17.3
Atlantic Superior	Sulzer - 6RLA66	Diesel	1	6	11,095 bhp	1 cpp	17.3
Avataq	Hanshin - 6LF58	Diesel	1	6	6,000 bhp	1 cpp	16.2
Avenger IV	*(Tug / Barge, usually paired with Chief Wawatam or PML 9000)*						
	British Polar	Diesel	2	9	2,700 bhp	1 cpp	12.0
Badger	Skinner Engine Co.	Steeple Compound Uniflow	2	4	8,000 ihp	2	18.4
Barbara Andrie	*(Tug / Barge, usually paired with A-390)*						
	GM Electro-Motive Div. 16-645-EF	Diesel	1	16	2,000 bhp	1	
Birchglen	Sulzer 4RLB76	Diesel	1	4	10,880 bhp	1cpp	13.8
Biscayne Bay (USCG)	Fairbanks Morse - 10-38D8-1/8	Diesel	2	10	2,500 bhp	1	13.8
Bristol Bay (USCG)	Fairbanks Morse - 10-38D8-1/8	Diesel	2	10	2,500 bhp	1	13.8
Buffalo	GM - Electro-Motive Div. - 20-645-E7	Diesel	2	20	7,200 bhp	1 cpp	16.1
Burns Harbor	GM - Electro-Motive Div. - 20-645-E7	Diesel	4	20	14,400 bhp	2 cpp	18.4

Vessel Name	Engine Manufacturer & Model #	Engine Type	Total Engines	Total Cylinders	Rated HP	Total Props	Speed MPH
Calumet	Alco - 16V251E	Diesel	2	16	5,600 bhp	1	16.1
Camilla Desgagnés	Werkspoor - 12TM410	Diesel	1	12	7,797 bhp	1 cpp	16.7
Canadian Enterprise	M.A.N. - 7L40/45	Diesel	2	7	8,804 bhp	1 cpp	13.8
Canadian Leader	Canadian General Electric Co. Ltd.	Turbine	1	**	9,900 shp	1	19.0
Canadian Miner	Fairbanks Morse - 12-38D8-1/8	Diesel	4	12	8,000 bhp	1 cpp	15.0
Canadian Navigator	Doxford Engines Ltd. - 76J4	Diesel	1	4	9,680 bhp	1	16.7
Canadian Olympic	M.A.N. - 8L40/54A	Diesel	2	8	10,000 bhp	1 cpp	15.0
Canadian Progress	Caterpillar - 3612-TA	Diesel	2	12	9,000 bhp	1 cpp	15.5
Canadian Prospector	Gotaverken - 760/1500VGS6U	Diesel	1	6	7,500 bhp	1	16.1
Canadian Provider	John Inglis Co. Ltd.	Turbine	1	**	10,000 shp	1	17.3
Canadian Ranger	Sulzer - 5RND68	Diesel	1	5	6,100 shp	1 cpp	19.6
Canadian Transfer	Sulzer - 5RND68	Diesel	1	5	6,100 shp	1 cpp	18.4
Canadian Transport	M.A.N. - 8L40/45	Diesel	2	8	10,000 bhp	1 cpp	13.8
Capt. Henry Jackman	MaK - 6M552AK	Diesel	2	6	9,465 bhp	1 cpp	17.3
Cason J. Callaway	Westinghouse Elec. Corp.	Turbine	1	**	7,700 shp	1	16.1
Catherine Desgagnés	Sulzer - 6SAD60	Diesel	1	6	3,841 bhp	1	15.5
Cedarglen	B&W - 7-74VTBF-160	Diesel	1	7	8,750 bhp	1 cpp	15.5
Charles M. Beeghly	Rolls-Royce Bergen B32:40L6P	Diesel	2	6	8,160 bhp	1 ccp	17.0
Chi-Cheemaun	Caterpillar C280-6	Diesel	4	6	9,280 bhp	2	
Cleveland	*(Tug / Barge, paired with Cleveland Rocks)*						
	Caterpillar 3516-B	Diesel	2	16	5,000 bhp	2	
CSL Assiniboine	Pielstick - 10PC2-2V-400	Diesel	2	10	9,000 bhp	1 cpp	15.0
CSL Laurentien	Pielstick - 10PC2-2V-400	Diesel	2	10	9,000 bhp	1 cpp	16.1
CSL Niagara	Pielstick - 10PC2-2V-400	Diesel	2	10	9,000 bhp	1 cpp	15.0
CSL Tadoussac	Sulzer - 6RND76	Diesel	1	6	9,600 bhp	1	17.0
Cuyahoga	Caterpillar - 3608	Diesel	1	8	3,000 bhp	1 cpp	12.6
Des Groseilliers (CCG)	Alco - 16V251F	Diesel	6	16	17,700 bhp	2	18.6
Diamond Star	B&W - 6L35MC	Diesel	1	6	5,030 bhp	1 cpp	14.4
Dorothy Ann	*(Articulated Tug / Barge, paired with Pathfinder)*					2 Ulstein	
	GM - Electro-Motive Div. - 20-645-E7B	Diesel	2	20	7,200 bhp	Z-Drive	16.1
Edgar B. Speer	Pielstick - 18PC2-3V-400	Diesel	2	18	19,260 bhp	2 cpp	17.0
Edward L. Ryerson	General Electric Co.	Turbine	1	**	9,900 shp	1	19.0
Edwin H. Gott	Enterprise - DMRV-16-4	Diesel	2	16	19,500 bhp	2 cpp	16.7
Emerald Star	B&W - 6L35MC	Diesel	1	6	5,030 bhp	1 cpp	14.4
English River	Werkspoor - TMAB-390	Diesel	1	8	1,850 bhp	1 cpp	13.8
Everlast	*(Articulated Tug / Barge, paired with Norman McLeod)*						
	Daihatsu - 8DSM-32	Diesel	2	8	6,000 bhp	2	16.5
Federal Agno	Sulzer - 6RTA58	Diesel	1	6	9,500 bhp	1	16.7
Federal Asahi	B&W - 6S46MC-C	Diesel	1	6	10,710 bhp	1	16.1
Federal Hudson	B&W - 6S46MC-C	Diesel	1	6	10,710 bhp	1	16.1
Federal Hunter	B&W - 6S46MC-C	Diesel	1	6	10,710 bhp	1	15.5
Federal Kivalina	B&W - 6S46MC-C	Diesel	1	6	10,710 bhp	1	16.1
Federal Maas	B&W - 6S50MC	Diesel	1	6	11,640 bhp	1	16.1
Federal Mackinac	B&W - 6S46MC-C	Diesel	1	6	10,540 bhp	1	16.1
Federal Oshima	B&W - 6S46MC-C	Diesel	1	6	10,710 bhp	1	16.1
Federal Progress	Sulzer - 7RTA58	Diesel	1	7	15,116 bhp	1 cpp	16.8
Federal Rhine	B&W - 6S50MC	Diesel	1	6	11,640 bhp	1	16.1
Federal Rideau	B&W - 6S46MC-C	Diesel	1	6	10,710 bhp	1	16.1
Federal Saguenay	B&W - 6S50MC	Diesel	1	6	11,665 bhp	1	16.1
Federal Schelde	B&W - 6S50MC	Diesel	1	6	11,640 bhp	1	16.1
Federal St. Laurent	B&W - 6S50MC	Diesel	1	6	11,640 bhp	1	16.1
Federal Venture	Sulzer - 7RTA58	Diesel	1	7	15,116 bhp	1 cpp	16.9
Federal Welland	B&W - 6S46MC-C	Diesel	1	6	10,710 bhp	1	16.1
Federal Yukon	B&W - 6S46MC-C	Diesel	1	6	10,710 bhp	1	15.5
Frontenac	Sulzer - 6RND76	Diesel	1	6	9,600 bhp	1 cpp	17.0
George R. Pearkes (CCG)	Alco - 16V251F	Diesel	3	16	8,973 bhp	2	13.8
G.L. Ostrander	*(Articulated Tug / Barge, paired with Integrity)*						
	Caterpillar - 3608-DITA	Diesel	2	8	6,008 bhp	2	17.3
Gordon C. Leitch	Sulzer - 6RND76	Diesel	1	6	9,600 bhp	1 cpp	17.3
Grayfox	Caterpillar - 3512 TAC	Diesel	2	12	2,350 bhp.	2	20.7
Griffon (CCG)	Fairbanks Morse - 8-38D8-1/8	Diesel	4	8	5,336 bhp	2	12.7
H. Lee White	GM - Electro-Motive Div. - 20-645-E7B	Diesel	2	20	7,200 bhp	1 cpp	15.0
Halifax	John Inglis Co. Ltd.	Turbine	1	**	10,000 shp	1	19.6
Hamilton Energy	GM - Electro-Motive Div. - 12-534-E6	Diesel	1	12	1,500 bhp	1 cpp	13.8
Herbert C. Jackson	General Electric Co.	Turbine	1	**	6,600 shp	1	16.0
Hollyhock (USCG)	Caterpillar - 3608TA	Diesel	2	6	3,100 bhp	1 cpp	
Indiana Harbor	GM - Electro-Motive Div. - 20-645-E7	Diesel	4	20	14,400 bhp	2 cpp	16.1
Invincible	*(Articulated Tug / Barge, paired with McKee Sons)*						
	GM - Electro-Motive Div. - 16-645-E7B	Diesel	2	16	5,750 bhp	2	13.8
J. A. W. Iglehart	De Laval Steam Turbine Co.	Turbine	1	**	4,400 shp	1	15.0

Vessel Name	Engine Manufacturer & Model #	Engine Type	Total Engines	Total Cylinders	Rated HP	Total Props	Speed MPH
J. S. St. John	GM - Electro-Motive Div. - 8-567	Diesel	1	8	850 bhp	1	11.5
J. W. Shelley	Fairbanks Morse -10-38D8-1/8	Diesel	4	10	7,999 bhp	1cpp	13.8
Jade Star	B&W - 6L35MC	Diesel	1	6	5,030 bhp	1 cpp	14.4
James Norris	Canadian Vickers Ltd.	Uniflow	1	5	4,000 ihp	1	16.1
James R. Barker	Pielstick - 16PC2-2V-400	Diesel	2	16	16,000 bhp	2 cpp	15.5
Jane Ann IV	*(Articulated Tug / Barge, paired with Sarah Spencer)*						
	Pielstick - 8PC2-2L-400	Diesel	2	8	8,000 bhp	2	15.8
Jiimaan	Ruston Paxman Diesels Ltd.- 6RK215	Diesel	2	6	2,839 bhp	2 cpp	15.0
John B. Aird	MaK - 6M552AK	Diesel	2	6	9,460 bhp	1 cpp	13.8
John D. Leitch	B&W - 5-74VT2BF-160	Diesel	1	5	7,500 bhp	1 cpp	16.1
John G. Munson	General Electric Co.	Turbine	1	**	7,700 shp	1	17.3
John J. Boland	GM - Electro-Motive Div. - 20-645-E7B	Diesel	2	20	7,200 bhp	1 cpp	15.0
John Sherwin	Conversion from steam to diesel power begun in 2008 but suspended due to economy						
John Spence	*(Tug / Barge, usually paired with McAsphalt 401)*						
	GM Electro-Motive Div. 16-567-C	Diesel	2	16	3,280 bhp	2	13.8
Joseph H. Thompson Jr.	*(Articulated Tug / Barge, paired with Joseph H. Thompson)*						
	Caterpillar	Diesel	2			1	
Joseph L. Block	GM - Electro-Motive Div. - 20-645-E7	Diesel	2	20	7,200 bhp	1 cpp	17.3
Joyce L. VanEnkevort	*(Articulated Tug / Barge, paired with Great Lakes Trader)*						
	Caterpillar - 3612	Diesel	2	12	10,200 bhp	2 cpp	
Kaministiqua	Sulzer 4RLB76	Diesel	4	4	10,880 bhp	1cpp	15.5
Karen Andrie	*(Tug / Barge, usually paired with A-397)*						
	GM Electro-Motive Div. 16-567-BC	Diesel	2	16	3,600 bhp	2	19
Kathryn Spirit	Pielstick 10PC2-V-400	Diesel	2		8,000 bhp	1 ccp	19
Katmai Bay (USCG)	Fairbanks Morse - 10-38D8-1/8	Diesel	2	10	2,500 bhp	1	13.8
Kaye E. Barker	De Laval Steam Turbine Co.	Turbine	1	**	7,700 shp	1	17.3
Lee A. Tregurtha	Rolls-Royce Bergen B32:40L6P	Diesel	2	6	8,160 shp	1 ccp	17.0
Mackinaw (USCG)	Caterpillar - 3612	Diesel	3	12	9,119 bhp	2 Azipod	17.3
Manistee	GM - Electro-Motive Div. - 20-645-E6	Diesel	1	20	2,950 bhp	1	
Manitowoc	Alco - 16V251E	Diesel	2	16	5,600 bhp	1	16.1
Mapleglen	B&W - 6K67GF	Diesel	1	6	11,600 bhp	1	16.1
Maria Desgagnés	B&W - 6S42MC	Diesel	1	6	8,361 bhp	1 cpp	16.1
Maritime Trader	Fairbanks Morse -8-38D8-1/8	Diesel	4	8	5,332 bhp	1 cpp	16.1
Martha L. Black (CCG)	Alco - 16V251F	Diesel	3	16	8,973 bhp	2	13.8
Maumee	Nordberg - FS-1312-H5C	Diesel	1	12	3,240 bhp	1	11.5
Melissa Desgagnés	Allen - 12PVBCS12-F	Diesel	2	12	4,000 bhp	1 cpp	13.8
Mesabi Miner	Pielstick - 16PC2-2V-400	Diesel	2	16	16,000 bhp	2 cpp	15.5
Michigan	*(Articulated Tug / Barge, paired with Michigan)*						
	GM - Electro-Motive Div. - 20-645-E6	Diesel	2	16	3,900 bhp	2	13.2
Michipicoten	Bethlehem Steel Co.	Turbine	1	**	7,700 shp	1	17.3
Mississagi	Caterpillar - 3612-TA	Diesel	1	12	4,500 bhp	1 cpp	13.8
Mobile Bay (USCG)	Fairbanks Morse - 10-38D8-1/8	Diesel	2	10	2,500 bhp	1	13.8
Montrealais	Canadian General Electric Co. Ltd.	Turbine	1	**	9,900 shp	1	19.0
Nanticoke	Pielstick - 10PC2-2V-400	Diesel	2	10	10,700 bhp	1 cpp	13.8
Neah Bay (USCG)	Fairbanks Morse - 10-38D8-1/8	Diesel	2	10	2,500 bhp	1	13.8
Nordik Express	GM Electro-Motive Div. 20-645-E7	Diesel	2	20	7,200 bhp	2 ccp	16.0
Oakglen	B&W - 6K67GF	Diesel	1	6	11,600 bhp	1	15.5
Ojibway	2005 GE 7FDM EFI	Diesel	1	16	4,100 bhp	1 cpp	
Olive L. Moore	*(Tug / Barge, usually paired with Lewis J. Kuber)*						
	Alco 16V251	Diesel	2	16	5,830 bhp	1	
Paul H. Townsend	Nordberg TSM-216	Diesel	1	6	2,150 bhp	1	12.1
Paul R. Tregurtha	Pielstick - 16PC2-3V-400	Diesel	2	16	17,120 bhp	2 cpp	15.5
Peter R. Cresswell	MaK - 6M552AK	Diesel	2	6	9,460 bhp	1 cpp	13.8
Petite Forte	*(Tug / Barge, usually paired with St. Marys Cement)*						
	Ruston 8ATC	Diesel	2	8	4,200 bhp	1	15.5
Petrolia Desgagnés	B&W - 8K42EF	Diesel	1	8	5,000 bhp	1 cpp	16.4
Philip R. Clarke	Westinghouse Elec. Corp.	Turbine	1	**	7,700 shp	1	16.1
Pierre Radisson (CCG)	Alco - 16V251F	Diesel	6	16	17,700 bhp	2	18.4
Pineglen	MaK - 6M601AK	Diesel	1	6	8,158 bhp	1 cpp	15.5
Prentiss Brown	*(Articulated Tug / Barge, paired with St. Marys Conquest)*						
	GM Electro-Motive Div. 12-645-E2	Diesel	2	12	3,900 bhp	1	
Presque Isle	*(Integrated Tug / Barge paired with Presque Isle)*						
	Mirrlees Blackstone Ltd. - KVMR-16	Diesel	2	16	14,840 bhp	2 cpp	
Qamutik	Wartsila - 6R46	Diesel	1	6	7,383 bhp	1 cpp	16.7
Quebecois	Canadian General Electric Co. Ltd.	Turbine	1	**	9,900 shp	1	19.0
Rebecca Lynn	*(Tug / Barge, usually paired with A-410)*						
	GM Electro-Motive Div. 16-567-BC	Diesel	2	16	3,600 bhp	2	
Reliance	*(Tug / Barge, usually paired with PML9000)*						

Vessel Name	Engine Manufacturer & Model #	Engine Type	Total Engines	Total Cylinders	Rated HP	Total Props	Speed MPH
	A.B. Nohab SVI 16VS-F	Diesel	2	16	5,600 bhp	1 cpp	17.6
Richelieu	B&W - 6K67GF	Diesel	1	6	11,600 bhp	1	15.4
Robert S. Pierson	Alco - 16V251E	Diesel	2	16	5,600 bhp	1	17.8
Roger Blough	Pielstick - 16PC2V-400	Diesel	2	16	14,200 bhp	1 cpp	16.7
Rosaire A. Desgagnés	MaK - 6M43	Diesel	1	6	7,341 bhp	1 cpp	17.8
Rt. Hon. Paul J. Martin	Pielstick - 10PC2-V-400	Diesel	2	10	9,000 bhp	1 cpp	15.0
Saginaw	MaK - 6M43C	Diesel	1	6	8,160 bhp	1 cpp	
Saguenay	B&W - 6K67GF	Diesel	1	6	11,600 bhp	1	16.1
Sam Laud	GM - Electro-Motive Div. - 20-645-E7	Diesel	2	20	7,200 bhp	1 cpp	16.1
Samuel de Champlain	*(Articulated Tug / Barge, paired with Innovation)*						
	GM - Electro-Motive Div. - 20-645-E5	Diesel	2	20	7,200 bhp	2 cpp	17.3
Samuel Risley (CCG)	Wartsila - VASA 16V22HF	Diesel	2	16	7,590 bhp	2 cpp	17.3
Sarah Desgagnés	MaK - 7M43	Diesel	1	7	9,517 bhp	1 cpp	15.0
Sauniere	MaK - 6M552AK	Diesel	2	6	8,799 bhp	1 cpp	15.0
Sea Eagle II	*(Tug / Barge, usually paired with St. Marys Cement II)*						
	GM Electro-Motive Div. 20-645-E7	Diesel	2	20	7,200 bhp	2	13.8
Spruceglen	Sulzer 4RLB76	Diesel	1	4	10,880 bhp	1cpp	13.8
St. Clair	GM - Electro-Motive Div. - 20-645-E7	Diesel	3	20	10,800 bhp	1 cpp	16.7
St. Marys Challenger	Skinner Engine Co.	Uniflow	1	4	3,500 ihp	1	12.0
Ste. Claire	Toledo Ship Building Co.	Triple Exp.	1	3	1,083 ihp	1	
Stephen B. Roman (Total)		Diesel			5,996 bhp	1 cpp	18.4
Stephen B. Roman (Center)	Fairbanks Morse - 10-38D8-1/8	Diesel	2	10	3,331 bhp		
Stephen B. Roman (Wing)	Fairbanks Morse - 8-38D8-1/8	Diesel	2	8	2,665 bhp		
Stewart J. Cort	GM - Electro-Motive Div. - 20-645-E7	Diesel	4	20	14,400 bhp	2 cpp	18.4
Susan W. Hannah	*(Articulated Tug / Barge)*						
	GM - Electro-Motive Div. - 12-645-E5	Diesel	2	12	4,320 bhp	2	11.5
Thalassa Desgagnés	B&W - 8K42EF	Diesel	1	8	5,000 bhp	1 cpp	16.4
Tim S. Dool	MaK model 8M43C	Diesel	1	8	10,750 bhp	1 cpp	
Umiak I	M.A.N.-B&W - 7S70ME-C	Diesel	1	7	29,598 bhp	1 cpp	16.5
Undaunted	*(Articulated Tug / Barge, paired with Pere Marquette 41)*						
	GM - Cleveland Diesel Div. - 12-278A	Diesel	1	12	2,400 bhp	1	11.5
Umiavut	Hanshin - 6LF58	Diesel	1	6	6,000 bhp	1 cpp	16.2
Vega Desgagnés	Wartsila - 9R32	Diesel	2	9	7,560bhp	1 cpp	16.1
Victorious	*(Articulated Tug / Barge, paired with John J. Carrick)*						
	MaK - 6M25	Diesel	2	6	5,302 bhp	2 cpp	12.1
Victory	*(Articulated Tug / barge, usually paired with James L. Kuber)*						
	MaK - 6MU551AK	Diesel	2	6	7,880 bhp	2	16.1
Walter J. McCarthy Jr.	GM - Electro-Motive Div. - 20-645-E7B	Diesel	4	20	14,400 bhp	2 cpp	16.1
Wilfred Sykes	Westinghouse Elec. Corp.	Turbine	1	16	7,700 shp	1	16.1
William J. Moore	*(Tug / Barge, usually paired with McLeary's Spirit)*						
	GM Electro-Motive Div. 16-645-E	Diesel	2	16	4,000 bhp	2 cpp	15.5
Yankcanuck	Cooper-Bessemer Corp.	Diesel	1	8	1,860 bhp	1	11.5

2009 CALENDAR

MARINE HISTORICAL
SOCIETY OF DETROIT

Join now and receive our
full-color 12-month calendar

www.mhsd.org

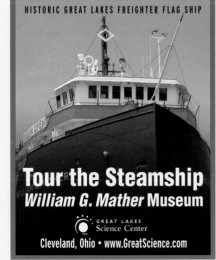

HISTORIC GREAT LAKES FREIGHTER FLAG SHIP

Tour the Steamship
William G. Mather Museum

GREAT LAKES
Science Center

Cleveland, Ohio · www.GreatScience.com

The Welland Canal

Lock up the perfect fun day out!

The **Welland Canals** were built to circumvent the mighty Niagara Falls. Marvel as lake and ocean freighters are raised and lowered in the locks on their journey between Lake Erie and Lake Ontario.

Welland Canals Centre at Lock 3
1932 Welland Canals Parkway,
St. Catharines, ON L2R 7K6
t 905-984-8880 ext. 226
toll free 1-800-305-5134
e museuminfo@stcatharines.ca
w www.stcatharineslock3museum.ca

THOROLD

Lock 7 Viewing Complex
50 Chapel Street South,
Thorold, ON L2V 2C6
t 905-680-9477
toll free 1-888-680-9477
e thoroldtourism@bellnet.ca
w www.thoroldtourism.ca

Call daily for ship schedules (April - December)

Motorcoach/Group Friendly!
Ship Viewing Platform - Always FREE!

Saltwater Fleets

Blacky, **on her maiden voyage through the Welland Canal.** *(Bill Bird)*

Listed after each vessel in order are: Type of Vessel, Year Built, Type of Engine, Maximum Cargo Capacity (at midsummer draft in long tons) or Gross Tonnage*, Overall Length, Breadth and Depth (from the top of the keel to the top of the upper deck beam). This list reflects vessels whose primary trade routes are on saltwater but which also regularly visit Great Lakes and St. Lawrence Seaway ports. It is not meant to be a complete listing of every saltwater vessel that could potentially visit the Great Lakes and St. Lawrence Seaway. To attempt to do so, given the sheer number of world merchant vessels, would be space prohibitive. Fleets listed may operate other vessels worldwide than those included herein; additional vessels may be found on fleet Web sites, which have been listed where available. Former names listed in boldface type indicate the vessel visited the system under that name.

Fleet # Vessel Name	Fleet Name	Type of Vessel	Year Built	Type of Engine	Cargo Cap. or Gross*	Overall Length	Breadth	Depth or Draft*
IA-1	**ALVARGONZALEZ NAVIGATION, GIJON, SPAIN**							
Covadonga		TK	2005	D	6,967	390' 09"	55' 05"	27' 07"
IA-2	**AMALTHIA MARINE INC., ATHENS, GREECE**							
Antikeri		BC	1984	D	28,788	606' 11"	75' 09"	48' 02"
(*LT Argosy* '84-'98, *Millenium Hawk* '98-'02, *Cashin* '02-'05)								
Seneca		BC	1983	D	28,788	606' 11"	75' 09"	48' 02"
(*Mangal Desai* '83-'98, *Millenium Eagle* '98-'02, *Stokmarnes* '02-'05)								
Tuscarora		BC	1983	D	28,031	639' 09"	75' 09"	46' 11"
(*Manila Spirit* '83-'86, *Rixta Oldendorff* '86-'06)								
IA-3	**AMERICAN CANADIAN CARIBBEAN LINE INC., WARREN, RHODE ISLAND, USA** (accl-smallships.com)							
Grande Caribe		PA	1997	D	97*	182' 07"	39' 01"	9' 10"
Grande Mariner		PA	1998	D	97*	182' 07"	39' 01"	9' 10"
Niagara Prince		PA	1994	D	99*	174' 00"	40' 00"	9' 00"
IA-4	**ANDERS UTKILENS REDERI AS, BERGEN, NORWAY** (utkilen.no)							
Sundstraum		TK	1993	D	4,737	316' 01"	50' 04"	26' 05"
(*Maj-Britt Terkol* '93-'96)								
IA-5	**ATHENA MARINE CO. LTD., LIMASSOL, CYPRUS**							
	FOLLOWING VESSELS UNDER CHARTER TO FEDNAV LTD.							
Federal Danube		BC	2003	D	37,372	652' 11"	78' 05"	50' 02"
Federal Elbe		BC	2003	D	37,372	652' 11"	78' 05"	50' 02"
Federal Ems		BC	2002	D	37,372	652' 11"	78' 05"	50' 02"
Federal Leda		BC	2003	D	37,372	652' 11"	78' 05"	50' 02"
Federal Patroller		BC	1999	D	17,451	469' 02"	74' 10"	43' 08"
(*Atlantic Pride* '99-'01, Seaboard Rover '01-'02, *Atlantic Patroller* '02-'05, African Patroller '05-'06)								
Federal Pioneer		BC	1999	D	17,451	469' 02"	74' 10"	43' 08"
(*Atlantic Pioneer* '99-'01, Seaboard Pioneer '01-'07)								
Federal Power		BC	2000	D	17,451	469' 02"	74' 10"	43' 08"
(*Atlantic Power* '00-'01, Seaboard Power '01-'07)								
Federal Pride		BC	2000	D	17,451	469' 02"	74' 10"	43' 08"
(*Atlantic Pride* '00-'01, Seaboard Rover '01-'02, *Atlantic Pride* '02-'05, Seabord Chile II '05-'06)								
Federal Weser		BC	2002	D	37,372	652' 11"	78' 05"	50' 02"
IA-6	**ATLANTSKA PLOVIDBA D.D., DUBROVNIK, REPUBLIC OF CROATIA** (www.atlant.hr)							
	FOLLOWING VESSEL CURRENTLY UNDER CHARTER TO FEDNAV LTD.							
Orsula		BC	1996	D	34,372	656' 02"	77' 01"	48' 10"
(*Federal Calumet* {2} '96-'97)								
IB-1	**B & N MOORMAN BV, RIDDERKERK, NETHERLANDS**							
Andromeda		GC	1999	D	6,663	388' 09"	49' 10"	27' 06"
IB-2	**BELUGA SHIPPING GMBH, BREMEN, GERMANY** (beluga-group.com)							
Beluga Constellation		BC	2006	D	12,476	524' 01"	70' 06"	30' 06"
Beluga Constitution		BC	2006	D	12,477	514' 04"	70' 06"	36' 06"
Beluga Efficiency		BC	2004	D	12,806	452' 09"	68' 11"	36' 01"
(*Beluga Efficiency* '04-'06, BBC Carolina '06-'07)								

| --- | --- | --- | --- | --- | --- | --- | --- | --- |
	Beluga Elegance	BC	2004	D	12,828	452' 09"	68' 11"	36' 01"
	Beluga Emotion	BC	2004	D	12,828	452' 09"	68' 11"	36' 01"
	(BBC Alabama '04-'04)							
	Beluga Endurance	BC	2005	D	12,782	452' 09"	68' 11"	36' 01"
	Beluga Energy	BC	2005	D	12,828	452' 09"	68' 11"	36' 01"
	Beluga Enterprise	BC	2005	D	12,744	452' 11"	70' 01"	36' 01"
	Beluga Eternity	BC	2004	D	12,782	452' 09"	68' 11"	36' 01"
	Beluga Expectation	BC	2005	D	12,744	452' 11"	70' 01"	36' 01"
	Beluga Federation	BC	2006	D	11,380	452' 11"	70' 01"	36' 01"
	Beluga Fighter	BC	2007	D	12,782	453' 00"	68' 11"	36' 01"
	Beluga Flirtation	BC	2007	D	12,782	426' 06"	70' 01"	36' 01"
	Beluga Formation	BC	2007	D	11,526	453' 00"	68' 11"	36' 01"
	Beluga Fusion	BC	2000	D	11,380	452' 11"	70' 01"	36' 01"
	Beluga Indication	BC	2005	D	11,380	452' 11"	70' 01"	36' 01"
	Beluga Recognition	BC	2005	D	11,380	452' 11"	70' 01"	36' 01"
	Beluga Recommendation	BC	2005	D	10,536	439' 04"	70' 06"	30' 06"
	Beluga Resolution	BC	2005	D	10,536	439' 04"	70' 06"	30' 06"
	Beluga Revolution	BC	2005	D	10,536	439' 04"	70' 06"	30' 06"
	BBC India	BC	1998	D	17,538	465' 10"	70' 06"	43' 08"
	(**Maria Green** '98-'04, **BBC India** '04-'08)							
	Margaretha Green	BC	2000	D	17,538	465' 10"	70' 06"	43' 08"
	(**Margaretha Green** '00-'00, Coral Green '00-'01, Nirint Voyager '01-'02, **Margaretha Green** '02-'04, Newpac Cumulus '04-'05)							
	Marion Green	BC	1999	D	17,538	465' 10"	70' 06"	43' 08"

IB-3 BERGSHAV MANAGEMENT AS, GRIMSTAD, NORWAY (bergshav.com)

	Bertina	TK	2006	D	13,157	421' 11"	67' 00"	37' 09"

IB-4 BERNHARD SCHULTE GROUP OF COMPANIES, HAMBURG, GERMANY (beschulte.de)

	Kristina Theresa	TK	2006	D	12,972	417' 04"	66' 11"	37' 09"
	(Songa Emerald '06-'06)							

IB-5 BIGLIFT SHIPPING BV, ROOSENDAAL, NETHERLANDS (www.bigliftshipping.com)

	Enchanter	HL	1998	D	12,950	452' 11"	74' 10"	42' 06"
	(**Sailor Jupiter** '98-'98)							
	Happy Ranger	HL	1998	D	15,065	454' 01"	74' 10"	42' 04"
	Tracer	HL	2000	D	8,874	329' 09"	73' 06"	26' 11"
	Tramper	HL	2000	D	8,874	329' 09"	73' 06"	26' 11"
	Transporter	HL	1999	D	8,469	329' 09"	80' 01"	36' 05"
	Traveller	HL	2000	D	8,874	329' 09"	73' 06"	26' 11"

IB-6 BLYSTAD TANKERS INC., OSLO, NORWAY (blystad.no)
FOLLOWING VESSELS CURRENTLY UNDER CHARTER TO SONGA SHIPMANAGEMENT

	Songa Crystal	TK	2006	D	12,800	417' 04"	66' 11"	37' 09"
	(Samho Crystal '06-'06)							
	Songa Pearl	TK	2008	D	17,539	472' 05"	74' 02"	41' 00"

IB-7 BOOMSMA SHIPPING BV, SNEEK, NETHERLANDS (boomsmashipping.nl)

	Frisian Spring	GC	2006	D	5,023	390' 01"	44' 00"	29' 10"
	Built: Port Weller Drydocks, Port Weller, ON							

IB-8 BRIESE SCHIFFAHRTS GMBH & CO. KG, LEER, GERMANY (briese.de)

	Bavaria	GC	1996	D	3,500	288' 09"	42' 00"	23' 04"
	(Geise '96-'96)							
	BBC Asia	GC	2003	D	7,530	393' 00"	66' 03"	32' 02"
	(Embse '03-'03)							
	BBC Atlantic	GC	2005	D	6,192	378' 11"	54' 02"	26' 01"
	(Westerriede '05-'05)							
	BBC Australia	GC	2005	D	7,530	393' 00"	66' 03"	32' 02"
	BBC Elbe	GC	2006	D	17,348	469' 07"	75' 11"	42' 08"
	(Horumersiel '06-'06)							

Tanker *Nordic Helsinki* in the Welland Canal. *(Matt Miner)*

Fleet #	Fleet Name / Vessel Name	Type of Vessel	Year Built	Type of Engine	Cargo Cap. or Gross*	Overall Length	Breadth	Depth or Draft*
	BBC Ems	GC	2006	D	17,348	469' 07"	75' 11"	42' 08"
	BBC Europe	GC	2003	D	7,409	391' 09"	66' 03"	32' 02"
	BBC France	GC	2005	D	4,309	324' 06"	45' 03"	24' 03"
	BBC Germany	GC	2002	D	7,530	393' 00"	66' 03"	32' 02"
	(BBC Germany '03-'06, Leda '06-'08)							
	BBC Iceland	GC	1999	D	4,806	330' 01"	54' 06"	26' 07"
	(Industrial Accord '99-'02)							
	BBC Mississippi	GC	2006	D	17,348	469' 07"	75' 11"	42' 08"
	(Greetsiel '06-'07)							
	BBC Scandinavia	GC	2007	D	7,530	393' 00"	66' 03"	32' 02"
	(Rysum '07-'07)							
	BBC Scotland	GC	2002	D	4,713	330' 01"	54' 06"	26' 07"
	BBC Shanghai	GC	2001	D	4,900	330' 01"	54' 06"	26' 07"
	(Baltic Sea '01-'01, BBC Shanghai '01-'03, TLI Aquila '03-'03)							
	BBC Venezuela	GC	1999	D	5,240	324' 10"	51' 11"	26' 07"
	(Fockeburg '99-'00, Global Africa '00-'01)							
	Borkum	GC	1994	D	18,355	486' 07"	74' 10"	40' 00"
	(Erna Oldendorff '94-'05)							
	Santiago	GC	1997	D	3,525	280' 10"	42' 00"	23' 04"
	Skaftafell	GC	1997	D	4,900	328' 01"	54' 06"	26' 07"
	(Launched as Torum, Industrial Harmony '97-'00, BBC Brazil '00-'03, Brake '03-'03, BBC Brazil '04-'04)							

IC-1 CANADA FEEDER LINES BV, GRONIGEN, NETHERLANDS *(www.canadafeederlines.eu)*

	CFL Prospect	GC	2007	D	6,500	388' 05"	43' 10"	29' 10"
	CFL Prudence	GC	2008	D	6,500	388' 05"	43' 10"	29' 10"

IC-2 CALLITSIS SHIP MANAGEMENT SA, PIRAEUS, GREECE

	Athanasios G. Callitsis	BC	1983	D	17,494	647' 08"	75' 09"	46' 11"
	(Punica '83-'96, Pintail '96-'07)							

IC-3 CANADIAN FOREST NAVIGATION (CANFORNAV) LTD., MONTREAL, QUEBEC, CANADA
(www.canfornav.com)
At press time, Canadian Forest Navigation Co. Ltd. had the following vessels under long or short-term charter. Please consult their respective fleets for details: Apollon, Blacky, Bluebill, Bluewing, Cinnamon, Eider, Gadwall, Garganey, Goldeneye, Greenwing, Mandarin, Milo, Miltiades, Orna, Pochard, Puffin, Redhead, Whistler, Wigeon, Woody

IC-4 CARISBROOKE SHIPPING, COWES, ISLE OF WIGHT, UNITED KINGDOM *(carisbrookeshipping.net)*

	Catharina-C	BC	1999	D	5,057	311' 04"	43' 04"	23' 05"
	Johanna-C	BC	1998	D	4,570	292' 00"	43' 02"	23' 05"
	Vanessa-C	BC	2003	D	10,500	477' 09"	60' 03"	33' 10"

IC-5 CANDLER SCHIFFAHRT GMBH, BREMEN, GERMANY

	Glory	BC	2005	D	7,378	381' 04"	59' 01"	34' 01"
	(FCC Glory '05-'06)							

IC-6 CHEMFLEET SHIPPING LTD., ISTANBUL, TURKEY *(chemfleet.org)*

	Sakarya	TK	2007	D	11,258	426' 06"	65' 00"	34' 01"
	(Sakarya-D '07-'08)							
	Zeynep A	TK	2007	D	10,500	425' 08"	64' 04"	34' 01"

IC-7 CHINA OCEAN SHIPPING CO., BEIJING, PEOPLE'S REPUBLIC OF CHINA *(www.cosco.com)*

	Yick Hua	BC	1984	D	28,086	584' 08"	75' 09"	48' 07"
	(Santa Lucia '84-'84, Pacific Defender '84-'85, Lori '85-'91)							

IC-8 CLIPPER GROUP AS, COPENHAGEN, DENMARK *(clipper-group.com)*

	Clipper Golfito	TK	2006	D	14,227	440' 02"	67' 03"	38' 01"
	Clipper Karen	TK	2006	D	11,259	382' 03"	65' 07"	38' 05"
	Clipper Katja	TK	2006	D	11,255	382' 03"	65' 09"	37' 05"
	Clipper Kira	TK	2007	D	11,259	382' 03"	65' 07"	38' 05"
	Clipper Klara	TK	2004	D	11,259	382' 03"	65' 09"	38' 05"
	Clipper Kristin	TK	2006	D	11,259	382' 03"	65' 07"	38' 05"

Fleet #	Fleet Name Vessel Name	Type of Vessel	Year Built	Type of Engine	Cargo Cap. or Gross*	Overall Length	Breadth	Depth or Draft*
	Clipper Krystal	TK	2006	D	11,259	382' 03"	65' 07"	38' 05"
	Clipper Kylie	TK	2007	D	11,259	382' 03"	65' 07"	38' 05"
	Clipper Lancer	TK	2006	D	10,098	388' 04"	62' 04"	33' 02"
	Clipper Leader	TK	2004	D	10,098	388' 04"	62' 04"	33' 02"
	(*Panam Trinity* '04-'06)							
	Clipper Leander	TK	2006	D	10,098	388' 04"	62' 04"	33' 02"
	Clipper Legacy	TK	2005	D	10,098	388' 04"	62' 04"	33' 02"
	Clipper Legend	TK	2004	D	10,098	388' 04"	62' 04"	33' 02"
	Clipper Loyalty	TK	2007	D	10,098	388' 04"	62' 04"	33' 02"
	Clipper Tasmania	TK	2007	D	12,800	417' 04"	67' 00"	37' 09"
	(*Swartberg* '07-'07, *Ruth Schulte* '07-'07)							
	Clipper Tobago	TK	1999	D	8,834	367' 05"	61' 08"	31' 08"
	(*Botany Treasure* '99-'06)							
	Clipper Trinidad	TK	1998	D	5,483	370' 09"	61' 08"	31' 08"
	(**Botany Trust** '98-'06)							
	Clipper Trojan	TK	1996	D	9,553	452' 09"	71' 06"	39' 08"
	(*Botany Trojan* '96-'98, *Stolt Trojan* '98-'04, **Botany Trojan** '04-'06)							
	Panam Atlantico	TK	2001	D	14,003	439' 08"	67' 03"	38' 01"
	Panam Flota	TK	1999	D	11,642	384' 06"	65' 07"	36' 09"

At press time, Clipper Group AS also had the following vessels under charter. Please consult their respective fleets for details: Magdalena Green, Makiri Green, Marinus Green, Marion Green, Marissa Green, Marlene Green

Fleet #	Fleet Name Vessel Name	Type of Vessel	Year Built	Type of Engine	Cargo Cap. or Gross*	Overall Length	Breadth	Depth or Draft*
IC-9	**COASTAL SHIPPING LTD., GOOSE BAY, NEWFOUNDLAND, CANADA**							
	Tuvaq	TK	1977	D	15,955	539' 08"	72' 10"	39' 04"
	(*Tiira* '02)							
IC-10	**COMMERCIAL FLEET OF DONBASS LLC, DONETSK, UKRAINE** (www.cfd.com.ua)							
	Berdyansk	BC	1977	D	27,559	584' 04"	75' 02"	48' 03"
	(*Baltic Skou* '77-'85)							
	Dobrush	BC	1982	D	28,136	644' 08"	75' 09"	46' 11"
	(**World Goodwill** '82-'85)							
	Makeevka	BC	1982	D	28,136	644' 08"	75' 09"	46' 11"
	(**World Shanghai** '82-'85)							

Saltwater tanker *Alessandro DP* on the St. Lawrence Seaway. *(Sam Lapinski)*

IC-11	**COMMERCIAL TRADING & DISCOUNT CO. LTD., ATHENS, GREECE**							
	Ira	BC	1979	D	26,697	591' 02"	75' 10"	45' 08"
	Ivi	BC	1979	D	26,697	591' 04"	75' 10"	45' 08"
IC-12	**COMMON PROGRESS COMPANIA NAVIERA SA, PIRAEUS, GREECE**							
	Kastor P	BC	1983	D	22,713	528' 03"	75' 07"	45' 07"
	(Sea Augusta '83-' 85, Jovian Lily '85-' 91)							
	Polydefkis P	BC	1982	D	22,713	528' 03"	75' 07"	45' 07"
	(Sea Astrea '82-' 85, Jovian Luzon '85-' 91)							
IC-13	**CRYSTAL POOL GROUP, HELSINKI, FINLAND** *(crystal.fi)*							
	Crystal Diamond	TK	2006	D	11,340	414' 00"	62' 04"	35' 01"
	Crystal Topaz	TK	2006	D	11,340	414' 00"	62' 04"	35' 01"
IC-14	**CSL GROUP INC., MONTREAL, QUEBEC, CANADA** *(csl.ca)*							
	MARBULK SHIPPING INC. – MANAGED BY CSL INTERNATIONAL INC.							
	PARTNERSHIP BETWEEN CSL INTERNATIONAL INC. AND ALGOMA CENTRAL CORP.							
	Ambassador	SU	1983	D	37,448	730' 00"	75' 10"	50' 00"
	Built: Port Weller Drydocks, Port Weller, ON (**Canadian Ambassador** '83-' 85, **Ambassador** '85-' 00,							
	Algosea {2} '00-' 00)							
	Pioneer	SU	1981	D	37,448	730' 00"	75' 10"	50' 00"
	Built: Port Weller Drydocks, Port Weller, ON (**Canadian Pioneer** '81-' 86)							
IC-15	**CYPRUS MARITIME CO. LTD., ATHENS, GREECE**							
	Lake Superior	BC	1982	D	30,670	617' 04"	76' 00"	47' 07"
	(**Broompark** '82-' 99, **Millenium Raptor** '99-' 02, Cardinal '02-' 02)							
ID-1	**DE POLI TANKERS BV, SPIJKENISSE, NETHERLANDS**							
	Alessandro DP	TK	2007	D	17,096	453' 01"	75' 06"	40' 02"
	Laguna D	TK	2000	D	15,200	446' 02"	75' 06"	40' 02"
	(Jo Laguna D '00-' 05)							
ID-2	**DOUN KISEN CO. LTD., OCHI EHIME PREFECTURE, JAPAN**							
	Bright Laker	BC	2001	D	30,778	606' 11"	77' 05"	48' 11"
	FOLLOWING VESSEL UNDER CHARTER TO FEDNAV LTD.							
	Federal Kushiro	BC	2003	D	32,787	624' 08"	77' 05"	49' 10"
IE-1	**EASTWIND SHIP MANAGEMENT, SINGAPORE, SINGAPORE** *(eastwindgroup.com)*							
	Arabian Wind	TK	1987	D	17,484	496' 05"	73' 06"	39' 10"
	*(Akademik Vekua '87-' 94, **Vekua** '94-' 00, **Gali** '00-' 05)*							
	Seram Wind	TK	1987	D	16,970	497' 01"	73' 07"	39' 10"
	(**Ilya Erenburg** '87-' 07)							
	Silver Wind	TK	1988	D	17,485	496' 01"	73' 06"	39' 08"
	*(Kapitan Rudnyev '88-' 94, **Kapitan Rudnev** '94-' 03, **Lake Maya** '03-' 06, Songa Maya '06-' 06,*							
	Sichem Maya '06-' 07)							
	FOLLOWING VESSEL CURRENTLY UNDER CHARTER TO FEDNAV LTD.							
	Yamaska	BC	1984	D	28,303	580' 08"	75' 09"	47' 07"
	(**Vamand Wave** '84-' 07)							
	Yarmouth	BC	1985	D	29,462	600' 04"	76' 01"	48' 10"
	(**Paolo Pittaluga** '85-' 91, **Federal Oslo** '91-' 00)							
	Yellowknife	BC	1984	D	29,651	622' 00"	74' 08"	49' 08"
	(**Bihac** '84-' 93, **La Boheme** '93-' 95, Lindsey M. '98-' 99, Med Pride '99-' 01)							
	Yosemite	BC	1985	D	28,019	584' 08"	75' 11"	48' 05"
	(**Astral Mariner** '85-' 90, **Lake Challenge** '90-' 97, **Manila Angus** '97-' 98, **Darya Devi** '98-' 06)							
	Yucatan	BC	1996	D	30,838	606' 11"	77' 05"	48' 11"
	(**Golden Laker** '96-' 04)							
IE-2	**EGYPTIAN NAVIGATION CO., ALEXANDRIA, EGYPT** *(www.enc.com.eg)*							
	Ebn Al Waleed	GC	1988	D	12,800	433' 01"	67' 04"	40' 01"
IE-3	**EITZEN CHEMICAL ASA, OSLO, NORWAY** *(eitzen-chemical.com)*							
	Fen	TK	2006	D	12,956	417' 04"	66' 11"	37' 09"
	(*Launched as Songa Onyx*, **Brovig Ocean** '06-' 07, **Liquid Blue** '07-' 07)							

Fleet #	Fleet Name / Vessel Name	Type of Vessel	Year Built	Type of Engine	Cargo Cap. or Gross*	Overall Length	Breadth	Depth or Draft*
	Glen	TK	2005	D	12,956	417' 04"	66' 11"	37' 09"
	(Launched as Songa Pearl, **Brovig Fjord** *'06-'07)*							
	Moor	TK	2006	D	12,956	417' 04"	66' 11"	37' 09"
	(Brovig Sea '06-'06, Songa Saphire '06-'07, **Liquid Elegance** *'07-'07)*							
	Nordic Helsinki	TK	2007	D	13,034	421' 11"	67' 00"	37' 09"
	(Spectator '07-'07)							
	North Fighter	TK	2006	D	19,932	474' 05"	77' 09"	42' 08"
	Sichem Aneline	TK	1998	D	8,941	378' 03"	61' 00"	33' 08"
	(Alexander '98-'04, Garonne '04-'04, Gironde '04-'05, **Songa Aneline** *'04-'05)*							
	Sichem Beijing	TK	2007	D	13,141	421' 11"	67' 11"	37' 09"
	Sichem Challenge	TK	1998	D	17,485	382' 06"	62' 04"	33' 02"
	(Queen of Montreaux '98-'99, **North Challenge** *'99-'06, Songa Challenge '06-'07)*							
	Sichem Defiance	TK	2001	D	17,369	442' 11"	74' 10"	41' 00"
	*(***North Defiance** *'01-'06,* **Songa Defiance** *'06-'07)*							
	Sichem Eva	TK	1988	D	17,485	496' 10"	73' 06"	39' 08"
	(Yakov Sverdlov '88-'94, **Jakov Sverdlov** *'94-'03, Songa Eva '03-'06)*							
	Sichem Manila	TK	2007	D	13,141	421' 11"	66' 11"	37' 09"
	Sichem Melbourne	TK	2007	D	12,936	417' 04"	67' 00"	37' 09"
	Sichem Mumbai	TK	2006	D	13,141	421' 11"	66' 11"	37' 09"
	Sichem New York	TK	2007	D	12,956	417' 04"	66' 11"	37' 09"
	Sichem Onomichi	TK	2005	D	13,105	421' 11"	67' 00"	37' 09"
	Sichem Padua	TK	1993	D	9,214	382' 06"	62' 04"	33' 02"
	(Anne Sif '93-'01, Sichem Anne '01-'02)							
	Sichem Palace	TK	2004	D	8,807	367' 05"	62' 04"	32' 10"
	Sichem Paris	TK	2008	D	13,079	421' 11"	67' 00"	37' 09"
	Sichem Peace	TK	2005	D	8,807	367' 05"	62' 04"	32' 10"
	Sichem Princess Marie-Chantal	TK	2003	D	7,930	370' 09"	60' 00"	31' 06"
	Sichem Singapore	TK	2006	D	13,141	421' 11"	66' 11"	37' 09"
IE-4	**ELDER SHIPPING LTD., LONDON, UNITED KINGDOM**							
	Balticland	BC	1977	D	17,161	511' 10"	73' 10"	45' 11"
	(Pollux '77-'88, Baltikum '88-'89, **Pollux** *'89-'90,* **Nomadic Pollux** *'90-'04)*							

Flinterland on the St. Marys River with a cargo of windmill parts. *(Roger LeLievre)*

Fleet #	Fleet Name Vessel Name	Type of Vessel	Year Built	Type of Engine	Cargo Cap. or Gross*	Overall Length	Breadth	Depth or Draft*
IE-5	**EMIRATES TRADING AGENCY LLC, DUBAI, UNITED ARAB EMIRATES**							
	Siam Star	BC	1984	D	29,617	587' 03"	75' 11"	47' 07"
	(Trident Mariner '84-'01, Taxideftis '01-'06)							
IE-6	**EMPROS LINES SHIPPING CO., ATHENS, GREECE**							
	Adamastos	BC	1986	D	17,792	479' 00"	74' 10"	40' 01"
	(Clipper Bueno '86-'93, Clipper Atria '93-'95)							
IE-7	**ENZIAN SHIPPING AG, BERNE, SWITZERLAND** *(www.enzian-shipping.com)*							
	Celine	BC	2001	D	8,600	423' 03"	52' 00"	32' 00"
	Sabina	BC	2000	D	9,231	416' 08"	52' 00"	32' 00"
	(Greta-C '00-'00)							
	SCL Bern	BC	2005	D	12,680	459' 03"	70' 06"	38' 03"
	(SCL Bern '05-'05, SITC Bern '05-'06)							
IE-8	**EURONAV NV, ANTWERP, BELGUIM** *(euronav.com)*							
	Cap Charles	TK	2006	D	159,049	899' 07"	157' 07"	76' 01"
	Cap Diamant	TK	2001	D	149,996	898' 11"	173' 11"	76' 09"
	Cap Georges	TK	1998	D	147,444	898' 11"	156' 10"	74' 10"
	Cap Guillaume	TK	2006	D	159,049	899' 07"	157' 07"	76' 01"
	Cap Lara	TK	2007	D	159,049	899' 07"	157' 07"	76' 01"
	Cap Laurent	TK	1998	D	147,444	898' 11"	156' 10"	74' 10"
	Cap Leon	TK	2003	D	159,049	899' 07"	157' 07"	76' 01"
	Cap Philippe	TK	2006	D	159,049	899' 07"	157' 07"	76' 01"
	Cap Pierre	TK	2004	D	159,049	899' 07"	157' 07"	76' 01"
IE-9	**EXECUTIVE SHIP MANAGEMENT LTD., SINGAPORE, SINGAPORE** *(executiveship.com)*							
	Chemical Trader	TK	2005	D	8,801	367' 05"	61' 04"	32' 10"
IF-1	**FAIRFIELD CHEMICAL CARRIERS, WILTON, CONNECTICUT, USA** *(fairfieldchemical.com)*							
	Fairchem Colt	TK	2005	D	19,998	477' 04"	77' 10"	43' 10"
IF-2	**FAR EASTERN SHIPPING CO. (FESCO), VLADIVOSTOK, RUSSIA** *(fesco.ru)*							
	Grigoriy Aleksandrov	BC	1986	D	24,105	605' 08"	75' 02"	46' 07"
	Khudozhnik Kraynev	BC	1986	D	24,105	605' 08"	75' 02"	46' 07"
IF-3	**FEDNAV LTD., MONTREAL, QUEBEC, CANADA** *(fednav.com)*							
	FEDNAV INTERNATIONAL LTD. - DIVISION OF FEDNAV LTD.							
	Federal Agno	BC	1985	D	29,643	599' 09"	76' 00"	48' 07"
	(Federal Asahi {1} '85-'89)							
	Federal Asahi {2}	BC	2000	D	36,563	656' 02"	77' 11"	48' 09"
	Federal Hudson {3}	BC	2000	D	36,563	656' 02"	77' 11"	48' 09"
	Federal Hunter {2}	BC	2001	D	36,563	656' 02"	77' 11"	48' 09"
	Federal Katsura	BC	2005	D	32,787	624' 08"	77' 05"	49' 10"
	Federal Kivalina	BC	2000	D	36,563	656' 02"	77' 11"	48' 09"
	Federal Maas {2}	BC	1997	D	34,372	656' 02"	77' 01"	48' 10"
	Federal Mackinac	BC	2004	D	27,000	606' 11"	77' 09"	46' 25"
	Federal Margaree	BC	2005	D	27,000	606' 11"	77' 09"	46' 25"
	Federal Nakagawa	BC	2005	D	36,563	656' 02"	77' 11"	48' 09"
	Federal Oshima	BC	1999	D	36,563	656' 02"	77' 11"	48' 09"
	Federal Progress	BC	1989	D	38,130	580' 07"	86' 07"	48' 08"
	(Northern Progress '89-'02)							
	Federal Rhine {2}	BC	1997	D	34,372	656' 02"	77' 01"	48' 10"
	Federal Rideau	BC	2000	D	36,563	656' 02"	77' 11"	48' 09"
	Federal Saguenay {2}	BC	1996	D	34,372	656' 02"	77' 01"	48' 10"
	Federal Sakura	BC	2005	D	32,787	624' 08"	77' 05"	49' 10"
	Federal Schelde {3}	BC	1997	D	34,372	656' 02"	77' 01"	48' 10"
	Federal Seto	BC	2004	D	36,563	656' 02"	77' 11"	48' 09"
	Federal St. Laurent {3}	BC	1996	D	34,372	656' 02"	77' 01"	48' 10"
	Federal Venture	BC	1989	D	38,130	580' 07"	86' 07"	48' 08"
	(Northern Venture '89-'02)							

Clipper Legacy in the Welland Canal. (Alain Gindroz)

Fleet #	Fleet Name Vessel Name	Type of Vessel	Year Built	Type of Engine	Cargo Cap. or Gross*	Overall Length	Breadth	Depth or Draft*
	Federal Welland	BC	2000	D	36,563	656' 02"	77' 11"	48' 09"
	Federal Yukon	BC	2000	D	36,563	656' 02"	77' 11"	48' 09"

At press time, FedNav Ltd. also had the following vessels under charter. Please consult their respective fleets for details: Federal Danube, Federal Elbe, Federal Ems, Federal Fuji, Federal Kumano, Federal Kushiro, Federal Leda, Federal Manitou, Federal Matane, Federal Mattawa, Federal Miramichi, Federal Patroller, Federal Pioneer, Federal Power, Federal Pride, Federal Polaris, Federal Pride, Federal Seto, Federal Shimanto, Federal Weser, Federal Yoshino, Inviken, Orsula, Spar Garnet, Spar Jade, Spar Opal, Spar Ruby, Utviken, Yamaska, Yarmouth, Yellowknife, Yosemite, Yucatan

Fleet #	Fleet Name Vessel Name	Type of Vessel	Year Built	Type of Engine	Cargo Cap. or Gross*	Overall Length	Breadth	Depth or Draft*
IF-4	**FINBETA, SAVONA, ITALY** *(finbeta.com)*							
	Acquamarina	TK	2004	D	12,004	447' 10"	66' 11"	33' 10"
	Ocean Pride	TK	1997	D	14,015	465' 10"	72' 02"	36' 01"
	(Sapphire '97-' 04)							
	Turchese	TK	1999	D	12,004	447' 10"	66' 11"	33' 10"
IF-5	**FISSER & V. DOORNUM KG GMBH & CO., HAMBURG, GERMANY** *(fissership.com)*							
	Okapi	GC	1972	D	6,364	332' 10"	52' 07"	30' 03"
	(Imela Fisser '72-' 75, Boca Tabla '75-' 82, Tabla '82-' 86)							
	Pyrgos	GC	1972	D	6,364	332' 10"	52' 07"	30' 03"
	(Elisabeth Fisser '72-' 79, Villiers '79-' 86)							
IF-6	**FLINTER GRONINGEN BV (ANCORA AFS MGRS.), GRONINGEN, THE NETHERLANDS** *(flinter.nl)*							
	Flinterduin	GC	2000	D	6,359	364' 01"	49' 02"	26' 09"
	Flintereems	GC	2000	D	6,200	366' 07"	48' 08"	26' 09"
	Flinterland	GC	2007	D	7,705	393' 08"	49' 10"	27' 11"
	Flintermaas	GC	2000	D	6,200	366' 05"	48' 10"	26' 10"
	Flinterspirit	GC	2001	D	6,358	366' 07"	48' 08"	26' 09"
IF-7	**FORTUM OIL AND GAS OY, FORTUM, FINLAND** *(fortum.com)*							
	Purha	TK	2003	D	25,000	556' 01"	78' 00"	48' 11"
IF-8	**FRANCO COMPANIA NAVIERA SA, ATHENS, GREECE** *(franco.gr)*							
	Barbro	BC	1984	D	29,692	599' 09"	75' 09"	48' 07"
	*(**Olympic Dignity** '84-' 92, **Alam Sejahtera** '92-' 07)*							
	Stefania I	BC	1985	D	28,269	584' 08"	75' 11"	48' 05"
	*(**Astral Ocean** '85-' 95, Sea Crystal '95-' 97, **Stefania** '97-' 98)*							
IF-9	**FRANK DAHL SHIPPING, CUXHAVEN, GERMANY** *(dahl-shipping.com)*							
	FOLLOWING VESSELS UNDER CHARTER TO WAGENBORG SHIPPING							
	Finex	GC	2001	D	9,857	433' 10"	52' 01"	31' 08"
	*(**Volmeborg** '01-'06)*							
	Veerseborg	GC	1998	D	8,664	433' 10"	52' 01"	31' 08"
	*(**Veerseborg** '98-' 04, **Matfen** '04-' 07)*							
	Vossborg	GC	2000	D	8,737	433' 10"	52' 01"	31' 08"
	*(Vossborg '01-' 04, **Morpeth** '04-' 07)*							
IF-10	**FUKUJIN KISEN CO. LTD., OCHI EHIME PREFECTURE, JAPAN**							
	FOLLOWING VESSELS UNDER CHARTER TO FEDNAV LTD.							
	Federal Kumano	BC	2001	D	32,787	624' 08"	77' 05"	49' 10"
	Federal Shimanto	BC	2001	D	32,787	624' 08"	77' 05"	49' 10"
	Federal Yoshino	BC	2001	D	32,787	624' 08"	77' 05"	49' 10"
IG-1	**GALATIA SHIPPING CO. SA, PIRAEUS, GREECE**							
	Panos G.	BC	1996	D	10,100	370' 09"	63' 08"	34' 01"
	(Ayutthaya Ruby '96-' 06)							
IG-2	**GREAT LAKES FEEDER LINES ULC, BURLINGTON, ONTARIO, CANADA**							
	Dutch Runner	RR	1988	D	3,056	275' 07"	52' 06"	20' 11"
	(North King '88-' 88, Dutch Runner '88-' 00, P&O Nedlloyd Douala '00-' 02)							

Fleet #	Fleet Name Vessel Name	Type of Vessel	Year Built	Type of Engine	Cargo Cap. or Gross*	Overall Length	Breadth	Depth or Draft*
IG-3	**GULMAR DENIZCILIK NAKLIYAT TICARET LTD., ISTANBUL, TURKEY**							
	Gulmar	BC	1981	D	27,048	627' 07"	75' 07"	44' 03"
	*(Oakstar '81-'82, **Soren Toubro** '82-'98, **Millenium Falcon** '98-'02, Giant '02-'04, Atlas Sun '04-'04)*							
IH-1	**HAPAG-LLOYD GMBH, HAMBURG, GERMANY** *(hapag-lloyd.com)*							
	Endurance	CO	1983	D	32,424	727' 02"	105' 08"	49' 03"
	(Tokyo Maru '83-'90, Alligator Joy '90-'95, CanMar Endeavour '96-'98, Contship Endeavour '98-'99, Cast Performance '99-'03, CanMar Endurance '03-'05, CP Endurance '05-'06)							
	Glory	CO	1979	D	18,643	580' 10"	88' 09"	44' 03"
	(Seatrain Saratoga '79-'80, TFL Jefferson '80-'86, Jefferson '86-'88, Asian Senator '88-'90, CMB Monarch '90-'91, Sea Falcon '91-'94, CanMar Glory '94-'05, CP Glory '05-'06)							
	Lisbon Express	CO	1995	D	34,330	709' 01"	105' 10"	62' 04"
	(CanMar Fortune '95-'03, Cast Prospect '03-'05, CP Prospector '05-'06)							
	Mississauga Express	CO	1998	D	40,879	803' 10"	105' 08"	62' 05"
	(CanMar Pride '98-'05, CP Pride '05-'06)							
	Montreal Express	CO	2003	D	47,840	964' 11"	106' 00"	60' 00"
	(CanMar Spirit '03-'05, CP Spirit '05-'06)							
	Ottawa Express	CO	1998	D	40,879	803' 10"	105' 11"	62' 05"
	(CanMar Honour '98-'05, CP Honour '05-'06)							
	Power	CO	1982	D	32,207	730' 00"	105' 10"	61'08"
	(America Maru '82-'90, Alligator Excellence '90-'95, CanMar Success '98-98, Contship Success '98-'99, Cast Power '99-'03, Montreal Senator '03-'05, CP Power '05-'06)							
	Toronto Express	CO	2003	D	47,840	964' 11"	106' 00"	60' 00"
	(CanMar Venture '03-'05, CP Venture '05-'06)							
	Triumph	CO	1978	D	18,643	580' 10"	88' 10"	44' 04"
	(Seatrain Independence '78-'81, Dart Americana '81-'87, American Senator '87-'89, CMB Marque '89-'90, CanMar Triumph '90-'05, CP Triumph '05-'06)							
	Valencia Express	CO	1996	D	34,330	709' 01"	105' 10"	62' 04"
	(CanMar Courage '96-'03, Cast Prominence '96-'05, CP Performer '05-'06)							
	Victory	CO	1979	D	18,643	580' 10"	88' 10"	44' 04"
	(Seatrain Chesapeake '79-'81, Dart Atlantica '81-'87, Singapore Senator '87-'89, American Senator '89-'90, CanMar Victory '79-'05, CP Victory '05-'06)							
IH-2	**HARBOR SHIPPING & TRADING CO. SA., CHIOS, GREECE**							
	Agios Minas	BC	1981	D	29,002	589' 11"	76' 01"	47' 07"
	*(**Violetta** '81-'86, **Capetan Yiannis** '86-'88, **Federal Nord** '88-'96, **Nordic Moor** '96-'98, **Chios Charity** '98-'07)*							
IH-3	**HARREN & PARTNER SCHIFFAHRTS GMBH, BREMEN, GERMANY** *(harren-partner.de)*							
	Palessa	HL	2000	D	7,069	387' 02"	64' 08"	31' 00"
	(Pantaleon '00-'00, Fret Moselle '00-'04)							
	FOLLOWING VESSELS UNDER CHARTER TO CANADIAN FOREST NAVIGATION LTD.							
	Pochard	BC	2003	D	35,200	631' 04"	77' 09"	50' 02"
	Puffin	BC	2003	D	35,200	629' 09"	77' 05"	50' 00"
IH-4	**HARTMANN REEDEREI, LEER, GERMANY** *(hartmann-reederei.de)*							
	OSC Vlistdiep	GC	2007	D	7,800	388' 11"	49' 10"	27' 09"
	(Launched as Vlistdiep)							
IH-5	**HELIKON SHIPPING ENTERPRISES LTD., LONDON, UNITED KINGDOM**							
	Elikon	BC	1980	D	16,106	582' 00"	75' 02"	44' 04"
	(Bailey '80-'89)							
IH-6	**HELLAS MARINE SERVICES LTD., PIRAEUS, GREECE** *(hellasmarine.gr)*							
	Sir Walter	BC	1996	D	18,315	486' 03"	74' 10"	40' 00"
	*(**Rubin Stork** '96-'03)*							
IH-7	**HERMANN BUSS GMBH, LEER, GERMANY** *(bussgruppe.de)*							
	Bornholm	BC	2006	D	7,869	388' 11"	49' 10"	27' 11"
IH-8	**HOLLAND SHIP SERVICE, THE NETHERLANDS** *(hollandshipservice.nl)*							
	FOLLOWING VESSELS UNDER CHARTER TO CLIPPER PROJECTS AS							
	Magdalena Green	BC	2001	D	17,538	465' 10"	70' 06"	43' 10"

Fleet #	Fleet Name / Vessel Name	Type of Vessel	Year Built	Type of Engine	Cargo Cap. or Gross*	Overall Length	Breadth	Depth or Draft*
	Makiri Green	BC	1999	D	17,538	465' 10"	70' 06"	43' 08"
	Marinus Green	BC	2000	D	17,538	465' 10"	70' 06"	43' 08"
	Marissa Green	BC	2001	D	17,538	465' 10"	70' 06"	43' 08"
	Marlene Green	BC	2001	D	17,538	465' 10"	70' 06"	43' 08"

II-1 ILVA SERVIZI MARITIME, MILAN, ITALY

Fleet #	Fleet Name / Vessel Name	Type of Vessel	Year Built	Type of Engine	Cargo Cap. or Gross*	Overall Length	Breadth	Depth or Draft*
	Sagittarius	BC	1987	D	29,365	613' 06"	75' 11"	46' 11"

II-2 INTERSEE SCHIFFAHRTS-GESELLSCHAFT MBH & CO., HAREN-EMS, GERMANY *(intersee.de)*

Fleet #	Fleet Name / Vessel Name	Type of Vessel	Year Built	Type of Engine	Cargo Cap. or Gross*	Overall Length	Breadth	Depth or Draft*
	Aachen	GC	2004	D	5,726	348' 02"	47' 03"	26' 07"
	(Lea '04-'04)							
	Amalia	GC	2006	D	5,726	348' 02"	47' 03"	26' 07"
	Amanda	GC	2005	D	5,726	348' 02"	47' 03"	26' 07"
	Anja	GC	1999	D	9,200	419' 06"	52' 00"	32' 00"
	(Anja '99-'01, TMC Brazil '01-'02)							
	Annalisa	GC	2000	D	8,737	433' 10"	52' 01"	31' 08"
	(Malte Rainbow '00-'03)							
	Carola	GC	2000	D	9,000	424' 08"	52' 00"	33' 04"
	(Beatrice '00-'00)							
	Jana	GC	2001	D	8,994	433' 09"	52' 01"	31' 08'
	(Chandra Kirana '01-'01)							
	Julia	GC	2006	D	5,726	348' 02"	47' 03"	26' 07"
	Julietta	GC	2002	D	10,500	468' 02"	59' 10"	33' 04"
	Katja	GC	2000	D	9,000	424' 08"	52' 00"	33' 04"
	(Katja '00-'01, MSC Apapa '01-'02)							
	Lara	GC	1998	D	5,500	330' 10"	49' 01"	27' 07"
	Nicola	GC	2000	D	5,050	312' 02"	43' 02"	23' 05'
	Nina	GC	1998	D	5,726	329' 09"	49' 03"	27' 07"
	(Nina '98-'98, Melody '98-'02)							
	Rebecca	GC	2002	D	10,500	468' 02"	59' 10"	33' 04"
	Serena	GC	2004	D	10,500	468' 02"	59' 10"	33' 04"
	Sofia	GC	2005	D	5,726	348' 02"	47' 03"	26' 07"
	Tatjana	GC	2000	D	9,000	424' 08"	52' 00"	33' 04"
	(Tatjana '00-'02, TMC Brazil '02-'02)							
	Thekla	GC	2003	D	8,994	433' 09"	52' 01"	31' 08"
	(Suryawati '03-'03)							
	Uta	GC	2007	D	11,211	477' 09"	59' 10"	33' 10"
	Victoria	GC	2004	D	10,500	468' 02"	59' 10"	33' 04"
	Winona	GC	2003	D	10,000	433' 09"	52' 06"	32' 10"
	(Vermontborg '03-'03)							
	Xenia	GC	2003	D	10,500	468' 02"	59' 10"	33' 04"

II-3 INTERSHIP NAVIGATION CO. LTD., LIMASSOL, CYPRUS *(intership-cyprus.com)*
THE FOLLOWING VESSELS UNDER CHARTER TO FEDNAV LTD.

Fleet #	Fleet Name / Vessel Name	Type of Vessel	Year Built	Type of Engine	Cargo Cap. or Gross*	Overall Length	Breadth	Depth or Draft*
	Federal Patriot	BC	2002	D	17,477	469' 02"	74' 10"	43' 08"
	*(Atlantic Progress '02-'03, **BBC Russia** '03-'08)*							
	Federal Pendant	BC	2003	D	17,477	469' 02"	74' 10"	43' 08"
	*(**Atlantic Pendant** '03-'05, **BBC Korea** '05-'08)*							

II-4 IONIA MANAGEMENT SA, PIRAEUS, GREECE

Fleet #	Fleet Name / Vessel Name	Type of Vessel	Year Built	Type of Engine	Cargo Cap. or Gross*	Overall Length	Breadth	Depth or Draft*
	Alkyon	BC	1981	D	18,277	487' 05"	73' 06"	38' 05"
	(Rich Arrow '81-'89, Pisagua '89-'95)							

II-5 ISKO MARINE SHIPPING CO., ISTANBUL, TURKEY

Fleet #	Fleet Name / Vessel Name	Type of Vessel	Year Built	Type of Engine	Cargo Cap. or Gross*	Overall Length	Breadth	Depth or Draft*
	Global Carrier	HL	1982	D	9,864	403' 06"	67' 08"	33' 10"
	*(**Titan Scan** '82-'02, Scan Trader '02-'03, Global Traveller '03-'04, Taipan Scan '04-'05)*							

IJ-1 JO TANKERS BV, SPIJKENISSE, NETHERLANDS *(jotankers.com)*

Fleet #	Fleet Name / Vessel Name	Type of Vessel	Year Built	Type of Engine	Cargo Cap. or Gross*	Overall Length	Breadth	Depth or Draft*
	Jo Spirit	TK	1998	D	6,248	352' 02"	52' 02"	30' 02"
	(Proof Spirit '98-'98)							

Fleet #	Fleet Name / Vessel Name	Type of Vessel	Year Built	Type of Engine	Cargo Cap. or Gross*	Overall Length	Breadth	Depth or Draft*
IJ-2	**JSM SHIPPING GMBH & CO., JORK, GERMANY**							
	BBC England	GC	2003	D	10,300	465' 10"	59' 10"	33' 04"
	(Frida '03-'04)							
	S Pacific	GC	2004	D	10,385	468' 02"	59' 10"	24' 02"
	(Ile de Molene '03-'04)							
IJ-3	**JUMBO SHIPPING CO. SA, ROTTERDAM, NETHERLANDS** *(jumboshipping.nl)*							
	Daniella	HL	1989	D	7,600	322' 09"	60' 03"	37' 02"
	(Stellaprima '89-'90)							
	Fairlane	HL	2000	D	7,123	361' 03"	68' 05"	44' 03"
	Fairlift	HL	1990	D	7,780	330' 08"	68' 10"	43' 08"
	Fairload	HL	1995	D	5,198	314' 00"	60' 03"	37' 02"
	Fairmast	HL	1983	D	6,375	360' 11"	67' 09"	34' 05"
	Fairpartner	HL	2004	D	10,975	469' 06"	86' 11"	44' 03"
	Fairplayer	HL	2007	D	10,975	469' 06"	86' 11"	44' 03"
	Jumbo Challenger	HL	1983	D	6,375	360' 11"	63' 10"	34' 05"
	Jumbo Javelin	HL	2004	D	10,975	469' 06"	86' 11"	44' 03"
	Jumbo Jubilee	HL	2008	D	10,975	469' 06"	86' 11"	44' 03"
	Jumbo Spirit	HL	1995	D	5,198	314' 00"	60' 03"	37' 02"
	Jumbo Vision	HL	2000	D	7,123	361' 03"	68' 05"	44' 03"
	Stellanova	HL	1996	D	5,198	314' 00"	60' 03"	37' 02"
	Stellaprima	HL	1991	D	7,780	330' 08"	68' 10"	43' 08"
IK-1	**KENT LINE, SAINT JOHNS, NEW BRUNSWICK, CANADA** *(kentline.com)*							
	Kent Timber	BC	1999	D	20,427	488' 10"	75' 09"	44' 03"
	(Antonie Oldendorff '99-'05)							
	Kent Trader	BC	1986	D	7,879	403' 07"	75' 06"	34' 06"
	(Scol Enterprise '86-'86, Weser-Importer '86-'88, Abitibi Claiborne '88-'01, Weser-Importer '01-'02, Normed Antwerp '02-'03)							
IK-2	**KNUTSEN O.A.S. SHIPPING AS, HAUGESUND, NORWAY** *(knutsenoas.com)*							
	Ellen Knutsen	TK	1992	D	17,071	464' 03"	75' 07"	38' 09"
	Sidsel Knutsen	TK	1993	D	22,625	533' 03"	75' 06"	48' 07"
	Synnove Knutsen	TK	1992	D	17,071	464' 03"	75' 07"	38' 09"
	Turid Knutsen	TK	1993	D	22,625	533' 03"	75' 06"	48' 07"
IK-3	**KREY SCHIFFAHRTS GMBH & CO. KG, SIMONSWOLDE, GERMANY** *(krey-schiffahrt.de)*							
	BBC Ontario	GC	2004	D	12,711	452' 10"	68' 11"	36' 01"
IL-1	**LATVIAN SHIPPING CO., RIGA, LATVIA** *(lscsm.lv)*							
	Dzintari	TK	1985	D	17,585	497' 00"	73' 06"	39' 10"
	(Moris Bishop '85 -'91)							
	Zanis Griva	TK	1985	D	17,585	497' 00"	73' 06"	39' 10"
	(Zhan Griva '85 -'91)							
IL-2	**LAURANNE SHIPPING BV, GHENT, NETHERLANDS** *(lauranne-shipping.com)*							
	LS Christine	TK	2007	D	8,400	411' 05"	59' 01"	27' 07"
	(Christine H '07 -'07)							
	LS Jacoba	TK	2006	D	15,602	485' 07"	70' 10"	37' 01"
	(Jacoba H '06 -'06)							
IL-3	**LAURIN MARITIME (AMERICA) INC., HOUSTON, TEXAS, USA** *(www.laurinmar.com)*							
	Mountain Blossom	TK	1986	D	19,993	527' 07"	74' 11"	39' 04"
	Swan Lake	TK	1982	D	10,579	445' 04"	62' 04"	33' 04"
	*(**Aurum** '82-'97)*							
IL-4	**LEHMANN REEDEREI, LUEBECK, GERMANY** *(hans-lehmann.de)*							
	Hans Lehmann	GC	2007	D	12,000	460' 04"	64' 07"	34' 05"
IL-5	**LIETUVOS JURU LAIVININKYSTE (LITHUANIAN SHIPPING CO.), KLAIPEDA, LITHUANIA** *(ljl.lt)*							
	Deltuva	BC	1994	D	16,906	490' 02"	75' 04"	39' 08"
	*(**Clipper Eagle** '82-'97)*							

Ziemia Cieszynska leaves the Iroquois Lock. *(Ron Walsh)*

	Raguva	BC	1994	D	16,906	490' 02"	75' 04"	39' 08"
	(Clipper Falcon '94-'08)							
	Staris	BC	1985	D	9,650	403' 06"	65' 08"	50' 09"
	(Abitibi Concord '85-'92, Concord '92-'94, Abitibi Concord '94-'96, Concord '96-'02)							
IL-6	**LIAMARE SHIPPING BV, MAARTENSDIJK, NETHERLANDS** *(liamareshipping.nl)*							
	Liamare	GC	1999	D	5,842	351' 03"	50' 02"	27' 03"
	(Ameland '99-'07)							
IL-7	**LINDOS MARITIME LTD., PIRAEUS, GREECE** *(greatlakescruiseco.com/clelia)*							
	Clelia II	PA	1990	D	2,420	289' 09"	50' 03"	27' 07"
	(Renaissance Four '90-'90)							
IM-1	**MARLOW NAVIGATION CO. LTD., LIMASSOL, CYPRUS** *(marlownavigation.com.cy)*							
	BBC Rosario	GC	2007	D	12,872	452' 09"	68' 11"	36' 01"
IM-2	**MURMANSK SHIPPING CO., MURMANSK, RUSSIA** *(msco.ru)*							
	Aleksandr Suvorov	BC	1979	D	19,885	531' 06"	75' 02"	44' 05"
	Mikhail Strekalovskiy	BC	1981	D	19,252	531' 06"	75' 02"	44' 05"
IN-1	**NAVARONE SA MARINE ENTERPRISES, LIMASSOL, CYPRUS**							
	FOLLOWING VESSELS UNDER CHARTER TO CANADIAN FOREST NAVIGATION LTD.							
	Blacky	BC	2008	D	30,801	607' 04"	77' 09"	47' 11"
	Bluebill	BC	2004	D	37,200	632' 10"	77' 09"	50' 10"
	Bluewing	BC	2002	D	26,747	611' 00"	77' 09"	46' 07"
	Cinnamon	BC	2002	D	26,747	611' 00"	77' 09"	46' 07"
	Greenwing	BC	2002	D	26,747	611' 00"	77' 09"	46' 07"
	Mandarin	BC	2003	D	26,747	611' 00"	77' 09"	46' 07"
IN-2	**NAVEMAR SpA, NAPLES, ITALY** *(navemar.it)*							
	BBC Finland	GC	2000	D	7,650	353' 06"	59' 09"	33' 02"
	(Norderney '00-'00)							
IN-3	**NAVIGATION MARITIME BULGARE LTD., VARNA, BULGARIA** *(navbul.com)*							
	Kamenitza	BC	1980	D	24,150	605' 08"	75' 00"	46' 05"
	Kapitan Georgi Georgiev	BC	1980	D	24,150	605' 08"	75' 00"	46' 05"
	Kom	BC	1997	D	13,971	466' 02"	72' 10"	36' 05"
	Malyovitza	BC	1982	D	24,456	605' 08"	75' 02"	46' 07"
	Milin Kamak	BC	1979	D	25,857	607' 07"	75' 02"	46' 07"
	Perelik	BC	1998	D	13,887	466' 02"	72' 10"	36' 05"
	Persenk	BC	1998	D	13,900	466' 02"	72' 08"	36' 04"
IN-4	**NOVOROSSIYSK SHIPPING CO. (NOVOSHIP), NOVOROSSIYSK, RUSSIA** *(novoship.ru)*							
	Vladimir Vysotskiy	TK	1988	D	16,970	497' 01"	73' 07"	39' 10"
IO-1	**OCEAN FREIGHTERS LTD., PIRAEUS, GREECE**							
	Pontokratis	BC	1981	D	28,738	590' 02"	75' 11"	47' 07"
	Pontoporos	BC	1984	D	29,155	590' 02"	75' 11"	47' 07"
IO-2	**OCEANEX INC., MONTREAL, QUEBEC, CANADA** *(oceanex.com)*							
	Cabot {2}	RR	1979	D	7,132	564' 09"	73' 11"	45' 09"
	Oceanex Avalon	CO	2005	D	14,747	481' 11"	85' 00"	45' 11"
	Oceanex Sanderling	RR	1977	D	15,195	364' 01"	88' 05"	57' 07"
	(Rauenfels '77-'80, Essen '80-'81, Kongsfjord '81-'83, Onno '83-'87, ASL Sanderline '87-'08)							
IO-3	**OLYMPIC SHIPPING AND MANAGEMENT SA, MONTE CARLO, MONACO** *(olyship.com)*							
	Calliroe Patronicola	BC	1985	D	29,640	599' 09"	75' 11"	48' 07"
	Olympic Melody	BC	1984	D	29,640	599' 09"	75' 11"	48' 07"
	(Olympic Memory '84-'84)							
	Olympic Mentor	BC	1984	D	29,640	599' 09"	75' 11"	48' 07"
	*(Calliroe Patronicola '84-'84, **Patricia-R.** '84-'88)*							
	Olympic Merit	BC	1985	D	29,640	599' 09"	75' 11"	48' 07"
	Olympic Miracle	BC	1984	D	29,640	599' 09"	75' 11"	48' 07"

IO-4	**OMICRON SHIP MANAGEMENT INC., MOSCHATO, GREECE**							
	Starlight	BC	1984	D	28,354	644' 06"	75' 06"	46' 11"
	(Noble River '84-'86, Helena Oldendorff '86-'06)							
IO-5	**ONEGO SHIPPING & CHARTERING, RHOON, NETHERLANDS** *(onegoshipping.com)*							
	Onego Merchant	BC	2004	D	7,800	393' 08"	49' 10"	27' 09"
	Onego Trader	BC	2003	D	7,800	393' 08"	49' 10"	27' 09"
	Onego Traveller	BC	2004	D	7,800	393' 08"	49' 10"	27' 09"
IO-6	**OSTERSTORMS REDERI AS, NORRKOPING, SWEDEN** *(externwebb.osterstroms.com)*							
	Emsmoon	GC	2000	D	6,359	366' 08"	49' 01"	32' 02"
	(Morgenstond III '00-'05)							
IP-1	**PARAKOU SHIPPING LTD., HONG KONG, PEOPLE'S REPUBLIC OF CHINA** *(parakougroup.com)*							
	FOLLOWING VESSELS UNDER CHARTER TO CANADIAN FOREST NAVIGATION LTD.							
	Eider	BC	2004	D	37,272	655' 10"	77' 09"	50' 02"
	Gadwall	BC	2007	D	37,272	655' 10"	77' 09"	50' 02"
	Garganey	BC	2007	D	37,272	655' 10"	77' 09"	50' 02"
	Redhead	BC	2005	D	37,272	655' 10"	77' 09"	50' 02"
	Whistler	BC	2007	D	37,272	655' 10"	77' 09"	50' 02"
	Wigeon	BC	2007	D	37,272	655' 10"	77' 09"	50' 02"
IP-2	**PEARL SEAS CRUISES LLC, GUILFORD, CONNECTICUT, USA** *(pearlseascruises.com)*							
	Pearl Mist	PA	2009	D	700	325' 00"	55' 01"	15' 07"
IP-3	**PEROSEA SHIPPING CO. SA, PIRAEUS, GREECE**							
	Sea Force	TK	2006	D	13,500	421' 11"	66' 11"	37' 09"
IP-4	**POT SCHEEPVAART BV, DELFZIJL, NETHERLANDS**							
	FOLLOWING VESSELS UNDER CHARTER TO WAGENBORG SHIPPING							
	Doggersbank	GC	1996	D	4,149	294' 07"	44' 11"	23' 07"
	Kwintebank	GC	2002	D	8,664	433' 10"	52' 01"	31' 08"
	Varnebank	GC	2000	D	8,664	433' 10"	52' 01"	31' 08"
IP-5	**POLISH STEAMSHIP CO., SZCZECIN, POLAND** *(polsteam.com)*							
	Irma	BC	2000	D	34,946	655' 10"	77' 05"	50' 02"
	Iryda	BC	1999	D	34,946	655' 10"	77' 05"	50' 02"
	Isa	BC	1999	D	34,946	655' 10"	77' 05"	50' 02"
	Isadora	BC	1999	D	34,946	655' 10"	77' 05"	50' 02"
	Isolda	BC	1999	D	34,946	655' 10"	77' 05"	50' 02"
	Nida	BC	1993	D	13,756	469' 02"	68' 08"	37' 02"
	Nogat	BC	1999	D	17,064	488' 10"	75' 06"	39' 08"
	Odra	BC	1992	D	13,756	469' 02"	68' 08"	37' 02"
	(Odranes '92-'99)							
	Orla	BC	1999	D	17,064	488' 10"	75' 06"	39' 08"
	Pilica	BC	1999	D	17,064	488' 10"	75' 06"	39' 08"
	Pomorze Zachodnie	BC	1985	D	26,696	591' 06"	75' 10"	45' 07"
	Rega	BC	1995	D	17,064	488' 10"	75' 06"	39' 08"
	(Fossnes '95-'02)							
	Warta	BC	1992	D	13,756	469' 02"	68' 08"	37' 02"
	(Wartanes '92-'99)							
	Ziemia Chelminska	BC	1984	D	26,696	591' 06"	75' 10"	45' 07"
	Ziemia Cieszynska	BC	1993	D	26,264	591' 02"	75' 09"	45' 07"
	(Ziemia Cieszynska '93-'93, Lake Carling '93-'03)							
	Ziemia Gnieznienska	BC	1985	D	26,696	591' 06"	75' 10"	45' 07"
	Ziemia Gornoslaska	BC	1990	D	26,264	591' 02"	75' 09"	45' 07"
	(Ziemia Gornoslaska '90-'91, Lake Charles '91-'03)							
	Ziemia Lodzka	BC	1992	D	26,264	591' 02"	75' 09"	45' 07"
	(Ziemia Lodzka '92-'92, Lake Champlain '92-'03)							
	Ziemia Suwalska	BC	1984	D	26,696	591' 06"	75' 10"	45' 07"
	Ziemia Tarnowska	BC	1985	D	26,696	591' 06"	75' 10"	45' 07"
	Ziemia Zamojska	BC	1984	D	26,696	591' 06"	75' 10"	45' 07"

IP-6	**PRECIOUS SHIPPING PUBLIC CO. LTD., BANGKOK, THAILAND** *(preciousshipping.com)*							
	Manora Naree	BC	1980	D	29,159	590' 10"	75' 09"	47' 06"
	(High Peak '84 -'90, Federal Bergen '90 -'92, Thunder Bay '92-'93, Federal Bergen '93-'04							
IR-1	**REEDEREI ERWIN STRALMANN, MARNE, GERMANY** *(reederei-strahlmann.de)*							
	Alesia	GC	2008	D	7,574	380' 10"	51' 10"	29' 02"
IR-2	**REEDEREI KARL SCHLUTER GMBH & CO., RENDSBURG, GERMANY**							
	FOLLOWING VESSEL UNDER CHARTER TO FEDNAV LTD.							
	Federal Mattawa	GC	2005	D	18,825	606' 11"	77' 09"	46' 03"
IR-3	**RIGEL SCHIFFAHRTS GMBH, BREMEN, GERMANY** *(rigel-hb.com)*							
	Isarstern	TK	1995	D	17,078	528' 03"	75' 06"	38' 05"
	Weserstern	TK	1992	D	10,932	417' 04"	58' 01"	34' 09"
IR-4	**ROHDEN BEREEDERUNG GMBH & CO., HAMBURG, GERMANY** *(rohden.de)*							
	Agena	GC	2001	D	3,380	283' 06"	42' 00"	23' 04"
IS-1	**SEA OBSERVER SHIPPING SERVICES SA, PIRAEUS, GREECE**							
	Krios	BC	1983	D	12,319	423' 04"	65' 07"	36' 09"
	(Fjordnes '83-'87, Star Jay '87-'87, Elpis '87-'90, Kamtin '90-'96, Falknes '96-'00, Demi Green '00-'01, Lia '01-'03)							
IS-2	**SEASTAR NAVIGATION CO. LTD., ATHENS, GREECE**							
	FOLLWING VESSELS UNDER CHARTER TO CANADIAN FOREST NAVIGATION LTD.							
	Apollon	BC	1996	D	30,855	606' 11"	77' 05"	48' 11"
	(Spring Laker '96-'06)							
	Goldeneye	BC	1986	D	26,706	591' 06"	75' 09"	48' 07"
	(Sun Ocean '86-'93, Luna Verde '93-'00)							
	Milo	BC	1984	D	27,915	584' 00"	75' 10"	48' 05"
	(Silver Leader '84-'95, Alam United '95-'98, United '98-'00)							
	Miltiades	BC	1983	D	28,126	584' 06"	75' 07"	46' 09"
	(La Liberte '83-'87, Liberte '87-'88, Astart '88-'93, Ulloa '93-'00, Toro '00-'07)							
	Orna	BC	1984	D	27,915	584' 00"	75' 10"	48' 05"
	(St. Catheriness '84-'90, Asian Erie '90-'92, Handy Laker '92-'98, Moor Laker '98-'03)							
	Polydefkis	BC	1983	D	12,334	423' 03"	65' 08"	36' 09"
	(Falknes '83-'86, Fitnes '86-'88, Falknes '88-'93, Uri '93-'97, Daisy Gren '97-'00, Arklow Dawn '00-'03)							
	Woody	BC	1984	D	25,166	593' 02"	75' 09"	47' 07"
	(High Light '84-'90, Scan Trader '90-'95, Asia Trader '95-'96, NST Challenge '96-'03)							
IS-3	**SERROMAH SHIPPING BV, ROTTERDAM, NETHERLANDS** *(serromahshipping.com)*							
	Oriental Kerria	TK	2004	D	14,298	440' 02"	67' 04"	38' 01"
IS-4	**SHIH WEI NAVIGATION CO. LTD., TAIPEI, TAIWAN** *(www.swnav.com.tw)*							
	Fodas Pescadores	BC	2001	D	11,600	387' 02"	64' 04"	36' 01"
	Royal Pescadores	BC	1997	D	18,369	486' 01"	74' 10"	40' 00"
IS-5	**SICILNAVI S.R.L., PALERMO, ITALY**							
	Vindemia	TK	1979	D	3,603	295' 11"	44' 07"	21' 04"
IS-6	**SIOMAR ENTERPRISES LTD., PIRAEUS, GREECE**							
	Island Skipper	BC	1984	D	28,031	584' 08"	76' 02"	48' 05"
	Island Triangle	BC	1984	D	28,031	584' 08"	76' 02"	48' 05"
	(Island Gem '84-'07)							
IS-7	**SPAR SHIPPING AS, BERGEN, NORWAY** *(sparshipping.com)*							
	FOLLOWING VESSELS UNDER CHARTER TO FEDNAV LTD.							
	Spar Garnet	BC	1984	D	30,674	589' 11"	75' 09"	50' 10"
	(Mary Anne '84-'93, Federal Vigra '93-'97)							
	Spar Jade	BC	1984	D	30,674	589' 11"	75' 10"	50' 11"
	(Fiona Mary '84-93, Federal Aalesund '93-'97)							
	Spar Opal	BC	1984	D	28,214	585' 00"	75' 10"	48' 05"
	(Lake Shidaka '84-'91, Consensus Atlantic '91-'92, Federal Matane '92-'97, Matane '97-'97)							

Odra near the Soo Locks. (Roger LeLievre)

Algoma Spirit, built in Croatia, is the former saltie *Sandviken.* (Kent Malo)

Lake Superior now sails as *Saguenay* for Canada Steamship Lines. (Roger LeLievre)

	Spar Ruby	BC	1985	D	28,259	584' 08"	75' 11"	48' 05"
	(Astral Neptune '85-'92, Liberty Sky '92-'98, Manila Bellona '98-'98, Solveig '98-'00)							
IS-8	**STARMARINE MANAGEMENT INC., ATHENS, GREECE**							
	Elpida	GC	1984	D	30,850	617' 04"	75' 11"	47' 07
	(Radnik '84-'96, Grant Carrier '96-'01, Chios Sailor '01-'07)							
IS-9	**STOLT PARCEL TANKERS INC., GREENWICH, CONNECTICUT, USA** (stolt-nielsen.com)							
	Stolt Kite	TK	1992	D	4,735	314' 11"	49' 06"	26' 05
	(Randi Terkol '92-'96)							
IS-10	**STX PAN OCEAN SHIPPING CO. LTD., SEOUL, SOUTH KOREA** (stxpanocean.co.kr)							
	Pan Voyager	BC	1984	D	29,433	589' 11"	78' 01"	47' 07"
IS-11	**SUNSHIP & MLB M. LAUTERJUNG, EMDEN, GERMANY** (sunship.de)							
	FOLLOWING VESSELS UNDER CHARTER TO FEDNAV LTD.							
	Federal Manitou	BC	2004	D	27,000	606' 11"	77' 09"	46' 03"
	Federal Matane	BC	2004	D	27,000	606' 11"	77' 09"	46' 03"
	Federal Miramichi	BC	2004	D	27,000	606' 11"	77' 09"	46' 03"
IT-1	**TEO SHIPPING CORP., PIRAEUS, GREECE**							
	Antalina	BC	1984	D	28,082	584' 08"	75' 10"	48' 05"
	(Union Pioneer '84-'88, Manila Prosperity '88-'89, Consensus Sea '89-'92, Wiltrader '92-'94)							
IT-2	**THALKAT SHIPPING SA, PIRAEUS, GREECE**							
	Dora	BC	1981	D	21,951	508' 06"	75' 00"	44' 07"
	(Verdant '81-'87, Luntian '87-'93, Verdin '93-'94, Oak '94-'02)							
IT-3	**THENAMARIS SHIPS MANAGEMENT INC., ATHENS, GREECE** (thenamaris.gr)							
	Seaguardian II	BC	1984	D	28,251	639' 09"	75' 10"	46' 11"
	(Seamonarch '84-'86, Sea Master II '86-'88, Sea Monarch '88-'97, Sealuck V '97-'00,							
	Seaharmony II '00-'01, Seamonarch II '01-'02)							
	Sealink	BC	1983	D	28,234	639' 09"	75' 10"	46' 11"
	(Seaglory '83-'86, Sea Star II '86-'97)							
IT-4	**TORVALD KLAVENESS GROUP, OSLO, NORWAY** (www.klaveness.com)							
	KCL Barracuda	CC	1984	D	17,722	482' 11"	74' 11"	40' 01"
	(Kiwi Star '84-'03, Thai Ho '03-'04)							
IT-5	**TRADEWIND TANKERS SL, BARCELONA, SPAIN** (tradewindtankers.com)							
	Tradewind Union	TK	1997	D	10,600	387' 02"	63' 08"	34' 01"
	(Southern Lion '97-'03)							
IT-6	**TRANSADRIATIC, UMAG, REPUBLIC OF CROATIA**							
	Orfea	GC	1977	D	9,008	416' 08"	61' 03"	32' 06"
	(Washington '77-'99, Orlec '99-'06)							
IU-1	**UNION MARINE ENTERPRISES SA OF PANAMA, PIRAEUS, GREECE**							
	Capetan Michalis	BC	1981	D	28,600	593' 02"	75' 09"	47' 07"
	(Vasiliki '81-'85)							
IV-1	**VENUS ENTERPRISE SA, VOULA, GREECE**							
	Sea Veteran	BC	1981	D	30,900	617' 05"	76' 01"	47' 07"
	(Nosira Sharon '81-'89, Berta Dan '89-'93, Gunay-A '93-'06)							
IV-2	**VIKEN SHIPPING AS, BERGEN, NORWAY** (vikenshipping.com)							
	FOLLOWING VESSELS UNDER CHARTER TO FEDNAV LTD.							
	Federal Fuji	BC	1986	D	29,643	599' 09"	76' 00"	48' 07"
	Federal Polaris	BC	1985	D	29,643	599' 09"	76' 00"	48' 07"
	Inviken	BC	1986	D	30,052	621' 05"	75' 10"	47' 11"
	(Bar '86-'97)							
	Utviken	BC	1987	D	30,052	621' 05"	75' 10"	47' 11"
	(Bijelo Polje '87-'92, C. Blanco '92-'95)							

Fleet #	Fleet Name Vessel Name	Type of Vessel	Year Built	Type of Engine	Cargo Cap. or Gross*	Overall Length	Breadth	Depth or Draft*
IW-1	**W. BOCKSTIEGEL REEDEREI KG, EMDEN, GERMANY** (reederei-bockstiegel.de)							
	BBC Campana	GC	2003	D	12,837	452' 09"	68' 11"	36' 01"
	(Asian Cruiser '03-'03)							
	BBC Delaware	GC	2004	D	12,782	453' 00"	68' 11"	24' 07"
	BBC Italy	GC	2001	D	7,820	353' 00"	59' 09"	33' 02"
	(BBC Italy '99-'01, Buccaneer '01-'03)							
	BBC Maine	GC	2007	D	12,792	444' 05"	68' 11"	36' 01"
	BBC Mexico	GC	2001	D	5,018	330' 08"	53' 10"	26' 11"
	(Deborah '01-'01)							
	BBC Peru	GC	2001	D	7,598	351' 01"	59' 09"	33' 02"
	BBC Plata	GC	2005	D	12,837	452' 09"	68' 11"	36' 01"
	(Asian Voyager '05-'05)							
	BBC Spain	GC	2001	D	7,598	351' 01"	59' 09"	33' 02"
	BBC Zarate	GC	2007	D	12,834	452' 09"	68' 11"	36' 01"
IW-2	**WAGENBORG SHIPPING BV, DELFZIJL, NETHERLANDS** (wagenborg.com)							
	Americaborg	GC	2007	D	17,356	469' 02"	70' 06"	43' 08"
	Asiaborg	GC	2007	D	17,356	469' 02"	70' 06"	43' 08"
	Australiaborg	GC	2007	D	17,356	469' 02"	71' 04"	43' 08"
	Dagna	GC	2005	D	6,000	363' 05"	45' 11"	26' 08"
	Diezeborg	GC	2000	D	8,867	437' 08"	52' 00"	32' 02"
	Dintelborg	GC	1999	D	8,867	437' 07"	52' 00"	32' 02"
	(Dintelborg '00-'01, MSC Dardanelles '01-'04)							
	Dongeborg	GC	1999	D	8,867	437' 08"	52' 00"	32' 02"
	Drechtborg	GC	2000	D	8,865	437' 08"	52' 02"	32' 02"
	(Drechtborg '00-'00, MSC Skaw '00-'02, Drechtborg '02-'03, Normed Rotterdam '03-'05)							
	Egbert Wagenborg	GC	1998	D	9,141	441' 05"	54' 02"	32' 02"
	*(Maasborg '98-'98, **Egbert Wagenborg** '98-'02, MSC Bothnia '02-'03)*							
	Kasteelborg	GC	1998	D	9,150	427' 01"	52' 01"	33' 06"
	Keizersborg	GC	1996	D	9,150	427' 01"	52' 01"	33' 06"
	Koningsborg	GC	1999	D	9,150	427' 01"	52' 01"	33' 06"
	Kroonborg	GC	1995	D	9,085	428' 10"	52' 02"	33' 06"
	Loireborg	GC	2008	D	7,350	401' 04"	47' 03"	26' 07"
	Marneborg	GC	1998	D	9,141	441' 05"	54' 02"	32' 02"
	(Marneborg '98-'04, Normed Istanbul '04-'06)							
	Medemborg	GC	1997	D	9,141	441' 05"	54' 02"	32' 02"
	*(**Arion** '97-'03)*							
	Metasborg	GC	2002	D	9,141	441' 05"	54' 02"	32' 02"
	Michiganborg	GC	1999	D	9,141	441' 05"	54' 02"	32' 02"
	Moezelborg	GC	1999	D	9,141	441' 05"	54' 02"	32' 02"
	Morraborg	GC	1999	D	9,141	441' 05"	54' 02"	32' 02"
	Munteborg	GC	1996	D	9,141	441' 05"	54' 02"	32' 02"
	*(**Munteborg** '96-'00, MSC Baltic '00-'04)*							
	Nassauborg	GC	2006	D	16,615	467' 06"	72' 02"	39' 04"
	Prinsenborg	GC	2003	D	16,615	467' 06"	72' 02"	39' 04"
	Vaasaborg	GC	1999	D	8,664	433' 10"	52' 01"	31' 08"
	Vancouverborg	GC	2001	D	9,857	433' 10"	52' 01"	31' 08"
	Vechtborg	GC	1998	D	8,664	433' 10"	52' 01"	31' 08"
	Victoriaborg	GC	2001	D	9,857	433' 10"	52' 01"	31' 08"
	(Volgaborg '01-'01)							
	Virginiaborg	GC	2001	D	9,857	433' 10"	52' 01"	31' 08"
	Vlistborg	GC	1999	D	8,664	433' 10"	52' 01"	31' 08"
	Voorneborg	GC	1999	D	8,664	433' 10"	52' 01"	31' 08"
	Voosborg	GC	2000	D	8,664	433' 10"	52' 01"	31' 08"
	*(Voosborg '00-'04, **Morpeth** '04-'04)*							

At press time, Wagenborg Shipping also had the following vessels under charter. Please consult their respective fleets for details: Doggersbank, Finex, Kwintebank, Varnebank, Veerseborg, Vossborg, Zeus

Fleet #	Fleet Name Vessel Name	Type of Vessel	Year Built	Type of Engine	Cargo Cap. or Gross*	Overall Length	Breadth	Depth or Draft*
IW-3	**WAKER SHIPPING BV, DELFZIJL, NETHERLANDS** *FOLLOWING VESSEL UNDER CHARTER TO WAGENBORG SHIPPING*							
	Zeus	GC	2000	D	9,150	427' 01"	52' 01"	33' 06"
IW-4	**W-O SHIPPING GMBH, HAREN-EMS, GERMANY** *(w-o-shipping.com)*							
	W-O Topa	TK	2002	D	10,600	416' 06"	64' 04"	30' 08"
	(Veronica P G '02-'03, Topa '03-'04, Veronica P G '04-'08)							
IY-1	**YAHATA KISEN CO. LTD., OCHI EHIME PREFECTURE, JAPAN**							
	Lodestar Grace	TK	2002	D	14,298	439' 08"	67' 03"	38' 01"
IY-2	**YARDIMCI SHIPPING GROUP, ISTANBUL, TURKEY** *(www.yardimci.gen.tr)*							
	CT Cork	TK	2008	D	10,303	383' 10"	68' 11"	31' 02"
IY-3	**YILMAR SHIPPING & TRADING LTD., ISTANBUL, TURKEY** *(yilmar.com)*							
	YM Jupiter	TK	2007	D	15,995	393' 08"	57' 09"	27' 11"

Liamare, **built in 1999, is registered in The Netherlands.** *(Roger LeLievre)*

GROH'S PHOTOGRAPHY
Great Lakes Freighter Images

Peter Francis Groh - Photographer and Owner
1815 Tivoli Lane
Sheboygan, WI 53081
(920)-918-3402
pfgroh@grohs-photography.com
www.flickr.com/photos/greatlakesships/

www.grohs-photography.com

SHIPS IN ACTION ON THE GREAT LAKES!

GREAT LAKES SHIPS

THE DVD / VIDEO SERIES

Each video features 15 ships in action as seen on various Great
Lakes, ports, river and locks. The U.S. & Canadian flagged
boats include: ★ Classic Lakers ★ Steamers ★ Self-Unloaders
★ Tankers ★ 1000 Foot Super Lakers. Plus ship info & history.

— VOLUMES 1-10 • DVD & Limited VHS —
65 MIN. EACH • COLOR • LIVE AUDIO • NARRATION

☐DVD   *Only* $24⁹⁵ EACH   Buy 2 or More Titles
-OR-
☐LIMITED VHS   *Only* $22⁹⁵ EACH

Plus S&H: One $6 • Two $7 • Three FREE
Wisconsin Residents add 5.5% sales tax

COMING SOON!
★ Lake Superior Sight Seeing Travel Guide Vol. 1-2
★ Lake Superior Lighthouses ★ Waterfalls

PLETS EXPRESS
P.O. Box 217 • Altoona, WI 54720 • 715-833-8899

www.pletsexpress.com

Get Up Close and Personal

Sault Ste. Marie provides
visitors with the best vantage
points for viewing the ships
that ply the waters of the
Great Lakes. Join us for an up
close and personal view of the
Soo Locks during Engineers Day:
June 26, 2009.

Logon to: saultstemarie.com
for details, lodging information
and more things to do in the Soo.

Sault
Ste Marie
PURE MICHIGAN℠

AV

— VANTAGE POINT —

Acheson Ventures of Port Huron, Michigan, invites you to Vantage Point. Visit our BoatNerd.com HQ, then grab a bite to eat and relax at the Great Lakes Maritime Center. Watch the freighters go by while enjoying free Wi-Fi access.

THE COFFEE HARBOR

- **Fresh-cut Fries**
- **Ice Cream**
- **Freighter Info**
- **Family Fun**
- **Free Wi-Fi**

810.985.4817

— HIGHLANDER SEA —

This ship offers opportunities for character development, teamwork, and community citizenship for the people of Port Huron, in particular it's youth, through leadership and training. As Port Huron's flagship, the ship berths in this maritime capital.

- **Tours**
- **Day Sails**
- **Private Charters**
- **Educational Programs**

810.966.3488

www.AchesonVentures.com

MEANINGS OF BOAT WHISTLES

1 SHORT: I intend to leave you on my port side (answered by same if agreed upon).

2 SHORT: I intend to leave you on my starboard side (answered by same if agreed upon). (Passing arrangements may be agreed upon by radio. If so, no whistle signal is required.)

5 OR MORE SHORT BLASTS SOUNDED RAPIDLY: Danger.

1 PROLONGED: Vessel leaving dock.

3 SHORT: Operating astern propulsion.

1 PROLONGED, SOUNDED AT INTERVALS OF NOT MORE THAN 2 MINUTES: Vessel moving in restricted visibility.

1 SHORT, 1 PROLONGED, 1 SHORT: Vessel at anchor in restricted visibility (optional). May be accompanied by the ringing of a bell on the forward part of the ship and a gong on the aft end.

3 PROLONGED and 2 SHORT: Salute (formal).

1 PROLONGED and 2 SHORT: Salute (commonly used).

3 PROLONGED and 1 SHORT: Internationl Shipmasters' Association member salute.

(Wade P. Streeter)

GREAT LAKES LOADING PORTS

Iron Ore
Duluth, Minn.
Superior, Wis.
Two Harbors, Minn.
Marquette, Mich.
Escanaba, Mich.

Petroleum
Sarnia, Ont.
E. Chicago, Ind.

Limestone
Port Inland, Mich.
Cedarville, Mich.
Drummond
 Island, Mich.
Calcite, Mich.
Rogers City, Mich.
Stoneport, Mich.
Marblehead, Ohio

Coal
Superior, Wis.
S. Chicago, Ill.
Toledo, Ohio
Sandusky, Ohio
Ashtabula, Ohio
Conneaut, Ohio

Grain
Thunder Bay, Ont.
Duluth, Minn.
Milwaukee, Wis.
Superior, Wis.
Sarnia, Ont.
Toledo, Ohio
Port Stanley, Ont.
Owen Sound, Ont.

Cement
Charlevoix, Mich.
Alpena, Mich.

Salt
Goderich, Ont.
Windsor, Ont.
Cleveland, Ont.
Fairport, Ohio

Frontenac unloading grain at Port Colborne. (Alain Gindroz)

MODELS & MORE AT YOUR GREAT LAKES SUPERSTORE

www.GreatLakesFreighters.com

We Specialize in Kits & Custom Models of Great Lakes Freighters

VIDEOS
CLOTHING
GIFTS

(440) 298-1243
5305 EMERSON RD.
MADISON, OH 44057

www.greatlakesfreighters.com
www.bearcomarine.com

DOOR COUNTY Maritime MUSEUM
& Lighthouse Preservation Society, Inc.

Tour the Tug JOHN PURVES

Freshwater Fury!
Held Over!

Don't miss *The Great Lakes' Perfect Storm!*

www.dcmm.org
On the waterfront - Sturgeon Bay, WI

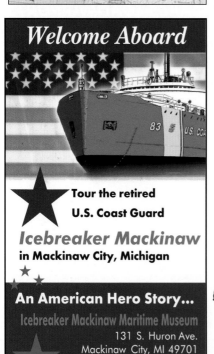

Welcome Aboard

Tour the retired
U.S. Coast Guard
Icebreaker Mackinaw
in Mackinaw City, Michigan

An American Hero Story...

Icebreaker Mackinaw Maritime Museum
131 S. Huron Ave.
Mackinaw City, MI 49701
phone: 231-436-9825
www.TheMackinaw.org

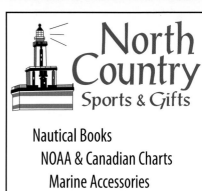

North Country Sports & Gifts

Nautical Books
NOAA & Canadian Charts
Marine Accessories
Gifts ... and more

103 N. Ontario St.   906-297-6461
De Tour Village, Michigan
www.NoCoSports.com

- 1917 Great Lakes freighter
- 20,000 sq.-foot indoor maritime museum
- Aquariums stocked with Great Lakes fish
- Over 100 exhibits including the lifeboats from the freighter EDMUND FITZGERALD

MUSEUM SHIP VALLEY CAMP

SAULT HISTORIC SITES
40 YEARS 1967~2007

TOWER OF HISTORY

Open Mid-May through Mid-October
Free Parking • Buses Welcome
www.saulthistoricsites.com

admin@saulthistoricsites.com
(888) 744-7867

George Kemp Downtown Marina
~AND~
Water Street Historic Block

- Modern Facilities • Internet Access
- Walking distance to local attractions
- Historic Homes open for viewing

- Express Elevator
- Museum exhibits
- Up to 20-mile panoramic view
- Excellent freighter watching!

FOLLOWING THE FLEET

These prerecorded messages help track vessel arrivals and departures.

Algoma Central Marine	(905) 988-2665	ACM vessel movements
Boatwatcher's Hotline	(218) 722-6489	Superior, Wis., Duluth, Two Harbors, Taconite Harbor and Silver Bay, Minn.
CSX Coal Docks/Torco Dock	(419) 697-2304	Toledo, Ohio, vessel information
DMIR Ore Dock	Discontinued	Duluth vessel information
Eisenhower Lock	(315) 769-2422	Eisenhower Lock vessel traffic
Michigan Limestone docks	(989) 734-2117	Calcite, Mich., vessel information
Michigan Limestone docks	(906) 484-2201	Ext. 503 – Cedarville, Mich., passages
Presque Isle Corp.	(989) 595-6611	Stoneport, Mich., vessel information
Soo Traffic	(906) 635-3224	Previous day – St. Marys River
Superior Midwest Energy Terminal (SMET)	(715) 395-3559	Superior, Wis., vessel information
Thunder Bay Port Authority	(807) 345-1256	Thunder Bay, Ont., vessel info
Great Lakes Fleet	(800) 328-3760	Ext. 4389 – GLF vessel movements
Upper Lakes Group	(905) 988-2665	ULG vessel movements
Vantage Point, Boatnerd World HQ	(810) 985-9057	St. Clair River traffic
Welland Canal tape	(905) 688-6462	Welland Canal traffic

With an inexpensive VHF scanner, boat watchers can tune to ship-to-ship and ship-to-shore traffic using the following frequency guide.

Commercial vessels only	Ch. 13 – 156.650 MHz	Bridge-to-bridge communications
Calling/distress only	Ch. 16 – 156.800 MHz	Calling/distress only
Commercial vessels only	Ch. 06 – 156.300 MHz	Working channel
Commercial vessels only	Ch. 08 – 156.400 MHz	Working channel
Supply boat at Sault Ste. Marie, Mich.	Ch. 08 – 156.400 MHz	Supply boat *Ojibway*
DeTour Reef – Lake St. Clair Light	Ch. 11 – 156.550 MHz	Sarnia Traffic - Sect. 1
Long Point Light – Lake St. Clair Light	Ch. 12 – 156.600 MHz	Sarnia Traffic - Sect. 2
Montreal – mid-Lake St. Francis	Ch. 14 – 156.700 MHz	Seaway Beauharnois – Sect. 1
Mid-Lake St. Francis – Bradford Island	Ch. 12 – 156.600 MHz	Seaway Eisenhower – Sect. 2
Bradford Island – Crossover Island	Ch. 11 – 156.550 MHz	Seaway Iroquois – Sect. 3
Crossover Island to Cape Vincent	Ch. 13 – 156.650 MHz	Seaway Clayton – Sect. 4 St. Lawrence River portion
Cape Vincent – mid-Lake Ontario	Ch. 13 – 156.650 MHz	Seaway Sodus – Sect. 4 Lake Ontario portion
Mid-Lake Ontario – Welland Canal	Ch. 11 – 156.550 MHz	Seaway Newcastle – Sect. 5
Welland Canal	Ch. 14 – 156.700 MHz	Seaway Welland – Sect. 6
Welland Canal to Long Point Light	Ch. 11 – 156.550 MHz	Seaway Long Point – Sect. 7
Montreal Traffic	Ch. 10 – 156.500 MHz	Vessel traffic
St. Marys River Traffic Service	Ch. 12 – 156.600 MHz	Soo Traffic, Sault Ste. Marie, MI
Lockmaster, Soo Locks	Ch. 14 – 156.700 MHz	Soo Lockmaster (call WUE-21)
Coast Guard traffic	Ch. 21 – 157.050 MHz	United States Coast Guard
Coast Guard traffic	Ch. 22 – 157.100 MHz	United States Coast Guard
U.S. mailboat, Detroit, MI	Ch. 10 – 156.500 MHz	Mailboat *J. W. Westcott II*

News ☙ Photos ☙ Information

BoatNerd.com

Great Lakes & Seaway Shipping On-Line Inc.

A.B.M. Marine
Thunder Bay, ON

Algoma Central Corp.
St. Catharines, ON

Algoma Central Corp.
St. Catharines, ON

American Canadian Caribbean Line Inc.
Warren, RI

American Marine Constructors
Benton Harbor, MI

American Steamship Co.
Williamsville, NY

Andrie Inc.
Muskegon, MI

Apostle Islands Cruise Service
Bayfield, WI

Arnold Transit Co.
Mackinac Island, MI

Basic Towing Inc.
Escanaba, MI

Bay City Boat Line
Bay City, MI

Bay Shipbuilding Co.
Sturgeon Bay, WI

Beaver Island Boat Co.
Charlevoix, MI

Billington Contracting Inc.
Duluth, MN

Blue Heron Co.
Tobermory, ON

Buffalo Public Works Dept.
Buffalo, NY

Busch Marine Inc.
Carrollton, MI

Calumet River Fleeting Inc.
Chicago, IL

Canada Steamship Lines Inc.
Montreal, QC

Canadian Coast Guard
Ottawa, ON

**Central Marine Logistics Inc.
Operator for ArcelorMittal**
Griffith, IN

Chicago Fire Department
Chicago, IL

Cleveland Fire Department
Cleveland, OH

Club Canamac Cruises
Toronto, ON

Columbia Yacht Club
Chicago. IL

Croisières AML Inc.
Québec, QC

Dan Minor & Sons Inc.
Port Colborne, ON

Dean Construction Co.
Belle River, ON

Detroit City Fire Department
Detroit, MI

Diamond Jack's River Tours
Detroit, MI

Dragage Verreault Inc.
Les Méchins, QC

Duc D'Orleans Cruise Boat
Corunna, ON

Durocher Marine
Cheboygan, MI

Eastern Upper Peninsula Transportation Authority
Sault Ste. Marie, MI

Edward E. Gillen Co.
Milwaukee, WI

Egan Marine Corp.
Lemont, IL

Equipments Verreault Inc.
Les Mechins, QC

Erie Sand & Gravel Co.
Erie, PA

Essroc Canada Inc.
Upper Lakes Group – Mgr.
North York, ON

Fraser Shipyards Inc.
Superior, WI

Gaelic Tugboat Co.
Detroit, MI

Gallagher Marine
Construction Inc.
Escanaba, MI

Gananoque Boat Line
Gananoque,ON

Geo. Gradel Co.
Toledo, OH

Goodtime Transit Boats Inc.
Cleveland, OH

Grand Portage /
Isle Royale Transportation Line
Superior, WI

Gravel & Lake Services Ltd.
Thunder Bay, ON

Gravel & Lake Services Ltd.
Thunder Bay, ON

Great Lakes Dock & Materials
Muskegon, MI

Great Lakes Fleet Inc.
Key Lakes Inc. – Mgr.
Duluth, MI

Great Lakes International
Towing & Salvage Ltd
Burlington, ON

Great Lakes Maritime Academy
Northwestern Michigan College
Traverse City, MI

Great Lakes Towing Co.
Cleveland, OH

Groupe C.T.M.A.
Cap-Aux-Meules, QC

HMC Ship Management Co.
Div. of Hannah Marine Corp.
Lemont, IL

Hamilton Port Authority
Hamilton, ON

Hannah Marine Corp.
Lemont, IL

Hannah Marine Corp.
Lemont, IL

Heritage Cruise Lines
St. Catharines, ON

Heritage Marine
Knife River, MN

Holly Marine Towing
Chicago, IL

Hornbeck Offshore Services
Covington, LA

Horne Transportation Ltd.
Wolfe Island, ON

Illinois Marine Towing Inc.
Lemont, IL

Inland Lakes Management Inc.
Alpena, MI

The Interlake Steamship Co.
Lakes Shipping Co.
Richfield, OH

Keystone Great Lakes Inc.
Bala Cynwyd, PA

Kindra Lake Towing LP
Downers Grove, IL

King Co. Inc.
Holland, MI

KK Integrated Shipping LLC
Menominee, MI

Lafarge Canada Inc.
Montreal, QC

Lafarge North America Inc.
Southfield, MI

Lake Michigan Carferry
Service Inc.
Ludington, MI

Laken Shipping Corp.
SMT (USA) Inc. – Mgr.
Cleveland, OH

Le Groupe Océan Inc.
Québec, QC

Lee Marine Ltd.
Sombra, ON

Lock Tours Canada
Sault Ste. Marie, ON

Lower Lakes Towing Ltd.
Port Dover, ON
Lower Lakes Transportation Co.
Cleveland, OH

Luedtke Engineering Co.
Frankfort, MI

M.C.M. Marine Inc.
Sault Ste Marie, MI

MacDonald Marine Ltd.
Goderich, ON

Madeline Island Ferry Line Inc.
LaPointe, WI

Maid of the Mist Steamboat Co. Ltd.
Niagara Falls, ON

Malcom Marine
St. Clair, MI

Manitou Island Transit
Leland, MI

Marine Tech Inc.
Duluth, MN

Mariposa Cruise Line
Toronto, ON

Maximus Corp.
Bloomfield Hills, MI

McAsphalt Marine Transportation
Scarborough, ON

McKeil Marine Ltd.
Hamilton, ON

McKeil Marine Ltd.
Hamilton, ON

McNally Construction Inc.
Hamilton, ON

Miller Boat Line
Put-in-Bay, OH

Montreal Port Authority
Montreal, QC

Museum Tug John Purves
Sturgeon Bay, WI

Museum Ship CCGC Alexander Henry
Kingston, ON

Museum Tug Edna G
Two Harbors, MN

Museum Ship HMCS Haida
Hamilton, ON

Museum Ship Keewatin
Douglas, MI

Museum Ships USS Little Rock USS The Sullivans
Buffalo, NY

Museum Ship Meteor
Superior, WI

Museum Ship City of Milwaukee
Manistee, MI

Museum Ship Milwaukee Clipper
Muskegon, MI

Museum Ships Norgoma (Sault Ste. Marie,ON)
Norisle (Manitowaning,ON)

Museum Ship Valley Camp
Sault Ste. Marie, MI

Museum Ship William A. Irvin
Duluth, MN

Museum Ships Willis B. Boyer (Toledo,OH)
William G. Mather (Cleveland,OH)

Muskoka Steamship Historical Society
Gravenhurst, ON

Nadro Marine Services Ltd.
Port Dover, ON

Nautica Queen Cruise Dining
Cleveland, OH

Norlake Transportation Co.
Port Colborne, ON

Ontario Ministry of Transportation
Downsview, ON

Osborne Companies Inc.
Grand River, OH

Owen Sound Transportation Co. Ltd.
Owen Sound, ON

Pere Marquette Shipping Co. Tug Undaunted
Ludington, MI

Port City Tug Inc.
Muskegon, MI

Provmar Fuels Inc.
Div. of Upper Lakes Group Inc.
Hamilton, ON

Purvis Marine Ltd.
Sault Ste. Marie, ON

Purvis Marine Ltd.
Sault Ste. Marie, ON

Rigel Shipping Canada Inc.
Shediac, NB

Roen Salvage Co.
Sturgeon Bay, WI

Ryba Marine Construction Co.
Cheboygan, MI

Selvick Marine Towing Corp.
Sturgeon Bay, WI

Shoreline Sightseeing Co.
Chicago, IL

Société des Traversiers
Du Québec
Québec, QC

Société Québecoise
D' Exploration Minière
Algoma Central Corp. – Mgr.
Sainte-Foy, QC

Soo Locks Boat Tours
Sault Ste. Marie, MI

St. Lawrence
Cruise Lines Inc.
Kingston, ON

St. Lawrence Seaway
Development Corp.
Massena, NY

St. Lawrence Seaway
Management Corp.
Cornwall, ON

St. Marys Cement Inc.
Toronto, ON

TGL Marine Holdings ULC
Toronto, ON

Thousand Islands & Seaway
Cruises
Brockville, ON

Thunder Bay Marine
Services Ltd.
Thunder Bay, On

Thunder Bay Tug
Services Ltd.
Thunder Bay, ON

Toronto Parks
& Recreation Department
Toronto, ON

Transport Desgagnés Inc.
Québec, QC

Transport Desgagnés Inc.
Québec, QC

Transport Igloolik Inc.
Montreal, QC

U.S. Army Corps of Engineers
Great Lakes & Ohio River Div.
Cincinnati, OH

United States Coast Guard
9th Coast Guard District
Cleveland, OH

United States
Environmental Protection Agency
Duluth, MN / Chicago, IL

United States
National Park Service
Houghton, MI

Upper Lakes Group Inc.
Toronto, ON

Upper Lakes Towing Co.
Escanaba, MI

Vanguard Shipping Inc.
Ingleside, ON

Vista Fleet
Duluth, MN

Voyageur Marine Transport Ltd.
Ridgeville, ON

Wendella Boat Tours
Chicago, IL

Zenith Tugboat Co.
Duluth, MN

On ships, as on buildings, stacks are used to vent exhaust smoke and provide an air draft for the boilers, if a vessel is so-equipped. Most modern vessels don't need a traditional smokestack but usually carry one for sake of appearances.

HOUSEFLAGS OF THE GREAT LAKES AND SEAWAY FLEETS

Andrie Inc.
Muskegon, MI

Algoma Central Corp.
St. Catharines, ON

American Steamship Co.
Williamsville, NY

Canada Steamship Lines Inc.
Montreal, QC

Fednav Ltd.
Montreal, QC

Gaelic Tugboat Co.
Detroit, MI

**Great Lakes Fleet Inc.
Key Lakes Inc. – Mgr.**
Duluth, MN

Great Lakes Maritime Academy
Traverse City, MI

Great Lakes Shipwreck Historical Society
Sault Ste Marie, MI

Great Lakes Towing Co.
Cleveland, OH

Inland Lakes Management Inc.
Alpena, MI

**Interlake Steamship Co.
Lakes Shipping Co.**
Richfield, OH

J.W. Westcott Co.
Detroit, MI

LaFarge Canada Inc
Montreal, QC

Lake Michigan Carferry Service Inc.
Ludington, MI

Le Groupé Ocean Inc.
Quebec, QC

**Lower Lakes Towing Ltd.
Lower Lakes Transportation Co.**
Port Dover, ON / Williamsville, NY

McAsphalt Marine Transportation Ltd.
Scarborough, ON

McKeil Marine Ltd.
Hamilton, ON

Owen Sound Transportation Co. Ltd.
Owen Sound, ON

Pere Marquette Shipping Co.
Ludington, MI

Purvis Marine Ltd.
Sault Ste. Marie, ON

Seaway Marine Transport
St. Catharines, ON

Transport Desgagnés Inc.
Québec, QC

Upper Lakes Group Inc.
Toronto, ON

Vanguard Shipping (Great Lakes) Inc.
Ingleside, ON

Voyageur Marine Transport Ltd.
Ridgeville, ON

Wagenborg Shipping B.V.
Delfzijl, Netherlands

COLORS OF THE MAJOR SALTWATER FLEETS

Amalthia Maritime Inc.
Athens, Greece

Athena Marine Co. Ltd.
Limassol, Cyprus

Atlantska Plovidba
Dubrovnik, Croatia

B&N Moorman B.V.
Ridderkerk, Netherlands

Beluga Shipping GMBH
Bremen, Germany

Bernhard Schulte Group
Hamburg, Germany

Biglift Shipping BV
Roosendaal, Netherlands

Blystad Tankers Inc.
Oslo, Norway

**Briese Schiffahrts
GMBH & Co. KG**
Leer, Germany

**Canadian Forest
Navigation Co. Ltd.**
Montreal, QC

Carisbrooke Shipping PLC
Cowes, UK

China Ocean Shipping Group
Bejing, PRC

**Clipper Wonsild Tankers AS
Clipper Elite Carriers**
Copenhagen, Denmark

Coastal Shipping Ltd.
Goose Bay, ON

Commercial Fleet of Donbass
Donetsk, Ukraine

**Commercial Trading &
Discount Co. Ltd.**
Athens, Greece

**Common Progress Compania
Naviera SA**
Piraeus, Greece

Crescent Marine Services
Copenhagen, Denmark

Crystal Pool Group
Helsinki, Finland

Eastwind Ship Management
Singapore, Singapore

Eitzen Chemical ASA
Oslo, Norway

Enzian Shipping AG
Berne, Switzerland

Euronav NV
Antwerp, Belgium

F Ship Management SA
Piraeus, Greece

Far-Eastern Shipping Co.
Vladivostok, Russia

Fednav International Ltd.
Montreal, QC

Fednav International Ltd.
Montreal, QC

Finbeta
Savona, Italy

Fisser & V. Doornum Kg GMBH
Hamburg, Germany

Flinter Groningen B.V.
Groningen, Netherlands

Fortum Oil & Gas
Fortum, Finland

**Franco Compania
Naviera SA**
Athens, Greece

Great Lakes Feeder Lines
Burlington, ON, Canada

Hapag Lloyd
Hamburg, Germany

**Harbor Shipping &
Trading Co. S.A.**
Chios, Greece

Intersee Schiffahrts-Gesellschaft MbH & Co.
Haren-Ems, Germany

Intership Navigation Co. Ltd.
Limassol, Cyprus

Isko Marine (Shipping) Co. SA
Piraeus, Greece

Jo Tankers, B.V.
Spijkenisse, Netherlands

JSM Shipping
Jork, Germany

Jumbo Shipping Co. S.A.
Rotterdam, Netherlands

Kent Line
Saint Johns, NB, Canada

Knutsen O.A.S. Shipping
Haugesund, Norway

Krey Schiffahrts GMBH & Co.
Simonswolde, Germany

Liamare Shipping BV
Maartensdijk, Netherlands

Laurin Maritime Inc.
Houston, TX

Lietuvos Juro Laivininkyste (Lithuanian Shipping Co.)
Klaipeda, Lithuania

Lehmann Reederi
Lubeck, Germany

Marbulk Shipping Inc. CSL International Inc. Mgr
Beverly, MS

Murmansk Shipping Co.
Murmansk, Russia

Murmansk Shipping Co.
Murmansk, Russia

Navigation Maritime Bulgare Ltd.
Varna, Bulgaria

Novorossiysk Shipping (Novoship)
Novorossiysk, Russia

Oceanex Ltd.
Montreal, QC

Olympic Shipping and Management S.A.
Athens, Greece

Onego Shipping & Chartering
Rhoon, Netherlands

Perosea Shipping Co. SA
Piraeus, Greece

Polish Steamship Co.
Szczecin, Poland

Pot Scheepvaart BV
Delfzijl, Netherlands

Precious Shipping Public Co.
Bangkok, Thailand

Sea Observer Shipping Services
Piraeus, Greece

Seastar Navigation Co. Ltd.
Athens, Greece

Shih Wei Navigation Co.
Taipei, Taiwan

Siomar Enterprises Ltd.
Piraeus, Greece

Spar Shipping A.S.
Bergen, Norway

Stolt Parcel Tankers
Greenwich, CT

Teo Shipping Corp.
Piraeus, Greece

Thenamaris Ships Management Inc.
Athens, Greece

Torvald Klaveness Group
Oslo, Norway

Mon Marine Enterprises S.A.
Piraeus, Greece

Viken Shipping AS
Bergen, Norway

W. Bockstiegel Reederei KG
Emden, Germany

Wagenborg Shipping B.V.
Delfzijl, Netherlands

W-O Shipping GmbH
Harren-Ems, Germany

Yardimici Shipping Group
Istanbul, Turkey

FLAGS OF NATIONS
IN THE MARINE TRADE

Antigua & Barbuda

Argentina

Australia

Austria

Azerbaijan

Bahamas

Bahrain

Barbados

Belgium

Bermuda

Bosnia & Herzegovinia

Brazil

Canada

Cayman Islands

Chile

China

Cote D'Ivoire

Croatia

Cyprus

Czech Republic

Denmark

Dominican Republic

Ecuador

Egypt

Estonia

Fiji

Finland

France

Germany

Ghana

Greece

Guinea

Haiti

Honduras

Hong Kong

Hungary

Iceland

India

Indonesia

Ireland

Isle of Man

Israel

Italy

Japan

Korea-South

Latvia

Liberia

Lithuania

Luxembourg

Malaysia

Malta
 Marshall Islands
 Mexico
 Monaco
 Morocco

 Myanmar
 Netherlands
 Netherlands Antilles
 New Zealand
 Nicaragua

 N. Mariana Islands
 Norway
 Pakistan
 Panama
 Peru

 Philippines
 Poland
 Portugal
 Republic of South Africa
 Romania

 Russia
 Singapore
 Solomon Islands
 Spain
 St. Kitts Nevis

 St. Vincent & The Grenadines
 Sweden
 Switzerland
 Syria
 Taiwan

 Thailand
 Trinidad & Tobago
 Tunisia
 Turkey
 Ukraine

 United Kingdom
 United States
 Vanuatu
 Venezuela
 Yugoslavia

Other Flags of Interest

International Shipmaster's Association – Member Pennant

Canadian Coast Guard Ensign

Dangerous Cargo On Board

Pilot On Board

U.S. Coast Guard Auxiliary Ensign

U.S. Coast Guard Ensign

U.S. Army Corps of Engineers

St. Lawrence Seaway Development Corp.

St. Lawrence Seaway Management Corp.

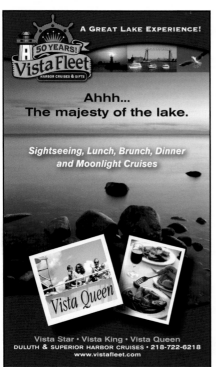

A GREAT LAKE EXPERIENCE!

Vista Fleet
50 YEARS!
HARBOR CRUISES & GIFTS

Ahhh...
The majesty of the lake.

*Sightseeing, Lunch, Brunch, Dinner
and Moonlight Cruises*

Vista Star • Vista King • Vista Queen
DULUTH & SUPERIOR HARBOR CRUISES • 218-722-6218
www.vistafleet.com

Lake Superior
MAGAZINE

Celebrating
30 Years
of Bringing Lake Superior
to the World

■ Maritime history & folklore books
■ Travel guides, maps, charts and more

Visit us at:
310 E. Superior St.
Duluth, MN 55802   Lake Superior
Port Cities Inc.

www.lakesuperior.com
1-888-BIG LAKE (888-244-5253)

Ship Watcher's
Paradise
located in beautiful Duluth, Minnesota

1-800-430-7437
www.southpierinn.com

Named *"Best
Waterfront
Hotel in
Minnesota
2007"* by the
Official Best Of!

SOUTH PIER INN
on the canal

The Original DVD Documentary

Don Hermanson's
ICEBREAKER
MACKINAW

*Join the last Captain
and crew during heavy
icebreaking on the Great Lakes
from the final breakout to
the decommissioning and
her final stop in
Mackinaw City, Michigan*

only
$22.95
includes
shipping!

Don Hermanson's
Keweenaw
Video Productions
PO Box 665
Houghton MI 49931
1-800-362-6088
Approx. 58 min

www.IcebreakerMackinaw.com

I want to...
ExperiencePortColborne.com

Sightsee   *Marvel*   *Reminisce*

Port Colborne

a community that loves your company

1-888-PORT-FUN

Experience the majesty & mystery of the
Shipwreck Coast at historic Whitefish Point

Step back in time & see....

Shipwreck Legends Come to Life

~ Marking the 30th Anniversary of the loss of the Edmund Fitzgerald

~ Experience the Haunting World of Shipwrecks - Interpretive Exhibits

~ National Historic Site - Oldest Active Light on Lake Superior

~ Restored 1861 Light Keepers Dwelling

~ Restored United States Coast Guard Boathouse -
Featuring History of Lifesaving on Lake Superior's
Shipwreck Coast

~ Shipwreck Coast Museum Store - One of the Finest
Maritime Gift Stores in Michigan

~ Overnight Accommodations Available - Stay in the
Adaptively Restored 1923 United States Coast Guard
Lifeboat Station Crews Quarters. Call 888-492-3747

~ Video Theater - Original Short Film on the History
of the Edmund Fitzgerald and Raising of the Bell

~ Boardwalk - Visitors Gain Access to View Lake
Superior's Shipwreck Coast

~ Whitefish Point Bird Observatory & Interpretive Center

SHIPWRECK
MUSEUM
AT WHITEFISH POINT

800-635-1742

www.shipwreckmuseum.com

Just 50 miles north of the Mackinac Bridge

50 Years
1959-2009
A Retrospective

Howard L. Shaw battles Rock Cut
ice in the late 1950s, helped by
the cutter **Arundel**. *(Tom Manse)*

Valley Camp **in service.** *(Tom Manse)*

***Valley Camp*
arriving at Sault
Ste. Marie in 1968.
Tom Manse on
deck (inset).**
(Roger LeLievre)

THE MAN WHO KNEW THE SHIPS

Know Your Ships
50 Years

This section is dedicated to Thomas Manse, who conceived and published our first edition in 1959. His passion was Great Lakes vessels, and he followed their movements with his camera for nearly 40 years. Thanks to his vision, "Know Your Ships" continues for new generations of boat watchers.

Tom had some help along the way. Volunteers such as John Bascom, Peter Worden, the Rev. Edward J. Dowling, the Rev. Peter Vanderlinden, Ed Wilson and John Vournakis were all invaluable early on. More recently, Jody Aho, Philip Clayton, Audrey LeLievre, Matt Miner, Gerry Ouderkirk, Neil Schultheiss, William Soleau, Wade P. Streeter, Franz VonRiedel, George Wharton and Chris Winters have made huge contributions. In addition, the work of many skilled marine photographers has appeared on these pages.

The readers who support "Know Your Ships" year after year deserve a special acknowledgment, as does the Web site BoatNerd.com, which has done more to build interest in boatwatching than its founder ever dreamed possible. There aren't enough master salutes in the world to thank everyone for how much they have done.

Roger LeLievre, Editor / Publisher

When Tom Manse launched a small booklet called *"Know Your Ships"* in 1959, the Great Lakes fleet numbered around more than 500 vessels operated by nearly 70 U.S. and Canadian companies. The steamer *Edmund Fitzgerald* was just a year old, the St. Lawrence Seaway was new, and several vessels up to 730 feet long were on the drawing boards to take advantage of the Seaway's maximum dimensions. Passenger ships still sailed the lakes, most vessels were powered by steam, iron ore had yet to be replaced by taconite, and the average cargo capacity per boat was around 20,000 tons.

Tom Manse, in his element.

Fifty years later, much has changed, from the size of the ships – some 1,000 feet long and capable of carring nearly 70,000 tons of cargo – to the size of the fleet itself. On the U.S. side of the lakes alone, there are now only about 145 major vessels sailing for just a handful of companies.

In these days of desktop publishing, it's hard to imagine someone beginning something like *"Know Your Ships"* with little more than a drafting table, an old camera and a dream. Yet that's just how *"KYS"* got its start.

Armed with a mid-1900s Kodak camera (the kind with a bellows that folded out from the front) that yielded black and white, postcard-sized negatives, Manse began shooting pictures of the passing freighter parade through the Soo Locks at Sault Ste. Marie, Mich., in the 1950s.

(Continued on Page 146)

Tom often said he started really concentrating on his photography in the mid-1950s because he feared that when the St. Lawrence Seaway opened, there would be wholesale scrappings of many familiar freighters. As it turned out, he was right. Manse set a goal of getting at least one photograph of all the ships sailing the lakes. In 1992, he estimated his collection at more than 25,000 negatives and slides. He made the trek from his home on Kimball Street in Sault Ste. Marie, Mich., to the Sugar Island ferry dock (we know it now by its official name, Mission Point) or to the end of the Soo Locks' West Pier, thousands of times over the years, just to see "what was coming."

That first issue of *"Know Your Ships"* was just 44 pages. Staple bound, it sold for 50 cents. Then – as now – it was conceived as a publication aimed at tourists, ship fans and people who lived along the water who wanted basic information about the ships that passed their shores.

Putting together early *"KYS"* editions was a labor-intense, time-consuming process. Any design work Manse did was by hand, using the drafting skills honed in his job as a machinist at Sault Ste. Marie's Michigan Northern (now Edison Sault) hydroelectric power plant. He would often look out the window and, spotting an unfamiliar stack marking on a vessel passing by, sketch the design, making a more accurate rendition later as he worked at night in his basement at home. That basement also contained a darkroom, barely big enough to turn around in, from which he turned out postcard-sized prints with a vintage contact printer.

Early 1960s Seaway visitor *La Chacra*. *(Tom Manse)*

Among the pictures included in that first edition was a cover shot of Canada Steamship Lines' steamer *Lemoyne*, downbound at Mission Point in early winter. In that issue, 25 U.S.-flagged vessel operators were referenced and a footnote indicated that approximately 70 freighters passed through the Soo Locks each day, a number hard to fathom now. According to the book, Pittsburgh Steamship Co. operated 57 boats; Canada Steamship Lines had 61.

Lemoyne **graced our first cover (top).**
Benson Ford **(above) was a typical
laker for many years before bigger
vessels, such as** *Edwin G. Gott* **(right, in
drydock), made their debut.**
*(Clockwise, Tom Manse,
Chris Winters, Tom Manse)*

In 1968, Manse left his job at the Edison hydro plant to direct the newly formed Le Sault de Sainte Marie Historic Sites and was a key figure in obtaining the obsolete lake boat *Valley Camp* for use as a museum in Sault Ste. Marie, Mich. It was a fitting new career for the man who knew the ships. But despite his love for the lakers, Tom never sailed on one. He often related an ill-fated attempt to ship out when he was a boy. "My father came right up the deck after me," he recalled.

Those who knew Tom knew he was a born salesman. He loved to talk steamboats, and he loved to load his car up with books and head to Port Huron or Duluth or the Welland Canal on sales trips. In the process, he made friends from one end of the lakes to the other. On Feb. 11, 1986, declared by the city of Sault Ste. Marie as "Tom Manse Day," the local paper editorialized: "He's almost like the prototypical weathered skipper – competent, grouchy, hard-bitten and experienced. ... He's talked ships and shipping every day of his life, and what he's forgotten is more than what most people could know in a lifetime."

Tom Manse passed away on April 27, 1994, at his home in Sault Ste. Marie, Mich., as the 35th edition of "Know Your Ships" rolled off the press.

WE'VE COVERED THE WATERFRONT

Cliffs Victory
(Peter Worden)

The pages that follow revisit some of the 2,000-plus images that have appeared in *"Know Your Ships"* over the past 50 years. What a challenge it was to choose from so many great photos! The sheer number of vessels that have appeared in these pages is as astonishing as the number of them that are no longer around.

It seems like only yesterday that boatwatchers – although they weren't yet defined as such – were viewing vessels such as the passenger liners *South American* or *Assiniboia*; the speedy *Cliffs Victory* or the Republic Steel triplets *Charles M. White, Tom M. Girdler* and *Thomas F. Patton;* or bulk carriers such as the *Benjamin F. Fairless, Renvoyle, Harry Coulby* or the ill-fated *Edmund Fitzgerald*, whose operator, Columbia Transportation Co. (later Oglebay Norton) was a recent corporate casualty. Other companies, now gone, were memorable too, ranging from family concerns such as the Misener, Paterson, Hindman, Reiss and Tomlinson fleets, to those operated by conglomerates such as Bethlehem, National and Republic Steel, the American and Imperial Oil companies and the Ford Motor Co.

Roger Blough and **John D. Leitch** meet on the St. Marys River. *(Roger LeLievre)*

JOHN D. LEITCH

ROGER BLOUGH
GREAT LAKES FLEET

Those boats and many others gave way over the years to new favorites, like the huge *Paul R. Tregurtha*, *Stewart J. Cort* and *Roger Blough*, as well as new companies such as Lower Lakes Towing and its subsidiaries. Classic lakers still in service, such as *Arthur M. Anderson*, *Lee A. Tregurtha* and *Edward L. Ryerson*, as well as long-established firms like the Interlake fleet and Canada Steamship Co. fleets, have helped bridge the decades.

What will the next 50 years bring? That's impossible to predict, of course. But won't it be fun to watch?

Meanwhile, please enjoy these images from our pages past.

– The "Know Your Ships" Crew

Middletown, seen from Columbia Star (right).
(Roger LeLievre)

Luxury liner North West, built in 1895. (Tom Manse Coll.)

CSL package freighter *Renvoyle*. *(Tom Manse)*

***Meaford* of 1906 passes Lime Island.** *(Roger LeLievre)*

***Mesabi Miner* in Detroit River ice.** *(Paul Beesley)*

John Roen V
(Tom Manse Coll.)

Calcite II **passes the Fort Gratiot Lighthouse at Port Huron.** *(Roger LeLievre)*

Bob Lo passenger steamer Ste. Claire in 1973. *(Roger LeLievre)*

William C. Selvick and Erindale. *(Andy LaBorde)*

Algolake on its maiden voyage in 1977. *(Tom Manse Coll.)*

Early Seaway saltie at Toledo in 1961.

City of Milwaukee
(Andy LaBorde)

Wilfred Sykes
(Roger LeLievre)

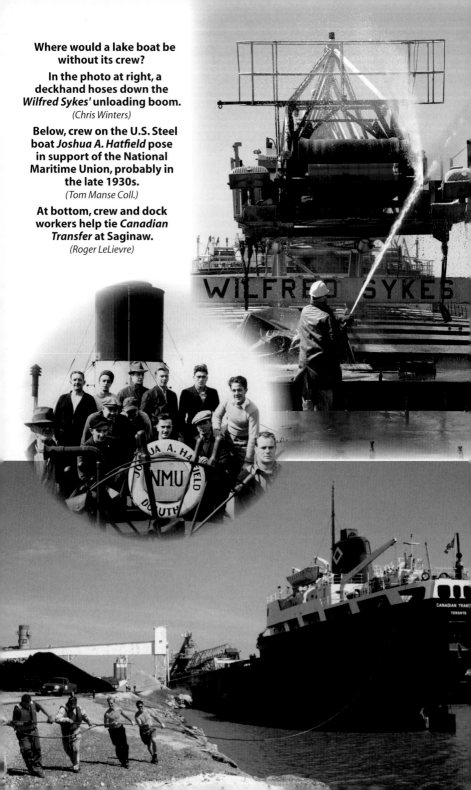

Where would a lake boat be without its crew?

In the photo at right, a deckhand hoses down the *Wilfred Sykes'* unloading boom.
(Chris Winters)

Below, crew on the U.S. Steel boat *Joshua A. Hatfield* pose in support of the National Maritime Union, probably in the late 1930s.
(Tom Manse Coll.)

At bottom, crew and dock workers help tie *Canadian Transfer* at Saginaw.
(Roger LeLievre)

Arthur M. Anderson upbound at sunset, 1971. (Roger LeLievre)

Lethbridge was one of many smaller canal steamers replaced by larger vessels when the Seaway opened.
(John Bascom)

Mapleglen, built as *Carol Lake* in 1960 and scrapped in 2003.
(Bob Campbell)

Tanker *Imperial London* in the early 1960s. *(Tom Manse)*

Michipicoten and *Paul R. Tregurtha* pass on the St. Marys River in 2003. *(Roger LeLievre)*

Teakglen makes her only trip under that name. She sails now as *Maritime Trader*. *(Jim Hoffman)*

Carferry *Viking* makes port at Manitowoc, Wis., in 1982 *(Andy LaBorde)*

Alexander Leslie, built in 1901 and sold for scrap in 1969. *(Roger LeLievre)*

Yankcanuck arrives at Sault Ste. Marie on its maiden voyage in 1963. *(Tom Manse)*

Tug *Dana T. Bowen* was named after a
Great Lakes author. *(Roger LeLievre)*

Engine room telegraph on
the *Wilfred Sykes*. *(Wade P. Streeter)*

Enders M. Voorhees loading grain at Cargill in Duluth. *(John Vournakis)*

Walter J. McCarthy Jr. passes Neebish Island in the lower St. Marys River. (Don Coles Great Lakes Aerial Photos – www.aerialpics.com)

Shenango II, which now sails as *Charles M. Beeghly.* (Tom Manse)

Lake Nipigon was renamed *Algonorth* in 1987.

Theoskepasti, an early Seaway visitor.

1960s artwork showing the Pittsburgh
Steamship fleet's *Benjamin F. Fairless*
after a visit from the supply boat *Ojibway*.

Col. James M. Schoonmaker
is now the musuem ship
Willis B. Boyer. *(Tom Manse)*

Passenger liner *Keewatin*. *(Tom Manse)*

John A. Holloway *(Tom Manse)*

Algowood **launch, 1980.** *(Bob Campbell)*

***Ernest R. Breech* in 1973.** *(Roger LeLievre)*

ERNEST R. BREECH

Cason J. Callaway was the first boat at Sault Ste. Marie in 1971. (Roger LeLievre)

**Gordon C. Leitch,
from a Welland
Canal lift bridge.**
(Roger LeLievre)

***Ernest T. Weir* sailed
later as *Courtney
Burton* and now as
American Valor.**
(Peter Worden)

**Converted from a World War II cargo vessel,
Charles M. White was scrapped in 1980.** (Tom Manse)

Tugs *Debbie Lyn* and *Ian Mac* at hard at work at Goderich. *(Roger LeLievre)*

***Algosteel* at anchor off Duluth.** *(Rod Burdick)*

MARINE MILESTONES

Edward L. Ryerson (Chris Winters)

1959-2009

By Jody Aho

1959: St. Lawrence Seaway opens. The bulk carrier *Seaway Queen*, named to honor the waterway, enters service. *"Know Your Ships"* publishes its first edition.

1960: *Edward L. Ryerson*, a favorite of boatwatchers, makes its maiden voyage.

1961: Many new vessels begin Great Lakes service from unlikely sources. Several World War II T-2 and T-3 tankers are converted to lakers, including *Leon Falk Jr.*, *Paul H. Carnahan*, *Pioneer Challenger* (later *Middletown* and now *American Victory*) and *Walter A. Sterling* (now *Lee A. Tregurtha*). On the Canadian side, *Hidja Marjanne* and *Northern Venture* are similar converts.

1962: The saltie *Montrose* sinks on July 30 after a collision in the Detroit River, near the Ambassador Bridge.

1963: Canadian shipbuilders add several new Seaway-size bulk carriers, among them *Murray Bay* (now *Canadian Provider*), *Black Bay*, *Baie St. Paul*, *Newbrunswicker*, *Quebecois*, *Frankcliffe Hall* (now *Halifax*) and *Silver Isle* (now *Algoisle*).

Walter A. Sterling
(Tom Manse)

Seaway Queen
(Rod Burdick)

Great Northern ore docks in Superior, Wis., in the 1960s. The coal dock on the left is now BNSF dock No. 5. The No. 1 dock, far right, was the one at which the *Edmund Fitzgerald* loaded her last cargo in November 1975. *(Tom Manse Coll.)*

Leecliffe Hall (Tom Manse)

Edmund Fitzgerald in 1975. *(Roger LeLievre)*

1964: The almost-new, 730-foot Canadian bulk carrier *Leecliffe Hall* sinks on Sept. 5 after a collision with the Greek ocean vessel *Apollonia*. This is the first loss of a maximum-sized Seaway bulker.

1965: The limestone carrier *Cedarville* goes down in the Mackinac Straits May 7 after a collision with the Norwegian vessel *Topdalsfjord*. Ten crew are lost.

1966: *Edmund Fitzgerald* becomes the first Great Lakes vessel to surpass the 26,000-ton mark for an iron ore cargo. The bulk carrier *Daniel J. Morrell* – one of the lakes' first 600-footers – breaks in half and sinks in Lake Huron on Nov. 29. Dennis Hale is the only survivor.

1967: Regular passenger service disappears from the lakes as the steamer *South American* is retired in October. The era of steam propulsion ends when *Feux-Follets* (now *Canadian Leader*) enters service, although many steamers continue in service. The self-unloader *Sylvania* is sunk at the dock in Port Huron after being struck by the *Renvoyle*.

Arthur B. Homer (Tom Manse Coll.)

Reiss Brothers
(Tom Manse)

Roger Blough at Duluth. (Kim Nolan)

1968: The Poe Lock at Sault Ste. Marie is opened by *Philip R. Clarke*, although it is not dedicated until 1969. The retired steamer *Valley Camp* becomes a marine museum at Sault Ste. Marie, Mich.

1969: The Reiss Steamship Co. is absorbed into the American Steamship Co., ending the presence of another historic Great Lakes fleet.

1970: *Arthur B. Homer* sets the record for the largest cargo carried on the Great Lakes, 27,550 gross tons of iron ore, breaking a record set by the *Edmund Fitzgerald* on August 10, 1969. The *Homer* would be the last non-1,000-footer to hold this record.

1971: The Wilson Marine Transit Co. and Republic Steel Co. disappear from the lakes. Their vessels are absorbed by other fleets. *Roger Blough* is nearly destroyed by an explosion and fire at the American Shipbuilding Co. yard in Lorain, Ohio, delaying her entry into service until the following June.

South American (Tom Manse Coll.)

Stewart J. Cort passes Detroit on its maiden voyage in 1972. *(Tom Manse Coll.)*

1972: *Stewart J. Cort*, at 1,000 feet long, enters service as the largest vessel on the lakes. She's the first of 13 such superships built over the next few years. *Sidney E. Smith, Jr.* sinks near the Bluewater Bridge in Port Huron after a collision with *Parker Evans* on June 5. *Charles M. Beeghly* is converted to a self-unloader.

1973: *Presque Isle* begins her career in December as the Great Lakes' second 1,000-footer.

1974: Year-round navigation attempts begin over the winter of 1974-75. *Algosoo*, the last laker built with the pilothouse forward and engines aft, makes its first trip. *Roy A. Jodrey* sinks in the Thousand Islands area on Nov. 21, 1974.

Cort's bow and stern sections, built on saltwater, head toward the lakes for mating to a prefab midsection.

Roy A. Jodrey *(Roger LeLievre)*

1975: *Edmund Fitzgerald* is lost on Lake Superior with all hands on Nov. 10.

1976: The Superior Midwest Energy Terminal opens in June. Shipments of low-sulfur coal begin immediately. Great Lakes vessels observe the U.S. Bicentennial with patriotic paint jobs.

1977: Two additional thousand-footers, *Mesabi Miner* and *Belle River* (now *Walter J. McCarthy, Jr.*), enter service, while two of the smallest and older operating vessels in the Kinsman fleet, the 552-foot *Paul L. Tietjen* and 545-foot *Harry L. Allen*, sail for the last time.

Charles M. Beeghly being lengthened at Superior, Wis., in 1972. *(Fraser Shipyard)*

Edwin H. Gott *(Eric Treece)*

1978: *George A. Stinson* (now *American Spirit*) enters service. *Harry L. Allen* is considered a total loss after being heavily damaged in the same fire that destroyed Capitol #4 grain elevator in Duluth on Jan. 21-22, 1978.

1979: *Edwin H. Gott* makes her maiden voyage on Feb. 16, the earliest (or latest) maiden voyage for any laker. This is the busiest year on record for the lakes, with more than 215 million tons of cargo handled.

1980: The Great Lakes shipping industry enters a recession, and many vessels older sail their last.

1981: *William J. De Lancey* (now *Paul R. Tregurtha*) sails on May 10, becoming the largest vessel on the Great Lakes. *Columbia Star* (now *American Century*), the last 1,000-footer built, other than tug-barge combinations, enters service May 30. The *John Sherwin* enters what turns out to be very long-term lay-up at Superior, Wis.

1982: Shipments of iron ore on the Great Lakes reach their lowest levels since the Great Depression. Many fleets have vessels laid up, including several of the 1,000-footers. The *Arthur M. Anderson*, *Cason J. Callaway*, *Philip R. Clarke* and *Armco* are converted to self-unloaders.

Ford Motor Co.'s _John Dykstra_. _(Peter Worden)_

Mesquite in 1965 _(USCG)_

Paterson's maiden voyage. _(Peter Worden)_

1983: The St. Lawrence Seaway carries its billionth ton of cargo.

1984: The Seaway celebrates its 25th anniversary. The Cleveland Cliffs Steamship Co. ceases operations. _E.G. Grace_ is the first of the World War II Maritime-class vessels sold for scrap.

1985: The last new Canadian bulker enters service. The _Paterson_ (now _Pineglen_) is also the last new vessel built at Collingwood Shipyards.

1986: The record for the largest cargo in a single trip is set in November when _Lewis Wilson Foy_ (now _American Integrity_) carries a cargo of 72,351 gross tons of pellets from Escanaba to Burns Harbor.

1987: The Great Lakes shipping industry comes out of its downturn. Before the slump ends, many familiar vessels have been sold for scrap.

1988: The Ford Motor Co. ceases operations at the end of the season, selling its three remaining vessels to the Interlake Steamship Co. Halco (Hall Corp. of Canada) also folds.

1989: The U.S. Coast Guard buoy tender _Mesquite_ is wrecked off the Keweenaw Peninsula. Her hull is later sunk for use as a recreational dive site.

1990: The tanker _Jupiter_ explodes at Bay City, Mich., Sept. 16 as it is unloading gasoline. The vessel is a complete loss.

J.W. Westcott II
(Mike Sipper)

Alpena at the Soo Locks. *(Roger LeLievre)*

1991: After a nearly 10-year lay-up, *Leon Fraser* re-enters service as the cement carrier *Alpena*.

1992: Carferry service resumes on Lake Michigan after the *Badger* is sold to the Lake Michigan Carferry Co.

1993: The Misener fleet folds at the end of the year.

1994: The 1,000-foot *Indiana Harbor* sets a new record for a single-trip Eastern coal shipment, 60,578 net tons. The carferry *Badger* becomes the only remaining coal-fired vessel on the lakes.

1995: Mailboat service on the Detroit River turns 100 years old. The *J.W. Westcott II* serves vessels with mail, newspapers and other goods. *J. Burton Ayers* returns to service as *Cuyahoga* for a new company, Lower Lakes Towing, which makes a success out of buying near-obsolete lakers and putting them back in service.

1996: The two-billionth ton of cargo passes through the St. Lawrence Seaway, carried by *Algosoo*.

1997: Overnight passenger service returns to the Great Lakes with the German-flagged, Bahamas-registered *c. Columbus*.

Cuyahoga on its namesake river. *(Dave Marcoux)*

E.M. Ford in Mackinaw Straits ice. *(Eric Treece)*

1998: The cement storage vessel *E.M. Ford* marks its 100th birthday.

1999: The 40th anniversary of the opening of the St. Lawrence Seaway is celebrated.

2000: Three U.S. Steel self-unloaders, *George A. Sloan*, *Myron C. Taylor* and *Calcite II*, sail their last for the company. In 2002, as *Mississagi*, *Calumet* and *Maumee*, they become part of the Lower Lakes Towing fleet. The self-unloading barge *Great Lakes Trader* enters service.

2001: The Canadian fleet Parrish & Heimbecker disappears from the lakes. Its steamers *Oakglen* and *Mapleglen* are sold to Canada Steamship Lines. *Windoc* is heavily damaged after a Welland Canal bridge is lowered prematurely on Aug. 11.

2002: N. M. Paterson & Sons exits the lake shipping business. The steamer *Kinsman Independent*, the last U.S.-flagged, non-self-unloading grain carrier, is laid up for the last time, ending an era. A number of lakers head for scrap, including the *Vandoc*, *Algogulf*, *Comeaudoc*, *Manitoulin* and *Algoriver*.

2003: *Seaway Queen*, *Mapleglen* and *Oakglen* are sold for scrap.

George A. Sloan
(John C. Meyland)

Damaged *Windoc* *(Dave Wobser)*

Joseph H. Frantz at Duluth. *(Dave Wobser)*

2004: The 1925-vintage *Joseph H. Frantz* sails for the last time, and the Steinbrenner-owned Kinsman Lines quits the Great Lakes shipping business.

2005: The Soo Locks celebrate 150 years.

2006: The Oglebay Norton Co., dating back to 1854, exits the shipping business; many of the vessels are sold to the American Steamship Co. The cement carrier *St. Marys Challenger* celebrates its 100th birthday as the oldest operating commercial steamboat in North America. The 1944-vintage icebreaker *Mackinaw* is retired, replaced by a new vessel of the same name. After years of lay-up, the *Edward L. Ryerson* re-enters service, to the delight of boatwatchers. Ed-heads

follow her every move, hoping for a salute from Capt. Eric Treece on the boat's booming steam whistles.

2007: The 1929-vintage *Calumet* is sold for scrap. Low water levels plague shippers, forcing them to reduce the amount of per-trip cargo carried.

2008: Many vessels lay up early as steel mills cut back production. The 50th anniversary of the 1958 loss of the *Carl D. Bradley* on Lake Michigan is observed.

2009: The St. Lawrence Seaway and *"Know Your Ships"* turn 50.

First *Mackinaw* convoys *Hagarty* in ice. *(USCG)* **Inset: New *Mackinaw* launched April 2, 2005.** *(Chris Winters)*

LOST ON THE LAKES

Edmund Fitzgerald
1958-1975

Orient Trader burns at Toronto in 1965. *(John Bascom)*

Daniel J. Morrell sank Nov. 29, 1966; 28 lost. *(Tom Manse)*

Cedarville sank May 7, 1965; 10 lost. *(Tom Manse)*

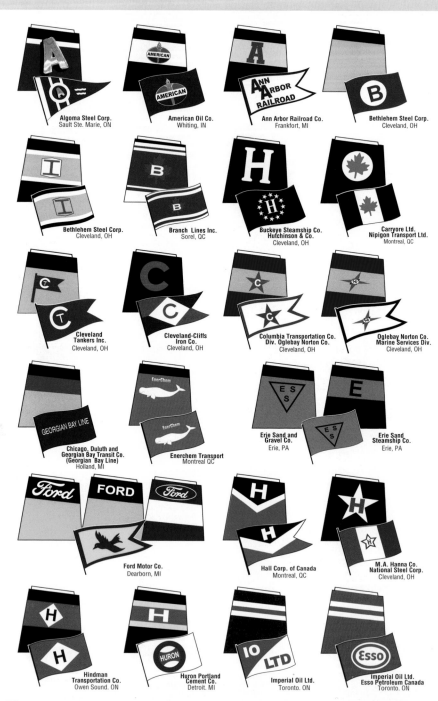

Algoma Steel Corp.
Sault Ste. Marie, ON

American Oil Co.
Whiting, IN

Ann Arbor Railroad Co.
Frankfort, MI

Bethlehem Steel Corp.
Cleveland, OH

Bethlehem Steel Corp.
Cleveland, OH

Branch Lines Inc.
Sorel, QC

Buckeye Steamship Co.
Hutchinson & Co.
Cleveland, OH

Carryore Ltd.
Nipigon Transport Ltd.
Montreal, QC

Cleveland Tankers Inc.
Cleveland, OH

Cleveland-Cliffs Iron Co.
Cleveland, OH

Columbia Transportation Co.
Div. Oglebay Norton Co.
Cleveland, OH

Oglebay Norton Co.
Marine Services Div.
Cleveland, OH

Chicago, Duluth and Georgian Bay Transit Co.
(Georgian Bay Line)
Holland, MI

Enerchem Transport
Montreal QC

Erie Sand and Gravel Co.
Erie, PA

Erie Sand Steamship Co.
Erie, PA

Ford Motor Co.
Dearborn, MI

Hall Corp. of Canada
Montreal, QC

M.A. Hanna Co.
National Steel Corp.
Cleveland, OH

Hindman Transportation Co.
Owen Sound. ON

Huron Portland Cement Co.
Detroit. MI

Imperial Oil Ltd.
Toronto. ON

Imperial Oil Ltd.
Esso Petroleum Canada
Toronto. ON

SEAWAY STACKS AND HOUSEFLAGS

have disappeared from the scene over the past 50 years.

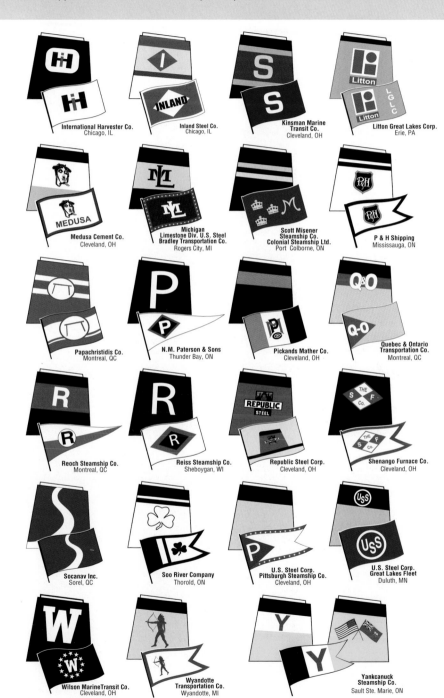

International Harvester Co.
Chicago, IL

Inland Steel Co.
Chicago, IL

Kinsman Marine
Transit Co.
Cleveland, OH

Litton Great Lakes Corp.
Erie, PA

Medusa Cement Co.
Cleveland, OH

Michigan
Limestone Div. U.S. Steel
Bradley Transportation Co.
Rogers City, MI

Scott Misener
Steamship Co.
Colonial Steamship Ltd.
Port Colborne, ON

P & H Shipping
Mississauga, ON

Papachristidis Co.
Montreal, QC

N.M. Paterson & Sons
Thunder Bay, ON

Pickands Mather Co.
Cleveland, OH

Quebec & Ontario
Transportation Co.
Montreal, QC

Reoch Steamship Co.
Montreal, QC

Reiss Steamship Co.
Sheboygan, WI

Republic Steel Corp.
Cleveland, OH

Shenango Furnace Co.
Cleveland, OH

Socanav Inc.
Sorel, QC

Soo River Company
Thorold, ON

U.S. Steel Corp.
Pittsburgh Steamship Co.
Cleveland, OH

U.S. Steel Corp.
Great Lakes Fleet
Duluth, MN

Wilson MarineTransit Co.
Cleveland, OH

Wyandotte
Transportation Co.
Wyandotte, MI

Yankcanuck
Steamship Co.
Sault Ste. Marie, ON

Southdown Challenger at sunset.
(Chris Winters)

INDEX TO ADVERTISERS

Thank you for supporting our advertisers!

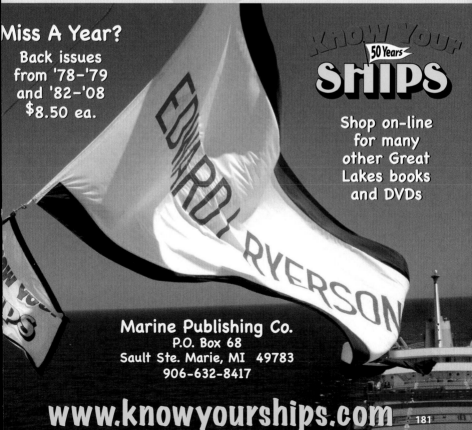

Miss A Year?
Back issues
from '78-'79
and '82-'08
$8.50 ea.

KNOW YOUR
50 Years
SHIPS

Shop on-line
for many
other Great
Lakes books
and DVDs

Marine Publishing Co.
P.O. Box 68
Sault Ste. Marie, MI 49783
906-632-8417

www.knowyourships.com

SHIP SIGHTINGS

Record your own vessel
observations here

DATE	NAME	LOCATION / DETAILS

DATE	NAME	LOCATION / DETAILS

The Auto Ferry Redefined

The Lake Express began service in 2004 as the first high speed auto ferry to operate between U.S. ports. Since then the Lake Express has delighted travelers with modern speed and comfort and an unrivaled experience.

For schedules, rates and more information:
www.lake-express.com

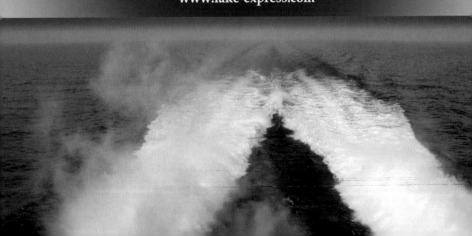